Margaret Beaufort

For Grandad

ABOUT THE AUTHOR

Elizabeth Norton gained her first degree from the University of Cambridge, and her Masters from the University of Oxford. Her other books include *England's Queens: The Biography*, *Anne Boleyn: Henry VIII's Obsession*, *Jane Seymour: Henry VIII's True Love*, *Anne of Cleves: Henry VIII's Discarded Bride*, *Catherine Parr* (all published by Amberley Publishing) and *She Wolves: The Notorious Queens of England*. She is currently writing a biography of Henry VIII's mistress, Bessie Blount, also for Amberley. She lives in Kingston Upon Thames.

Margaret Beaufort

Mother of the Tudor Dynasty

ELIZABETH NORTON

AMBERLEY

With thanks to Pembroke Castle

Cover illustrations: Front and back flap: Photograph © John Foley (www. imaginegallery.co.uk).

This edition first published 2011

Amberley Publishing
The Hill, Stroud
Gloucestershire, GL5 4EP

www.amberleybooks.com

British Library Cataloguing in Publication Data.
A catalogue record for this book is available from the British Library.

ISBN 978 1 4456 0578 4

Typesetting and Origination by Amberley Publishing.
Printed in Great Britain.

CONTENTS

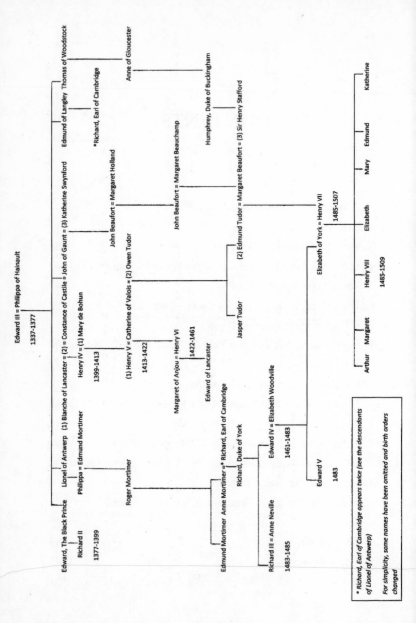

1. Margaret's royal descent.

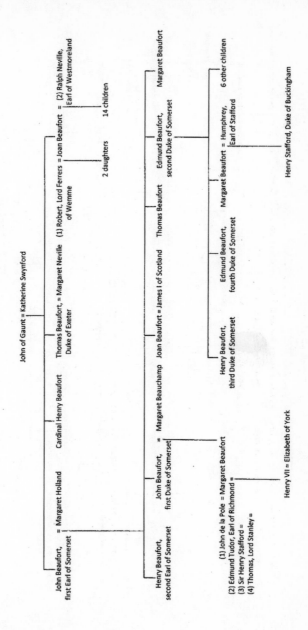

2. The Beaufort family.

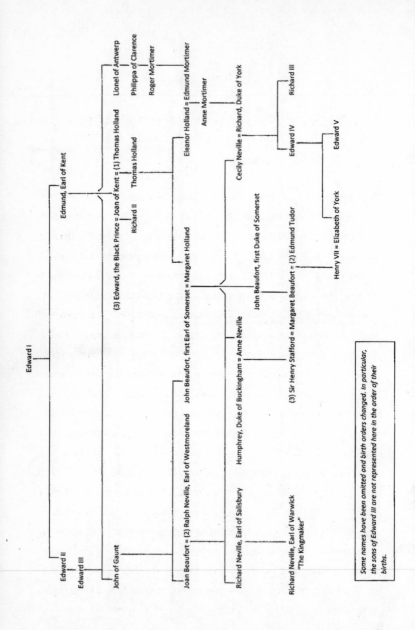

3. Margaret's links to the House of York.

A BEAUFORT HEIRESS: 1443-1444

At a sermon given in memory of Margaret Beaufort in 1509, her friend, John Fisher declared, 'Dare I say of her, she never yet was in that prosperity, but the greter it was, the more alwaye she dredde the adversyte.' Margaret was observed to weep at the coronation of her son, Henry VII, and at the marriage of her grandson, Prince Arthur, and the coronation of her younger grandson, Henry VIII. These were not tears of joy, and as Fisher observed, 'whereyn she had full grete joy, she let not to saye, that some adversyte wolde follow. So that eyther she was in sorrowe by reason of the present adversytes; or else whan she was in prosperyte, she was in drede of the adversyte for to come'. The idea of Fortune's wheel, with its random changes from prosperity to disaster, was a popular one in medieval England, and Margaret Beaufort, with her long and turbulent life, saw herself, and was seen by others, as the living embodiment of the concept. Margaret was the mother of the Tudor dynasty in England, and it was through her that Henry VII was able to bid for the throne and gather enough strength to claim it. She knew times of great prosperity and power, but also times of deep despair. These were, to a large extent, products of the period in which Margaret lived, and her family, the Beauforts, had also suffered and prospered from Fortune's random spin in the years before her birth.

Margaret Beaufort was born on 31 May 1443 at Bletso in Bedfordshire, a manor that belonged to her mother, Margaret Beauchamp, the daughter and heiress of Sir John Beauchamp of Bletso. Margaret was named after her mother, who had been a widow at the time of her marriage to John Beaufort, Earl, and later Duke, of Somerset. Margaret Beauchamp was of gentry, rather than noble stock, and she had previously been the wife of Sir Oliver St John, who died in 1438 and by whom she had seven children. She was not a particularly good match for Somerset, but by the time of their marriage in 1439, he was already a bachelor in his late thirties, and she was the most prestigious wife he could find.

Fortune's wheel was not kind to John Beaufort, Duke of Somerset. He was the second son of John Beaufort, 1st Earl of Somerset, and succeeded to the earldom on the death of his elder brother in 1418, when he was still a child. The Beaufort family enjoyed a somewhat uncertain status in England. The 1st Earl of Somerset was the eldest son of John of Gaunt, Duke of Lancaster (the third surviving son of Edward III) by Katherine Swynford. Katherine was the daughter of a knight from Hainault who served Edward III's queen, Philippa of Hainault, in England, and she was placed in her youth with Blanche, Duchess of Lancaster, the first wife of John of Gaunt. Katherine married an English knight, but she remained with John of Gaunt's family, and around the time that he married his second wife, Constance of Castile, she became his mistress. The affair between John of Gaunt and Katherine Swynford lasted throughout his second marriage and was common knowledge in England from at least 1375. The couple had four children, who were given the surname 'Beaufort' after one of John of Gaunt's continental possessions. They were openly acknowledged by John but, due to their illegitimate birth, had no rights of inheritance. This changed in 1396, when 'the duke of Lancastre, for the love he had to his chyldren, he wedded their mother the lady Katheryn of Ruet, wherof there was moche marveyle bothe in Englande and in Fraunce, for she was but of base lynage, in regarde to the two other wyves'. The marriage of John of Gaunt and Katherine Swynford shocked England but did not, in itself, legitimise their children. John of Gaunt, as the then eldest surviving son of Edward III and one of the most powerful men in Europe, was determined to improve his children's status, and he obtained the Pope's consent to the legitimisation of the Beauforts. Whilst this ensured that, in the eyes of the Church, the subsequent marriage removed the stain of bastardy from the four Beauforts, under English law, they remained illegitimate. John of Gaunt was able to persuade his nephew, Richard II, to pass a statute in 1397, in which he declared,

> Richard, by the grace of God, King of England and of France, and Lord of Ireland, to our most dear kinsmen the noble men John [Beaufort], knight, Henry, clerk, Thomas, young gentleman, and to the beloved noble woman, Joan Beaufort, young lady, children of our most dear uncle the noble man John, Duke of Lancaster, our lieges, greeting and benevolence of our royal majesty. Since we thought in our inner contemplation, how ceaselessly and with what honours we have been blessed by the paternal and sincere affection of our uncle, and by the maturity of his counsel, we thought it fitting and worthy that with our knowledge of his merits and contemplation of the grace of persons, we should confer the blessing of our special prerogative and of our favour and grace on you who shine by the quality of your great worth and the honesty of your life and manners, and are sprung from royal stock, and

endowed with many virtues and signs of divine favour. Therefore, yielding to the prayers of our uncle, your father, with whom it is said, you bear a defect of birth ... we wish nevertheless that whatsoever honours, dignities, pre-eminencies, status, ranks, and offices, public and private, perpetual and temporal, feudal and noble there may be ... whether held immediately or directly from us ... you may receive, hold, enjoy, and exercise, as fully, freely, and lawfully as if you were born in lawful wedlock.

Richard concluded by confirming that 'we legitimate you ... and any children that you may have', and he imposed no limits on the Beaufort's new status. By the statute of 1397, the Beauforts were legally to be considered as legitimate as their elder half-brother, Henry, Earl of Derby, and the other children of John of Gaunt's first two marriages. As a further mark of their status and royal favour, Richard II created the eldest Beaufort, John, Earl of Somerset. Although John of Gaunt had only one legitimate son before the legitimisation of the Beauforts, he had no real dynastic need of further sons, as his heir, Henry, Earl of Derby, was a mature man with a large family of his own. It is therefore most likely that, as one contemporary, the chronicler Jehan Froissart, suggested, John of Gaunt was motivated by affection for his new wife and their children. John did not long survive his marriage, and his Will is a testament to his love for the children of all three of his marriages. He left bequests to all his children and to Katherine Swynford, although he asked to be buried beside his first wife, Blanche, in St Paul's Cathedral.

Although John of Gaunt sought to provide for his Beaufort children, his main efforts were directed towards his heir, Henry, Earl of Derby, and he secured a marriage for him with Mary de

Bohun, one of the greatest heiresses in England. Even in his father's lifetime, Henry came into conflict with his cousin, Richard II, and following John of Gaunt's death in 1399, he returned from a continental exile to depose his cousin, taking the throne as Henry IV. With the accession of Henry IV, the Beauforts, as the half-siblings of the King, naturally came to a degree of prominence. A near contemporary of Henry, John Capgrave, declared that he wore the crown 'not so much by right of descent as by the election of the people', and it was certainly the case that there were people in England with a stronger hereditary claim than Henry IV. In spite of the defects in his own claim, Henry was not prepared to consider the possibility of the Beauforts inheriting the crown, and he inserted a clause into the statute of 1397 declaring that they were legitimate in all matters, save with regard to the inheritance of the throne. The legality of this insertion is debatable, and it does not appear to have been enacted by parliament. However, it did, in the eyes of many, prejudice any claim to the throne that the Beauforts could make. By the time of Margaret Beaufort's birth, the Beauforts were recognised as close kin to the ruling Lancastrian dynasty, but their position with regard to the crown was distinctly uncertain. In other respects, however, Henry IV was prepared to favour his Beaufort half-siblings, and in 1404, for example, he agreed to grant the Earl of Somerset £1,000 a year until he could be provided with lands to maintain his position. Somerset's daughter, Joan Beaufort, was also considered a suitable bride for James I of Scotland, whom she married during the reign of Henry VI in 1424.

Margaret's grandfather, John, Earl of Somerset, died in 1410 and was succeeded by his eldest son. Eight years later, on the death of his elder brother, Margaret's father succeeded to the family earldom and estates. The second John Beaufort endured something of a wasted life. Only three years after he became Earl of Somerset, when he was still aged under twenty, he travelled to France in the company of his stepfather, Thomas, Duke of Clarence, the brother of Henry V. Clarence was one of the leading English commanders in the Hundred Years War, which had begun in the fourteenth century when Edward III claimed the throne of France through his mother, Isabella of France. Clarence and Somerset served together at the Battle of Baugé in 1421, which proved to be one of the few defeats suffered by Henry V's army during his successful conquest of France. The battle was a disaster, and Clarence and a number of other prominent members of the English nobility were killed. Somerset and his younger brother Thomas were captured, and both entered a long and frustrating imprisonment in France. There is evidence that both brothers fiercely resented their imprisonment. For example, in 1427, they jointly petitioned parliament and the Duke of Gloucester, who ruled as protector for the young king, Henry VI, to ask that an agreement be put into effect so that they could be released in exchange for the imprisoned Duke of Bourbon. This agreement came to nothing, although Thomas Beaufort was eventually released in 1430. Somerset, as the elder brother, was a more valuable prisoner, and as the highest ranking English prisoner taken by the French, it took seventeen years for his ransom to be agreed. Whilst he was imprisoned, he was overshadowed at the English court by his younger brother, Edmund Beaufort.

Somerset returned to England after seventeen years and immediately set about establishing himself as a leading nobleman and landowner. He had been young and inexperienced when he was imprisoned, and upon his release, he found the challenge of his role as a landowning lord beyond his capabilities.

According to the *Crowland Chronicle Continuations*, on his return to England, Somerset resolved to take personal control of his manor of Deeping in Lincolnshire:

> And the whole multitudes of the district flocked forth to meet him, each one endeavouring to be avenged upon his neighbour, and thinking himself fortunate in being enrolled among the number of his servants. The people of Depyng were especially elated, as though a prophet had arisen amongst them; escorting him about on every side, promising great things, and suggesting still more; while by the voice of a herald they proclaimed him lord of the whole marsh. Upon this, his heart was elevated to a lofty pitch, and, being puffed up by the great applause of the populace, his horn was exalted too greatly on high. Forthwith, tolls were levied by his servants in the vills; and the cattle of all were driven away from the marshes, and, when driven as far as Depyng, were there detained; nor were they allowed to be redeemed without a payment and acknowledgement of him as lord of the demesne.

Somerset also upset the abbot of the neighbouring Crowland Abbey by raising an embankment and refusing to allow goods to be transported to the monastery over his lands. The indignant abbot complained directly to the King, to Somerset's fury.

Somerset had been forced to pay a large ransom to secure his release from France, and this may have been behind his attempts to extract the maximum profit from Deeping and his other lands. He certainly drove a hard bargain when, in 1443, it was suggested that he lead a military expedition in France. Following his accession to the throne, Henry V had renewed the Hundred Years War against France with great success, and by the time of his death in 1422, he had been recognised as heir to the French throne. With Henry

V's early death, his infant son, Henry VI, inherited his claims, and he was proclaimed as King of France on the death of his maternal grandfather, Charles VI. Initially, with France governed by Henry VI's uncle, the Duke of Bedford, the English were able to maintain their grip on the conquered kingdom. However, by the early 1440s, the tide of the war had firmly turned against them. In 1443, the English council determined to send an army to defend Gascony, which had been in English hands since the twelfth century, and Somerset was selected to be the commander.

The choice of Somerset to lead an important military expedition was an odd one, as, apart from a brief experience of war in his late teens, he had no military experience. By 1443, Henry VI, who was the only child of his parents' marriage, had few relatives, and the English royal family was greatly depleted. Somerset, with his Lancastrian blood, was therefore almost certainly selected due to his position on the fringes of the royal family rather than due to any ability that he had shown. The choice proved to be disastrous.

Somerset was not entirely enthusiastic about the campaign, and he drove a hard bargain with the royal council. Henry VI agreed to create his cousin Duke of Somerset, with precedence over all other dukes save the King's uncle, the Duke of Gloucester, and the royally descended Duke of York, who was leading a campaign in Normandy. Somerset also received an annual income of 600 marks, after his initial demands for 1,000 marks were rejected, and was created Earl of Kendal. For Somerset, this was an acknowledgement of his royal blood, and he was satisfied with all that was granted, also receiving the confirmation that he would be in overall authority in any part of France 'in the whiche my said Lorde of York cometh not'. One final point over which Somerset bargained was in relation to the child that his wife was expecting that summer. Somerset knew that it was possible that he would not survive the campaign, and he was anxious to ensure that Margaret Beauchamp retained custody of their expected child and, also, their lands and their disposal in marriage. This again was granted, and the birth of Margaret Beaufort on 31 May, less than three weeks before the day appointed for the expedition, may account for the fact that Somerset did not meet with his army as planned. Personal business may also have delayed matters, and that summer, he met with the abbot of Crowland at Corfe Castle in Dorset in an attempt to bring their dispute to an end. Somerset was in no hurry to reach an agreement, but he was finally persuaded to write to his seneschal ordering him not to interfere with the abbey or its servants until the matter could be fully settled on his return. Somerset missed the next date scheduled for his campaign to begin, and around 9 July, the council lost patience, informing him that the delay was costing the king £500 a day and ordering him to depart. He finally joined his army at the end of July and took up his commission as 'lieutenant and captain-general of France and Gascony'. He immediately caused a major diplomatic incident by taking his army into Brittany, an ally of England, and pillaging the towns and countryside. It seems unlikely that Somerset could have failed to realise that he had crossed into Brittany, and his actions demonstrate his shortcomings as a military commander. Duke Francis I of Brittany immediately complained to Henry VI, declaring that Somerset had entered like a conqueror and threatening to abandon his alliance with the English. With difficulty, the Breton alliance was salvaged, but not before Somerset had extracted a tribute payment from the duchy. His expedition proved to be utterly ineffective, and he was summoned home in disgrace, having cost the crown over £26,000.

Somerset appears not to have realised quite how furious the King and council were, and the *Crowland Chronicle Continuations* tell us that he returned 'amid much pomp to England'. He was soon made aware of the anger directed at him when he was refused an audience with the King, instead being banished from court. A chastened Somerset returned to his West Country estates, aware that his career was over and that he was facing a charge of treason. According to the *Crowland Chronicle Continuations*, which appears to be a reliable source for Somerset and his family,

> The noble heart of a man of such high rank upon his hearing this most unhappy news [i.e., his banishment], was moved to extreme indignation; and being unable to bear the stain of so great a disgrace, he accelerated his death by putting an end to his existence, it is generally said; preferring thus to cut short his sorrow, rather than pass a life of misery, labouring under so disgraceful a charge.

Somerset died just under a year after the birth of his only child. The charge of suicide cannot be substantiated, but it is certainly a possibility, as he was in the greatest disgrace. Margaret Beaufort had no memory of her father, but she was later associated with Crowland Abbey and would have heard the rumours about her father's death. In commenting on Somerset's death, the Crowland chronicler recited a prophecy about the duke, declaring that it had been foreseen that 'hardly for twice two years endured John's pride of power'. As a sign of her sympathy for her father, Margaret later paid for a grand tomb to mark his grave and that of her mother at Wimborne Minster in Dorset. Even from her infancy, Margaret Beaufort's life was subject to the jubilation and miseries of Fortune's wheel, and she reached her first birthday as both the daughter of a disgraced probable suicide and one of the greatest heiresses in England.

2

FIRST MARRIAGE: 1444-1453

With the disgrace and early death of her father, Margaret, who was only days away from her first birthday, was left in a precarious position. Before he left for France, Margaret's father had secured the King's agreement that, in the event of his death, his wife would be left with custody of their child. Whilst Somerset's younger brother, Edmund Beaufort, inherited the Somerset earldom and some estates entailed on the male line, Margaret was left very wealthy, and certain members of the court began to look greedily towards her wardship and eventual marriage.

Although Somerset had secured the King's agreement to Margaret's wardship remaining with her mother, following his disgrace, the King and his council were in no mood to grant the family any favours. In the medieval period, when a minor inherited land, their wardship and the rights to their marriage immediately passed to the king. This meant that the king could benefit from the revenues of the estates during the heir's minority and arrange their marriage, something that could be very lucrative. Wardships were frequently given as rewards to favoured members of the court, and within weeks of Somerset's death, Henry VI had granted Margaret's wardship to his most favoured councillor, William de la Pole, Earl of Suffolk, declaring to his chancellor, the Archbishop of Canterbury, that:

Right Reverend fader in God, right trusty and right welbeloved, we grete you wel. And for asmoche as oure Cousin the Duc of Somerset is nowe late passed to God's mercy, the whiche hath a doughter and heir to succede after hym of ful tender age, called Margarete. We, considering the notable service that oure Cousin therl of Suffolk hath doon unto us, and tendering hym therfore the more specially as reason wol, have of oure grace and especialle propre mocion and mere deliberacion graunted unto hym to have the warde and mariage of the said Margarete, withouten eny thing therfore unto us or oure heires yielding. Wherfore we wol and charge you that unto oure said Cousin of Suffolk ye do make, upon this oure graunte, lettres patents souffisant in lawe and in deue forme; and that ye faille not hereof, As we specially truste you, and as ye desire to do unto us singuleir plesir, and that ye send unto us oure said lettres patents seeled by the berer of thees.

Perhaps as a concession to his earlier promise to Somerset, the King allowed Margaret to remain in her mother's household during her childhood, a departure from the common practice, which generally saw an heir raised in the household of the person who held their wardship.

Margaret's wardship was granted to the most powerful man in England, as the Earl (who would later be created first a marquess and then a duke) of Suffolk was commonly believed to control the King. Henry VI had come to the throne in his infancy and, by 1444, had ruled the kingdom personally for some years. Even during his lifetime, Henry VI had a poor reputation with his subjects. One contemporary record, for example, states that two husbandmen from Sussex, John and William Merfeld, were arrested for stating in the market place that 'the king was a natural fool and would often hold a staff in his hands with a bird on the end, playing therewith as a fool, and that another king must be ordained to rule the land, saying that the king was no person able to rule the land'. A number of other hostile sources implied that the King was a simpleton and unfit to rule, with Jean de Waurin, for example, declaring that he was simple-minded and ruled like a child. The truth of this is difficult to judge, although the King is unlikely to have suffered from a learning disability, as he is known to have mastered both French and Latin. No mental deficiency was noted in the instructions given to Henry's guardian, the Earl of Warwick, in 1428, when the boy king was seven years old. The earl was instructed 'to remain about the king's person, to do his utmost in teaching him good manners, literature, languages, nurture and courtesy and other studies necessary for so great a prince'. It is clear that the boy was considered to be normal enough, although, as he aged, he was noted to take a simplistic and overly earnest approach to the world, declaring, for example, when he was sixteen, that he would avoid the sight and conversation of women and 'affirming these to be the work of the devil' before quoting from the gospel that to look at a woman with the eye was to commit adultery with the heart. The King was renowned for his piety and, according to his supporter, John Blacman,

[Henry] once complained heavily to me in his chamber at Eltham, when I was alone there with him studying his holy books, and giving ear to his wholesome advice and the sighs of his most deep devotion, [concerning] a knock on his door by a certain mighty duke of the realm: the king said, 'They so interrupt me that, whether by day or night, I can hardly snatch a moment for reading the holy scripture without disturbance'.

Henry was not unintelligent, but in many matters, he was childlike and easily led. He was entirely unsuited to the role of a medieval king, and he relied heavily on a handful of advisors, the most unpopular of whom was Suffolk.

Margaret's guardian, William de la Pole, Earl, and later Duke, of Suffolk, came from a family of wool merchants in Kingston-upon-Hull who had made their fortune and been ennobled some years before his birth in 1396. The family were viewed as upstarts by many of the traditional nobility, although they were connected with the Lancastrian royal family through Suffolk's marriage to Alice Chaucer, the granddaughter of Katherine Swynford's sister. Suffolk was, first and foremost, a courtier, and Henry VI had quickly come to rely on his advice after declaring his majority, making him chamberlain of England and employing him as his ambassador in France in 1444 whilst the King's marriage was negotiated. It was Suffolk who acted as Henry's proxy in his marriage ceremony with Margaret of Anjou, and he and his wife escorted the new queen to England, earning her esteem.

Margaret Beauchamp was an heiress in her own right and she raised both Margaret and the children of her first marriage at her manors of Bletso and Maxey. Few details survive of Margaret Beaufort's upbringing, but it is apparent that she developed a strong bond with her St John half-siblings. Margaret created an embroidery showing the descent of the St John family during her childhood, and in her later life, she always took an interest in the family. For example, after 1504, she appointed her nephew, John St John, as her chamberlain and also named him as an executor of her Will. She arranged a marriage for one of her nephews with the royally descended Margaret Plantagenet, daughter of the Duke of Clarence.

There is also some evidence that Margaret enjoyed a warm relationship with her mother, who remarried in 1447, taking Lionel, Lord Welles, as her third husband. Margaret Beauchamp was a shrewd woman and, as the Crowland Chronicler noted, took an active and firm interest in the management of her estates:

The lady duchess Margaret, her mother, held the said lordship of Depyng in dower for many years, during which she survived: besides which, she continued to retain full possession thereof, all the days of her life, a period of nearly thirty years, both in exacting amercements for trespasses, levying for repairs of the embankments, and taking poundage for animals, in such manner as she had found the same rights appendant to the said marsh lands on the day of her husband's death.

Margaret Beaufort was accused of acquisitiveness in her later life, and in this, she was a similar character to her mother. Although the Crowland Chronicler was generally favourable in his references to Margaret's mother, in one entry he did note with censure that, with regard to an area of marshland that was disputed by Margaret Beauchamp and the abbey, she kept it in her possession with the markers and other boundaries being removed so that it was impossible for anyone to remember where the boundary had originally been. For the most part, Margaret Beauchamp was a friend of Crowland Abbey, and in 1465, the chronicler recorded evidence of the closeness between mother and daughter:

In the same year, also, the duchess, Lady Margaret, relict of John, the illustrious duke of Somerset, one who had always proved gracious and favourably disposed to our monastery, and who, as we have already mentioned, had received the manor of Depyng as a part of her dower, while staying at her castle of Maxay, was desirous, in a spirit of extreme devoutness, to be commended to our prayers; upon which, she was readily admitted to be a sister of our chapter. Influenced by pious considerations, she also induced her daughter, the Lady Margaret, Countess of Richmond, and heir to the before-named manor of Depyng, (who had been married, as we have long before already mentioned, to the lord Henry, the illustrious son of the duke of Buckingham), to become a sister along with her, and in like manner enjoy the benefit of our prayers. This was done, to the end that, being bound to us by such ties as these, she might be rendered more benevolent to us hereafter, and more complacent in every respect.

Margaret Beaufort was always affectionate to her maternal family, and it was her mother who would have been responsible for her early education.

The education of women was not routine in late medieval England, but there is a considerable body of evidence to show that Margaret Beaufort was well educated. John Fisher, Margaret's chaplain and friend in the last years of her life, commented on this in the sermon that he gave in memory of her:

Fyrst, she was of singular Wisedom, ferre passyng the comyn rate of women. She was good in remembraunce, and of holdyng memorye; a redye wytte she had also to conceive all thynges, albeit they were ryghte derke. Right studious she was in Bokes, which she had in grete number, both in Englysh and in Frenshe; and for her exercise, and for the profyte of other, she did translate divers maters of Devocyon out of Frensh into Englysh. Full often she complayned that in her youthe she had not given her to the understanding of Latin, wherein she had a lytell perceyvyng.

Whilst Margaret received little Latin tuition, her French education was first rate, and Fisher noted that she possessed a number of books in the language for her religious mediations and that she also employed herself in translating French works into English. In his dedication to the English translation of *The Hystorye of Kinge Blanchardyne and Queen Eglantyne his Wyfe,* the printer William Caxton asked Margaret 'to pardon me of the rude and common English, where as shall be found fault; for I confess me not learned, ne knowing the art of rhetorick, ne of such gay terms as now be said in these days and used'. Whilst Caxton, who benefitted from Margaret's patronage, naturally intended to flatter her, his comment does, again, suggest that she had a reputation for learning, and this accords with her later interest in book production, her translation works and her interest in Oxford and Cambridge Universities. Within her family circle, Margaret was known to value the written word, and the mother of her third husband, the Duchess of Buckingham, included a bequest in her Will 'to my daughter of Richmond [Margaret], a book of French called LUCUN; another book of French of epistles and gospels; and a primmer with clasps of silver gilt, covered with purple velvet'.

Whilst it is clear that Margaret's education was, by the standards of the time, extensive, particular attention would have been paid to instructing her in her future life as the wife of a nobleman. In his sermon on Margaret, John Fisher noted,

She was bounteous and lyberal to every Person of her Knowledge or acquaintance. Avarice and covetyse she most hated, and sorowed it full moche in all persons, but specially in ony that belong'd unto her. She was also of syngular easyness to be spoken unto, and full curtayse answere she would make to all that came unto her. Of mervayllous gentyleness she was unto all folks, but specially unto her owne whom she trusted and loved ryghte tenderly. Unkynde she wolde not be unto no creature, ne forgetfull of ony kyndness or servyce done to her before, which is no lytel part of veray nobleness. She was not vengeable, ne cruell; but redy anone to forgete and to forgyve injuryes done unto her, at the leest desyre or mocyon made unto her for the same. Mercyfull also and pyteous she was unto such as was grevyed and wrongfully troubled, and to them that were in Poverty, or sekeness, or ony other mysery.

To God and to the Chirche full obedient and tractable. Serchynge his honour and plesure full besyly. Awareness of her self she had alway to eschewe every thyng that myght dishonest ony noble woman, or disdayne her honour in ony condycyon.

Margaret was the highest ranking of Margaret Beauchamp's children from her three marriages, and she ensured that her daughter was raised to be aware of her status. Fisher felt that Margaret was a credit to her mother, declaring that she 'was a veray Doughter in all [noble manners]'. The shadow of her wardship must have hung over her early childhood however, and early in 1450, the Duke of Suffolk finally decided to make clear his plans for her.

During the early years of Henry VI's reign, his leading councillors had been his uncle, Humphrey, Duke of Gloucester, and his great uncle, Cardinal Beaufort. Beaufort had virtually retired from court before his death in April 1447, making room for Suffolk to increase his influence. Gloucester, who was disliked by his nephew, the King, also found his influence increasingly marginalised in the early years of the 1440s, and on 10 February, he was suddenly arrested and was found dead a few days later. Although Gloucester's death was announced to have been due to natural causes, it was widely rumoured that Suffolk had ordered his murder. When, shortly afterwards, Normandy fell whilst under the control of Margaret's uncle, Edmund Beaufort, who was Suffolk's ally, Suffolk became increasingly disliked.

By early 1450, Suffolk was aware that he was deeply unpopular, and on 28 January, the commons in parliament ordered his arrest and imprisonment in the Tower of London. He had originally intended to marry his eldest son, John de la Pole, to the wealthy heiress of the Earl of Warwick, whose wardship he had secured at a similar time to Margaret's. The Warwick heiress's early death threw these plans into disarray, and at some point between 28 January and 7 February 1450, in an attempt to increase his support and ensure that his family continued to benefit from Margaret's lands, he brought the two children together to be married. At the time of the marriage, John de la Pole was eight years old and Margaret only six, and the couple never lived together as husband and wife. Instead, it is likely that, once the ceremony had been performed, Margaret was returned to her mother's custody whilst Suffolk attempted to salvage his position as the most powerful man in England. Margaret was given no choice in the marriage, and it is possible that she never fully understood the ceremony that was performed, later referring to her second husband, Edmund Tudor, as her first. Whilst the marriage remained unconsummated and both children were below the age of consent, the marriage was, in any event, voidable, although Suffolk did go to the trouble of obtaining a dispensation from the Pope due to the blood relationship between Margaret and John.

Suffolk arranged the marriage solely in an attempt to secure the best possible match for his son, but this was not how many in England viewed it. By 1450, the English royal family was severely depleted and Henry VI had no children, siblings, first cousins or uncles remaining. In order to find a successor for the King from the house of Lancaster, it was necessary to look once again at the children of John of Gaunt, and assuming that the Beauforts were legally able to inherit the crown, this meant the descendants of John Beaufort, 1st Earl of Somerset. Margaret, as the only child of the 1st Duke of Somerset (the eldest son of the 1st earl to marry and produce a child), was potentially the heir to the throne after Henry VI, and this did not go unnoticed by Suffolk's opponents in England.

By ordering the marriage, Suffolk played into his enemies' hands. In early February, the commons prepared a bill of impeachment against the hated minister, accusing him of treason. The first charge claimed that Suffolk had conspired with the French to organise an invasion of England to destroy Henry VI:

> To the entente to make John, sonne of the same Duke, [King] of this your seid realme, and to depose you of your heigh regalie therof; the same Duke of Suffolk havyng thenne of your graunte the ward and mariage of Margarete, doughter and heire of John, the late Duke of Somerset, purposing here to marey to heis said sonne, presuming and pretendyng her to be nexte enheritable to the Corone of this your realme, for lak of issue of you Soverayn Lord, in accomplishement of heis seid traytours purpose and entent, wheroppon the same Duke of Suffolk, sith the tyme of his areste, hath do the seid Margarete to be maried to heis seid sonne.

Suffolk was further accused of handing France back to Henry's uncle, Charles VII of France, and giving the county of Maine to the Queen's father, the titular King of Sicily. The charge that Suffolk intended to place his son on the throne through his marriage to Margaret was the chief article laid against him, and it is clear that Margaret's position as the most likely heir to the House of Lancaster was widely known. The charges against Suffolk were clearly absurd, and whilst he was guilty of covetousness and mismanagement of the King's affairs, it is implausible that he would have conspired with the French king. The only precedent for a female sovereign in England had been the attempt of Henry I's daughter, the Empress Matilda, to assert herself as queen of England in the twelfth century, and whilst Matilda's son did eventually successfully press her claim, the empress's attempts to wear the crown had ushered in nearly two decades of civil war with her cousin, King Stephen. In his answer to the charges, Suffolk denied that Margaret was the heir to the throne and declared that his motivations for the marriage were merely financial and that he had hoped to marry his son to the wealthier heiress to the Earl of Warwick, only to be thwarted by her early death.

Margaret was still a young child at the time of Suffolk's impeachment, but her mother and those around her cannot but have been alarmed at the mention of her name in connection with his alleged treason. Suffolk put up a spirited defence to the charges against him, declaring that he would be heard by the King, and whilst the charges, if proved, would have merited death, the King instead ordered that Suffolk be banished from the realm for five years. Suffolk's banishment was a lenient sentence and one that was likely to have been ordered for his own protection, in the hope that, after a period in exile, the public resentment towards him would have been forgotten. On the eve of his departure from England on 30 April, Suffolk wrote a moving letter to his son, commanding him to obey the King and his mother in all things and to follow God's law, finishing

and last of alle, as hertily and as lovyngly as ever fader blessed his chld in erthe, I yeve you the blessyng of oure Lord and of me, which of his infynite mercy encrece you in alle vertu and good lyvyng. And that youre blood may by his grace from kynrede to kynrede multeplye in this erthe to hys servise, in such wyse as after the departyng from this wreched world here, ye and thei may glorefye hym eternally amongs his aungelys in hevyn.

Interestingly, the sons of John de la Pole would eventually attempt to lay claim to the crown, but this was not through Margaret Beaufort. Suffolk left for an exile in Flanders early in May 1450, but shortly after setting sail, his ship was intercepted by a privateer's ship, the *Nicholas of the Tower*. Suffolk was greeted with the words 'welcom, Traitor' and taken aboard the second vessel. After a mock trial by the sailors, he was beheaded with a rusty sword. His body was abandoned on the beach near Dover.

Suffolk's murder shocked England, and it must have appeared suddenly very dangerous to Margaret's mother for her daughter to be married to Suffolk's son and heir. In spite of this, Henry VI and his queen Margaret of Anjou retained their affection for the duke, and they continued to show favour to the family. Margaret remained with her mother throughout the duration of her marriage to John de la Pole, and she was a wife in name only. Finally, in early 1453, Lady Fortune span her wheel again, and she was summoned to court for the first time in order for her future to be decided.

3

SECOND MARRIAGE: 1453-1456

Following the Duke of Suffolk's murder, Margaret remained with her mother. The King did not, at first, show any interest in Margaret, although, with Suffolk's death, her wardship had once again passed to the crown. This changed in February 1453, when Margaret's mother was commanded to come to court, bringing her daughter with her in her train. For Margaret, the summons meant that Fortune's Wheel was about to turn again.

Margaret was still only nine years old at the time of the summons, and it would have been her first visit to court. On 23 April 1453, she and her mother attended the St George's Day celebrations of the Order of the Garter at Windsor Castle, and this may have been Margaret's first sight of the King. Henry VI was never the most prepossessing of kings, and his own wife, Margaret of Anjou, had failed to recognise him at their first meeting when he attended her dressed as a squire. In spite of this, he was a kindly figure and may have met with the young Margaret personally. Henry VI was certainly interested in his young cousin, and on 12 May 1453, he made her a grant of 100 marks to spend on clothes – a vast sum at the time. On the same occasion, he also granted Margaret's wardship to his half-brothers, Edmund and Jasper Tudor.

By the early 1450s, Henry VI had little close kin, and he began to show an increased interest in the children of his mother, Catherine of Valois. Catherine of Valois was the youngest daughter of Charles VI of France, and Henry V had demanded marriage to her as part of his attempt to win the French throne. The French had initially resisted Henry's demands, but after his successful military campaign, the marriage was agreed, in 1420, along with Charles VI's confirmation of Henry as his heir, an agreement that disinherited his son, the Dauphin. The couple married in May 1420, and early the next year, Catherine visited England for the first time. She remained in her husband's kingdom for the rest of the year, giving birth to the future Henry VI on 6 December 1421 before rejoining her husband in France the following May. With Henry V's early death on 31 August 1422, Catherine, who was only twenty-one, was left without a role in England, as her husband had declined to appoint her as either regent or guardian for their son. Nonetheless, she returned to England with the King's body and took up residence with her son. During the early years of the reign, she remained with him and she was an important figure in his upbringing, only obtaining her own household in 1430, when he was eight years old.

At some point either before or after she established her own household, Catherine secretly married a young Welshman who was in her service, Owen Tudor. Details of the marriage are scant, but one story claims that Owen, who was considerably beneath Catherine socially, first came to her attention when he fell into her lap during a dance. Another story suggested that Catherine caught sight of Owen whilst he was swimming and, attracted to him, asked to meet with him secretly. The marriage only became common knowledge after Catherine's death at Bermondsey Abbey on 3 January 1437, when she was discovered to have borne her husband four children: Edmund, Jasper, Owen and an unnamed daughter who died in her infancy. The younger Owen Tudor eventually became a monk. His two brothers were sent to be raised by Katherine de la Pole, the sister of the Duke of Suffolk, at Barking Abbey, where they were prepared for life as gentlemen. Their half-brother, Henry VI, was fond of them and, once they were adults, took them into his household. In 1452, he created his elder half-brother, Edmund, Earl of Richmond, and his younger half-brother, Jasper, Earl of Pembroke. He was also generous in his treatment of them, and when, in 1455, parliament passed an Act annulling any wardships granted in the previous five years in order to return revenue to the crown, Henry specifically exempted from this any wardships granted to the queen 'or of any Graunte made unto Edmond Erle of Richemond, and to Jasper Erle of Pembroke, of the kepyng of the Londes and Tenements and of the Heire of John late Duke of Somerset; and of the Mariage of Margarete Doughter and Heire of the seid late Duke'. Henry VI wanted to ensure that Margaret's future remained solely at the disposal of his half-brothers, whom he considered to be his closest kin.

By granting Margaret's wardship to his half-brothers, it is certain that the King intended a marriage between one of them and Margaret. In 1453, Edmund Tudor was aged around twenty-two, and as the elder brother, it was he who decided to marry Margaret in 1455, shortly after her twelfth birthday. Margaret later told her chaplain, John Fisher, that she was given a choice as to whether to marry John de la Pole (to whom she was actually already married) or Edmund Tudor:

She which as then was not fully nine years old, doubtfull in her mynde what she were best to do, asked counsayle of an old Gentlewoman whom she moche loved and trusted, which dyde advyse her to commend her self to St Nicholas the patron and

helper of all true maydens, and to beseche him to put in her mynde
what she were best to do. This counsayle she follow'd, and made
her Prayer so, full often; by specially that nyghte when she sholde
the morrowe after make answare of her mynde determynately. A
mervaylous thyng! that same nyght, as I have herde her tell many
a tyme, as she lay in Prayer, calling upon St Nicholas, whether
slepynge or wakeynge she could not assure, but about four of
the clocke in the mornynge, one appered unto her arrayed like a
Byshop, and naming unto her Edmonde, bad take hyme unto her
Husbande. And so by this meane she did enclyne her mynde unto
Edmonde, the Kyng's Broder, and Erle of Rychemonde.

Margaret was close to Fisher later in her life, and it is likely that
she genuinely believed that she had been told by a vision to accept
Edmund Tudor. It was fortunate, however, that she did indeed wish
to divorce her first husband and marry the King's half-brother, as,
in reality, she had no choice in the matter. It was Henry VI himself
who decided that Margaret should marry Edmund, and it is very
likely that, early in 1453, he was motivated by Margaret's royal
blood. Margaret's strong claim to be the heir to the Lancastrian
dynasty was well known, and Henry almost certainly considered
Edmund to be the best possible successor to the crown in the event
that he died childless.

Whilst Henry VI selected Edmund Tudor as a possible successor
through his marriage to Margaret, such a provision quickly became
unnecessary, and in the spring of 1453, the Queen, Margaret of
Anjou, announced her first pregnancy after several years of childless
marriage. Whilst this should have been a moment for Henry VI to
consolidate his position as King of England, public discontent at
his kingship soon began to gain momentum. On 16 July 1453, the

English army was decisively defeated at the Battle of Castillon by the French leaving the English in possession only of Calais on the Continent. This was a disaster for Henry VI, as, over the course of his thirty year reign, he had succeeded in losing an entire kingdom. He was devastated, and the news triggered an attack of a mental disorder that he had inherited from his grandfather, Charles VI of France, who was famously considered to be insane for much of his life. On 15 August 1453, Henry complained that he felt unusually tired, and he retired to bed early. According to *Whethamstede's Register*, during the night, 'a disease and disorder of such a sort overcame the king that he lost his wits and memory for a time, and nearly all his body was uncoordinated and out of control that he could neither walk, nor hold his head upright, nor easily move from where he sat'. Whilst seemingly conscious, Henry was unable to take in anything around him. On 13 October 1453, whilst he was still unresponsive, his wife gave birth to her only child in London, a son whom she named Edward.

Henry VI remained in an unresponsive state for some months and, disastrously for the Queen and her supporters, was unable to recognise the prince as his son. According to one contemporary account, Margaret of Anjou made strenuous efforts to secure the King's recognition of the child, aware that there were rumours that her pregnancy had been the result of an extramarital affair with Margaret Beaufort's uncle, Edmund Beaufort, Duke of Somerset:

> As touchyng tythynges, please it you to wite that at the Princes coming to Wyndesore, the Duc of Buk' toke hym in his armes and presented hym to the Kyng in godely wise, besechyng the Kyng to blisse hym; and the Kyng gave no answere. Natheless the Duk abode stille with the Prince by the Kyng; and whan he coude no

maner answere have, the Quene come in, and toke the Prince in hir armes and presented hym in like forme as the Duke had done, desiryng that he shuld blisse it; but alle their labour was in veyne, for they departed thens without any answere or counteaunce saving only yay ones he loked on the Prince and caste doune his eyene ayen, without any more.

By February 1454, when it was clear that the King's illness would be a long one, the Queen attempted to secure the regency, only for parliament to instead appoint Henry's cousin, Richard, Duke of York, as protector. York, who, like both Henry VI and Margaret Beaufort, was a descendant of Edward III, was an enemy of Margaret's uncle, Somerset, who had replaced Suffolk as the King's chief minister. York ordered Somerset's imprisonment in the Tower, and he was only released when Henry finally began to recover his wits at the end of 1454. He was able to wrest back authority from York, but it is clear that Henry's recovery was only a partial one, and his Queen, Margaret of Anjou, emerged as the real power behind the throne.

Margaret Beaufort's whereabouts are unrecorded during the period of her wardship with the Tudor brothers, although it is likely that she remained with her mother, continuing her education. Margaret's sympathies during the early years of the Wars of the Roses, which involved a dispute between the rival houses of Lancaster and York, would naturally have been with the King, her own close kinsman, and her uncle, the Duke of Somerset. She therefore cannot but have been alarmed when she heard that her uncle had been killed fighting against the Duke of York at the first Battle of St Albans in late May 1455 or that the King had been returned to York's custody and a second protectorate declared.

Events did not, however, directly affect her, and whilst her value as a potential royal claimant had been devalued to some extent by the birth of Prince Edward, she was still a wealthy heiress, and she was married to Edmund Tudor in November 1455.

Edmund Tudor is a shadowy character and little is known about his life. His tomb, which was originally in the House of Grey Friars at Carmarthen but was moved to St David's Cathedral following the dissolution of the monasteries, is marked by a brass showing an unprepossessing young man wearing armour. This is the only known representation of Margaret's second husband, although it was not made in his lifetime, instead being produced during the reign of the couple's son, Henry VII. Edmund's epitaph also gives little detail about his life, merely declaring that 'under this marble stone here inclosed resteth the bones of that most noble lord Edmond Earl of Richmond father and brother to kings, the which departed out of this world in year of our lord God MCCCCLVI the third of the month of November: on whose soul Almighty Jesu have mercy'.

It is possible that Margaret Beaufort and Edmund Tudor might have been rather more closely related than previously realised. Edmund Tudor's birth was veiled in considerable secrecy, and he was not born in one of Catherine of Valois's own properties, with the Queen instead travelling to Much Hadham, a manor belonging to the Bishop of London in order to give birth in the greatest possible privacy. The name Edmund was an odd choice for Catherine of Valois and Owen Tudor and deserves some further comment. Before her relationship with Owen Tudor began, Catherine had been romantically linked with Margaret Beaufort's uncle, Edmund Beaufort, the future Duke of Somerset, and the pair had hoped to marry. Any man that Catherine married would become the King's stepfather, with a good claim to the regency during his minority. Beaufort was a controversial choice amongst the King's council, which was already deeply divided by a dispute between the King's uncle, the Duke of Gloucester, and his great uncle, Cardinal Beaufort. In 1426, parliament made a formal request to the regency council that they cease their refusals to allow Catherine to remarry. It is likely that Catherine petitioned parliament for their aid herself. Henry VI's council was determined to prevent Catherine from making any new marriage, and in the parliament of 1429 to 1430, a statute was passed legislating on the remarriage of dowager queens. The new law ordered that anyone who dared marry the Queen without the King's express permission would have his lands and property confiscated and effectively meant that Catherine could not remarry until Henry VI obtained his majority. This put an end to Beaufort's ambition to marry the Queen, but given the choice of the name Edmund for her eldest son by her second marriage, it is possible that she and Beaufort had already been lovers and that her relationship with Owen Tudor, a man of such low status that the advantages of a marriage to the Queen far outweighed the risks, may have proved necessary in order to ensure that Catherine did not bear an illegitimate child. This can only be speculation, but the choice of name is suggestive. Catherine certainly retained links with the Beaufort family during the rest of her life, and Cardinal Beaufort is known to have visited her at Waltham soon after Christmas 1430. She also had links with Thomas Chaucer, a descendant of Katherine Swynford's sister.

It is therefore not impossible that Margaret and her second husband might have been first cousins, although, if this was the case, it was not commented upon by contemporaries. Both Edmund and Jasper Tudor supported the Duke of York in his first protectorate, and during that period, Edmund received a grant of the manor and lordships of Kendal and Weresdale by parliament, although Jasper was present with the King at the first Battle of St Albans. York, Margaret and a number of other leading members of the nobility were also the co-heirs to the estates of the Earldom of Kent through their descent from the Holland family, and in 1455, Margaret and Edmund, along with York and the other co-heirs, co-petitioned the King in relation to the manors of Collingham and Bardsley and the advowson of the church in Middleton, which were part of the inheritance. This again suggests some degree of co-operation between the King's half-brothers and his Protector. In 1455, Edmund was sent to Wales to act as Henry VI's representative there, and it is likely that he took Margaret with him as his wife. Although, at twelve, Margaret was considered old enough to marry, she was physically small and underdeveloped and, to her contemporaries, would not have been considered ready to consummate her marriage. Legally, where a man married an heiress in the medieval period, he received a life interest in her estates once he had fathered a child by her. This almost certainly informed Edmund's decision to marry Margaret once she reached the age of twelve, and to the indignation of his contemporaries, he immediately consummated the marriage, with Margaret falling pregnant during the first half of 1456, traditionally whilst the couple were staying at Caldicot Castle in the Welsh Marches. The early consummation of the marriage shows an unpleasant side of Edmund Tudor's character, and it is clear that he was acquisitive to the point of disregarding his young wife's health and wellbeing. His actions placed her life, and the life of her child, in danger. Margaret's thoughts on the early consummation of her marriage can also be seen in her vocal opposition to the early marriage of her granddaughter and namesake, Princess Margaret.

She spoke of her concern that young Margaret's husband 'would not wait, but injure her, and endanger her health'. Margaret spoke from experience.

As it happened, Edmund Tudor was not destined to ever see his child. On 10 August 1456, he was captured at Camarthen Castle by Sir William Herbert, an ally of the Duke of York, and imprisoned. He was released soon afterwards but died at Carmarthen on 1 November 1456 after contracting the plague. Margaret was only thirteen at the time of her husband's early death and heavily pregnant. She was also acutely aware that, by virtue of her relationship to the Lancastrian dynasty, she was a figure of importance in the Wars of the Roses, and, in terror of her own life and that of her child, she immediately sought protection with her brother-in-law, Jasper Tudor, as she awaited the birth of her child.

4

MARGARET'S FIRST WIDOWHOOD: NOVEMBER 1456-JANUARY 1458

Edmund Tudor's sudden death came as a shock to Margaret, and she later admitted that she was terrified that she and her unborn child would also succumb to the plague. At the age of only thirteen, she found herself alone and unprotected in Wales whilst the dispute between the King and the Duke of York raged, and she took the only practical course, immediately travelling to her brother-in-law, Jasper Tudor, at Pembroke Castle to seek his protection.

Few houses in which Margaret lived survive, and Pembroke Castle, which can still be visited today, is therefore of interest. A near contemporary of Margaret's, the sixteenth-century antiquary John Leland, provided a description of the town and the castle, and from this, it is easy to see why Margaret felt secure there. According to Leland, the town was 'well waullid and hath iii Gates by Est, West and North'. The castle dominated the town and

stondith hard by the Waul on a hard Rokke, and is veri larg and strong, being doble wardid. In the utter Ward I saw the Chaumbre wher King Henri the VII was borne, in Knowlege wherof a Chymmeney is new made with the Armes and Badges of King Henri the VII. In the Botom of the great strong rownd Tower in the inner Ward is a mervelus Vault caullid the Hogan. The toppe of this round Towr is gatherid with a Rose of stone

almost in conum, the Top wherof is Keverid with a flat Mille
Stone.

According to tradition, Margaret was lodged in a chamber in the
outer ward of the castle, and it was there, on 28 January 1457, that
she gave birth to her first child: a son.

Margaret's son was born more than three months after his father's
death, and Margaret must have spent an anxious few months
awaiting the birth. The last few months of 1456 saw her fortunes at
their lowest ebb. Aged only thirteen, she had reason to be anxious
about the birth; pregnancy in a girl so young was generally looked
upon with disapproval. Margaret endured a long and arduous
labour, during which it was expected that both she and the child
would die. For Margaret, who was a pious woman, it may have
seemed miraculous that both she and her son survived, and she later
came to look back on the day of her son's birth as one of the best of
her life, reminiscing in a letter that she wrote to Henry VII after he
had become king, 'At Calais town, this day of St Anne's, that I did
bring into this world my good and gracious prince, king, and only
beloved son.' In the same letter, Margaret also referred to her son
as 'my dearest and only desired joy in this world' and, in an earlier
letter, declared that Henry was her 'own sweet and most dear King,
and all my worldly joy'. Margaret became utterly devoted to her son
from the moment that he was born, and this may have been due to
the fear that she felt after being widowed during her pregnancy and
the dangers of the birth. Whilst she was grateful to survive, however,
it is believed that the birth itself damaged Margaret, as there is no
record that she ever conceived another child, something that was
commonly attributed to her youth at the time of Henry VII's birth.

Margaret was living with her brother-in-law, Jasper Tudor, at the time of the birth, and it appears that he sought to influence her decisions regarding her son. The sixteenth-century Welsh chronicler Elis Gruffydd claimed that, at his baptism, Margaret's son was named Owen, and this was almost certainly Jasper's choice, as a tribute to his father, Owen Tudor, who was then still alive. It is likely that the first Margaret heard about the choice of name was at the baptism, and in this incident, it is possible to see her forceful and strong-willed character for the first time. The chronicler records that Margaret, on hearing the name, ordered the bishop conducting the christening to baptise her son again, this time with the name Henry. For Margaret, whose ancestry was, for the most part, English, Owen may have seemed an unsuitable name for her son, but she also had a practical reason for her choice of name. By naming her son after his uncle, King Henry VI, who was probably also his godfather, Margaret ensured that he had a powerful protector and firmly linked her child to his royal Valois family, rather than to his less prestigious Tudor kin.

During the reign of Henry VII, a number of attempts were made to stress Owen Tudor's noble lineage as a means of demonstrating that the members of the Tudor dynasty were as well born as their predecessors on the throne. Owen Tudor had indeed come from a prominent Welsh family, although he was not of princely rank. In spite of this, during Henry VII's reign, it was rumoured that Owen had been a descendant of the ancient kings of Britain, and it was with reference to this that Henry named his eldest son Arthur, as a reminder of the mythical British King Arthur. Jasper Tudor was proud of his family and birth, and in his Will, which he wrote during the reign of Henry VII, he left a sum of money for four priests to pray for 'the wele of my soul, and for the soul of my father; as also for the souls of Katherine, sometime Queen of England, my mother,

Edmund late Earl of Richmond my brother, and the souls of others my predecessors'. Henry Tudor never met any of the people to whom his uncle referred in his Will, but he benefitted his Tudor kin when he was in a position to do so. Whilst he was king, Henry VII ordered that ceremonies be kept to commemorate his father at Westminster Abbey annually on 3 November, and he also granted a yearly sum to the grey friars of Carmarthen in order for them to carry out a daily chantry mass for his father's soul. Henry VII also aided more distant members of the family. After his accession, he knighted his uncle, David Owen, an illegitimate son of Owen Tudor, and arranged for him to marry a Sussex heiress. The third son of Owen Tudor and Catherine of Valois, who became a monk in childhood, also received some benefit from his kingly nephew, and in his accounts for 1498, Henry VII recorded a payment of £2 'to Owen Tudder' as a reward. In 1502, he paid over three pounds 'to Morgan Kidwells for burying of Owen Tudder'. Henry always identified with his paternal family to some extent. It was, however, Margaret who would be the dominant family influence on Henry's life.

As a widow at the time of Henry's birth, Margaret was able to focus her attention fully on her son. Her feelings for Edmund Tudor are unclear, but it is unlikely that she had ever been in love with her husband, who was considerably older than her. Margaret had reason to worry about her child, as, according to his contemporary biographer Bernard Andreas, Henry was a delicate child. Andreas claimed that Margaret was devoted to raising Henry and that she kept him with her in an attempt to help build up his strength. For the most part, she and her son remained at Pembroke Castle, and they would often have been in each other's company. Margaret would have attended to Henry's early education, although, given his young age, she must also have found other ways to occupy herself.

Margaret was still only thirteen when Henry was born, but it is likely that his birth, coupled with the shock of the loss of her husband, caused her to grow up rapidly. Jasper Tudor did not marry until near the end of his life, and Margaret, as the highest ranking lady at Pembroke Castle, would have taken on the role of mistress of the household. In her later life, Margaret developed a great reputation for piety and charity, and it is likely that this was an interest of hers from early in her life.

Most details of Margaret's character come from her later life, but it is likely that, even during her first widowhood, she had begun to develop into one of the strongest-willed women of her time. In Margaret's funeral sermon preached by John Fisher, the bishop compared his patron to the Biblical Martha, claiming that she resembled her in a number of aspects of her life. Fisher first compared Margaret to Martha, who was the sister of Lazarus whom Jesus brought back from the dead, in relation to her noble birth and noble character. He claimed that Margaret was

bounteous and lyberal to every Person of her Knowledge or acquaintance. Avarice and Covetyse she most hated, and sorowed it full moche in all persons, but specially in ony that belong'd unto her. She was also of syngular Easyness to be spoken unto, and full curtayse answere she would make to all that came unto her. Of mervayllous gentyleness she was unto all folks, but specially unto her owne whom she trusted and loved ryghte tenderly. Unkynde she wolde not be unto no creature, ne forgetfull of ony kyndness or servyce done to her before, which is no lytel part of veray nobleness. She was not vengeable, ne cruell; but redy anone to forgete and to forgyve injuryes done unto her, at the leest desyre or mocyon made unto her for the same. Mercyfull also and pyteous she was unto such as was grevyed and wrongfully troubled, and to them that were in Poverty, or sekeness, or ony other mysery.

John Fisher, who admired Margaret and, in his earlier years, had depended on her patronage, obviously presented a very favourable picture of her. Little evidence survives of Margaret's character before she came to prominence during the reign of Richard III, but her decisive action following the death of her second husband, Edmund Tudor, demonstrate that she was determined. As events surrounding Margaret's third marriage show, she also had an independence of spirit, although, as John Fisher said, Margaret was loyal to her kin and helped them throughout her life, particularly in her promotion of her son. From the surviving evidence, it is also fair to say that she was not vengeful or cruel, although Fisher certainly omits some of the less attractive sides of her character. It is apparent, for example, that Henry VII's renowned acquisitiveness was a trait that he inherited from his mother.

Whilst Fisher ignored some of the more forceful aspects of Margaret's personality, he went into great detail about her piety, for which she was famous. Margaret was devout and, given her mother's own well-known devoutness, it is likely that this developed in her youth. Fisher claimed that she was 'to God and to the Chirche full obedient and tractable'. It is also possible to see something of Margaret's beliefs in the work that she chose to translate and publish after her son's accession. Her most famous translation project, *The Myrroure of Golde,* was divided into seven chapters, one for each day of the week. Chapter four in particular, which is headed 'How we ought to dispise and hate the worlde', perhaps best shows something of the rules by which Margaret attempted to live, and she was later renowned for her ascetic lifestyle. According to the book, which, although not written by Margaret, was chosen by her as a suitable work to translate into English from French, 'Saint John in his first canonyque shewyth us that we ought not to love the worlde ne the thingis that be in the worlde, and saithe in this maner, love ye not the worlde ne thingys that be therin, yf there be any that loveth the worlde the charite of God is not with hym'.

Margaret took her religious devotion beyond the more conventional piety of some of her peers, and Henry Parker, who was a member of her household during the last decade of her life, later recorded that 'her grace wolde often say, at her table when she heard that the great turke preuayled so aganest the crysten men, she wolde wyshe that she were a launder to them that shoulde go against them'. Margaret was charitable, and whilst much of her work would have been carried out in the last half of her life when her son was king, she had always been a wealthy woman, and it is likely that she was already engaged in benevolent activities in her youth. Fisher claimed that Margaret was responsible for the maintenance of twelve poor people and that she gave them lodging, food and clothing. She also visited them when they were ill to comfort them and help tend to them. She supported priests and is remembered as the foundress of an alms house built for women near the Chapel of St Anne at Westminster.

Although Margaret was constantly aware of the dangers of the political situation in England, at Pembroke, she would have been shielded from much of what was happening, and spending time with her son, the year after his birth might have been amongst the most peaceful of her life. As a widow and a wealthy heiress, however, Margaret knew that her peace was unlikely to last and that there was a constant danger that the King would force a new husband upon her. Within weeks of Henry's birth, Margaret had already decided to take decisive action, and by March or April of 1457, she had arranged her third marriage and promised that it would take place once the prescribed year of mourning for Edmund Tudor had come to an end. Unusually, Margaret selected her third husband herself, with only the advice of her brother-in-law, Jasper Tudor, to guide her.

5

THIRD MARRIAGE: 1458-1470

Although, with Henry's birth, Margaret had an heir for her estates, as a wealthy widow, she was still an attractive proposition. Any man that she married could look forward to a life interest in her lands, and it was only a matter of time before she married for a third time. Margaret was very aware that a husband was likely to be selected for her, as had happened on two previous occasions, if she did not take decisive action herself.

The obvious candidate for Margaret's third husband would have been Jasper Tudor, with whom she lived and who had an active interest, as Henry's uncle, in providing for his welfare. It is unclear whether this possibility ever crossed Margaret's and Jasper's minds, but if it did, they took no steps to try to achieve the marriage. Such a marriage would have placed the pair firmly within the forbidden degrees of consanguinity as far as the Church was concerned, as, through Margaret's marriage to Edmund, she and Jasper had become officially brother and sister. Such a prohibition was not insurmountable, and dispensations could be, and often were, obtained from the Church to allow a match. Margaret's own grandson, Henry VIII, for example, would later obtain a similar dispensation to marry his brother's widow, Catherine of Aragon. Given the fact that Margaret had borne Edmund a child, it is likely that the relationship between Margaret and Jasper would have been considered additionally close. There was therefore no guarantee that they would have received a dispensation, and if they ever thought of the match, they may have considered that the difficulties were too great to be ignored. Alternatively, they may simply have had no interest in marriage to each other, although it is very unlikely that Margaret met her third husband much before their wedding. Love, physical attraction and compatibility were very far from Margaret's thoughts when she began to contemplate a third marriage only weeks after the birth of her son, and both she and Jasper were determined to find her a husband who would protect Henry's interests.

Traditionally, women who had given birth underwent the ceremony of churching forty days after they had given birth, signalling their return to society. Henry was born on 28 January 1457, and in March, almost as soon as Margaret had been churched, she and Jasper travelled together from Pembroke to the Duke of Buckingham's manor of Greenfield, which was near Newport. Margaret and Jasper obviously felt that time was of the essence in the selection of her third husband, and they discussed the possibility of a match with the duke's second son, Henry Stafford. Terms were agreed quickly, and a dispensation for the marriage was granted on 6 April by the Bishop of Coventry and Lichfield.

Henry Stafford was around twenty years older than Margaret and in his early thirties when the match was arranged. As a younger son, he had little income, and a marriage with Margaret was an excellent one for him. Margaret is unlikely to have met Henry Stafford before the marriage was discussed, but she knew he was, in many ways, an appropriate choice for her. The couple were related twice. Stafford was a descendant of Thomas of Woodstock, the youngest son of Edward III and, like Margaret, he therefore had a claim to the throne. His mother, Anne Neville, was the daughter of Margaret's great aunt, Joan Beaufort, a considerably closer connection and one that meant that a dispensation was required. It is probable that Stafford was selected by Margaret and Jasper as a suitable husband due to the power of his father, Humphrey, Duke of Buckingham: he was the only peer in England who could hope to rival his brother-in-law, Richard, Duke of York.

The marriage had evidently been agreed by April when the dispensation was arranged, and it is likely that the terms of the marriage settlement were agreed at the same time. Details of these do not survive, but in his Will, which was made in August 1460, Stafford's father bequeathed 'to my son Henry cccc marks, to him and to my daughter Margaret, countess of Richmond, his wife'. It is likely that this 400 marks had been promised at the time of the marriage settlement and represented Henry Stafford's contribution to marital funds. It was a relatively small sum, and it is clear that Margaret's main motivation for the match was not financial support. Following the meeting at Greenfield, she returned to Pembroke Castle to spend the conventional year in mourning for Edmund Tudor and to start to raise her son. With the marriage agreed and with Buckingham's powerful protection, she was aware that there was no need to hurry the wedding.

Margaret finally married Henry Stafford on 3 January 1458, a few months before her fifteenth birthday. References to Henry Stafford, like those relating to so many important figures in Margaret's life, are scarce, as her third husband made little impact on the political situation in England. What evidence there is suggests that the marriage was a happy one. Both Margaret's parents-in-law referred to her as their daughter in their Wills, and whilst the Duke of Buckingham's bequest to his son and daughter-in-law was probably intended to fulfil his obligations under the couple's marriage contract, the bequest of Margaret's mother-in-law, which was of books to 'my daughter Richmond', was more personal. The Duchess of Buckingham was also fond enough of her daughter-in-law to lend her some of her valuable books, with accounts from Henry Stafford's receiver noting that Margaret ordered her servant, William Bailey, to return them, presumably when she had finished reading them. Henry Stafford's own Will survives; it was written after over thirteen years of marriage and shows the depth of feeling that existed between the couple:

Henry Stafford, knight, son to the noble Prince Humphrey, late Duke of Bucks, October 2d, 1471. My body to be buried in the College of Plecye. To buy xii marks worth of livelode by year, to be amortized for the finding of an honest and fitting priest to sing for my soul in the said college for evermore clx l.; to my son-in-law the Earl of Richmond, a trappur, four new horse harness of velvet; to my brother John Earl of Wiltshire, my bay courser; to Reynold Bray, my Receiver General, my grizzled horse; I bequeath the rest of my goods to my beloved wife Margaret Countess of Richmond, whom I likewise constitute my executrix.

Stafford's Will shows the regard in which he held Margaret, and it is likely that his reference to her as his 'beloved wife' was genuine. Margaret's feelings for Henry Stafford do not anywhere survive, but the marriage lasted considerably longer than her first two marriages, and she does appear to have been content. A further indication that the couple were close can be seen from the fact that they regularly travelled together. In the late 1460s, for example, they made a leisurely journey from the Midlands to London, stopping at a number of places on the way, including Huntingdon,

Royston, Ware and Waltham. The couple then spent three months in London before moving on to Woking, a manor that would become their main home together. The couple made regular visits to London throughout their marriage, as well as making progresses around their extensive estates, and it is clear, from this regular travel, that they enjoyed being in each other's company.

Soon after their marriage, Margaret and Henry Stafford set up home at Bourne in Lincolnshire, a manor that belonged to Margaret. This was a considerable distance from Pembroke, where Margaret had been living with her son. Although evidence is scant, it does not appear that she retained custody of her son. On 8 January 1458, in what was likely to have been a response to Margaret's marriage, Henry VI granted Henry Tudor's wardship jointly to Jasper Tudor and the Earl of Shrewsbury. Henry was certainly living at Pembroke Castle in 1461, and it is likely that he did not leave to live with his mother following her marriage, although it is clear that his mother and stepfather visited him. After a few years of marriage, Henry would also have taken on even greater significance for Margaret and Henry Stafford, as it would have become evident that they would have no children together. Stafford's bequest of some horse equipment to Margaret's son, which is one of only three bequests made to individuals, suggests that he was fond of his stepson and that he filled something of the gap left in Henry's life by the death of Edmund Tudor.

Stafford's accounts during the time of his marriage to Margaret show that he was often in ill health. He frequently sent to London for medicines, and there are a number of references to physicians in his records. He may have suffered from the condition St Anthony's Fire, which, in the fifteenth century, was considered to be a form of leprosy. This is suggested by the fact that he joined the confraternity of the leper hospital at Burton Lazars in Leicestershire. Margaret was also always devoted to St Anthony Abbott, the patron saint of those afflicted with skin complaints, and this, given that her devotion persisted into her later life, again suggests a fondness for her third husband that endured until well after his death. In spite of Stafford's ill health, the couple were able to regularly indulge in their favourite pastime of hunting, making a hunting trip, for example, in 1470 to the area around Windsor and Henley.

Margaret's marriage to Henry Stafford was, in part, a response to the troubled political climate in which she lived, and she sought a powerful protector for herself and her son. The dispute between the Houses of Lancaster and York continued to rage in the late 1450s. With Henry VI's illness in 1453 and 1454, his wife, Margaret of Anjou, emerged as the leader of the Lancastrian party in England, and her enemy, York's nephew by marriage, the Earl of Warwick, wrote in 1460 that 'our king is stupid and out of his mind; he does not rule but is ruled. The government is in the hands of the queen and her paramours'. Following the first Battle of St Albans, at which Margaret Beaufort's uncle, Edmund Beaufort, Duke of Somerset, had been killed, the King had been taken into York's custody and the duke had once again been declared protector. Margaret of Anjou continued to build up a powerbase, and in October 1458, after an attempt was made to assassinate Warwick in London, the earl fled to Calais where he began raising troops. His father, the Earl of Salisbury, headed north to raise an army there, whilst York went to Wales to muster support. Margaret of Anjou, determined to oppose them, went to Cheshire and began to raise troops under the banner of her son, the Prince of Wales.

Margaret Beaufort, as a member of the House of Lancaster and the sister-in-law of Henry VI, sympathised with the King, in spite of her kinship with York's wife, Cecily Neville, who was the daughter of her great aunt. Henry Stafford and his father were also connected to York through Cecily Neville, but they remained staunchly Lancastrian in their sympathies. In October 1459, Margaret of Anjou won a victory over the Yorkists when they fled in the face of her army in the Welsh Marches. In June 1460, her fortunes ebbed, and she was heavily defeated at the Battle of Northampton, at which the King was once again taken prisoner. The outcome of the battle was a disaster for the Lancastrian cause, and it also had personal consequences for Margaret and her husband. They received word that Henry Stafford's father, the Duke of Buckingham, had been killed in battle. This removed a powerful protector from the couple, and the duke was succeeded to his titles and estates by his five-year-old grandson, Henry Stafford's nephew Henry, 2nd Duke of Buckingham.

As a prisoner of the Yorkist party, Henry VI was taken to London. Success emboldened the Duke of York, and in October 1460, he returned to the capital. According to *Whethamstede's Register*,

The lord king [Henry VI] was assembled with the prelates, peers, and commons in parliament at Westminster, for the good government of the realm, soon, almost at the beginning of the parliament, the Duke of York, with the pomp of a great following, arrived in no small exultation of spirit; for he came with horns and trumpets and men at arms, and very many other servants. And entering the palace there, he marched straight through the great hall until he came to that solemn room where the king was accustomed to hold parliament with his commons. And when he arrived there, he advanced with determined step until he reached the royal throne, and there he laid his hand on the cushion or bolster, like a man about to take possession of his right, and kept his hand there for a short while. At last, drawing back, he turned his face towards the people, and standing still under the cloth of state, he looked attentively at the gazing assembly.

And while he stood there, looking down at the people, and awaiting their applause, Master Thomas Bourgchier, the Archbishop of Canterbury, came up, and, after a suitable greeting, asked him whether he wished to come and see the lord king. At this request the duke seemed to be irritated, and replied curtly in this way: 'I know of no person in this realm whom it does not behove to come to me and see my person, rather than I should go and visit him'.

York's conduct stunned those assembled, and it was a major departure from his previous actions. It was the moment that the course of the war turned from simply being concerned with dominance over the King and instead focused on who had the most right to wear the crown.

Richard, Duke of York, set out his claim to the throne to those who had assembled for the parliament. Although, on his paternal line, York was only a descendant of the fourth surviving son of Edward III, his maternal family was of more concern to the Lancastrian party. York's mother, Anne Mortimer, was the daughter of Roger Mortimer, Earl of March, who in turn had been the son of Philippa, the only child of Lionel of Antwerp, Duke of Clarence, the second son of Edward III. York's own father, Richard, Earl of Cambridge, had been executed in 1415 for plotting to put his brother-in-law, Edmund Mortimer, on the throne, and whilst the Mortimer claim had lain dormant since Edmund Mortimer's death, it had not been forgotten. Unlike France, England did not have the Salic law that barred a woman from either succeeding to the throne or transmitting her claim. Whilst, by the fifteenth century, no woman had successfully prosecuted a claim to the English throne, Henry II had claimed the throne through his mother in the twelfth century. There was therefore nothing in English law to bar first Philippa of Clarence and then her granddaughter, Anne Mortimer, from transmitting a valid claim to the throne.

Under the rules of heredity, there is no doubt that York had the strongest claim to the throne. However, Henry VI also had a strong claim, and according to his contemporary John Blacman, he set this out some years after York first stated his claim:

[When] King Henry was asked, during his imprisonment in the Tower, why he had unjustly claimed and possessed the crown of England for so many years, he would answer thus: 'My father was king of England and peaceably possessed the crown of England for the whole of his reign. And his father and my grandfather were kings of the same realm. And I, a child in the cradle, was peaceably and without any protest crowned and approved as king by the whole realm, and wore the crown of England some forty years, and each and all of my lords did me royal homage and plighted me their faith, as was also done to my predecessors.

For all his shortcomings as a king, Henry VI was still able to muster a considerable amount of support, and the idea of deposing him in 1460 was not popular. A compromise was therefore reached in which it was agreed that Henry VI would remain king for the duration of his life and that York would be his heir, disinheriting the Lancastrian Prince of Wales. York's triumph proved to be short-lived, and the Queen, on hearing of her son's disinheritance, marched north with an army of 20,000 men. On 31 December

1460, she met an army commanded by York and his brother-in-law, Salisbury, at Wakefield and won a great victory. York was killed during the course of the battle, whilst Salisbury, who was captured, was summarily executed. According to *Hall's Chronicle*, Margaret of Anjou could not resist displaying her triumph to the world, and her men 'came to the place wher the dead corps of the duke of Yorke lay, and caused his head to be stryken of, and set on it a croune of paper, and so fixed it on a pole, and presented it to the Quene'. Margaret had both York and Salisbury's heads set on poles above the gates of York before marching south in triumph.

Margaret of Anjou met a second Yorkist army at St Albans as she moved south, and she was once again victorious, taking possession of her husband, who had been taken out of London to appear as a puppet at the head of the Yorkist army. Outside London, however, Margaret of Anjou committed her greatest mistake, as she was persuaded not to enter the city by a deputation concerned by the damage that would be done by her army. Margaret instead moved north again, and within days, York's eldest son, Edward, Earl of March, had entered the capital and had himself declared king as Edward IV. On 29 March, Margaret of Anjou's army met the new king's in battle at Towton, and she was defeated. The Queen, her son and the hapless Henry VI were driven as fugitives towards Scotland.

The events of 1460 were dramatic and affected the lives of most people in England to some extent. Jasper Tudor remained loyal to his half-brother throughout the turmoil of the year, and in late January 1461, he moved towards the Herefordshire border raising troops in the company of his father, Owen Tudor. Whilst Edward IV concentrated his efforts on defeating Margaret of Anjou and the main Lancastrian army, he instructed his ally, Sir William Herbert to raise a force to face the Tudors. On 3 February 1461, the two armies met at Mortimer's Cross in Herefordshire in an engagement that proved to be disastrous for the Tudors. During the course of the battle, Owen Tudor was captured by Herbert and later executed on the orders of the Yorkist king. Jasper managed to escape and fled towards Pembroke Castle. Margaret, whose whereabouts during this period are not recorded, must have listened anxiously for news of all that was happening in Wales, and it is almost certain that the four-year-old Henry Tudor was present at Pembroke Castle during the turbulent events. Throughout much of the year, Jasper remained at large and loyal to his half-brother, but it soon became obvious that his position was unsustainable. On 30 September 1461, Pembroke Castle surrendered to Sir William Herbert, and the following month, Jasper sailed to Scotland to join Margaret of Anjou and Henry VI in their efforts to regain the English throne.

Margaret suffered troubles of her own during 1461, as both her husband, Henry Stafford, and her stepfather, Lord Welles, fought for Henry VI at Towton. If, as seems likely, Margaret's relationship with her third husband was a loving one, she must have been horrified to see him leave for battle, and it was a great relief when he returned to her unharmed, albeit as a member of the losing army. Margaret's mother did not prove so fortunate in her own husband, as Lord Welles fell in the field, leaving his widow to manage his estates on behalf of their young son, John. Margaret later secured an advantageous marriage for her youngest half-brother to Cecily of York, the daughter of Edward IV, and it is clear that she felt the same sense of responsibility towards him that she did for her elder St John half-siblings. He also paid her the compliment of making her one of the executors of his Will, demonstrating that the pair had a close relationship, and it is likely that Margaret was also grieved by her stepfather's death, as he must have played a prominent role in her early childhood. It was a relief for Margaret when, on 25 June 1461, Edward IV, who was in a mood to be conciliatory towards former Lancastrian supporters, granted Henry Stafford a pardon for opposing him at Towton, and whilst the couple would still have been uncertain about the favour in which they were held by the King, they were at least aware that Stafford would not face prosecution as a supporter of Henry VI.

Whilst Margaret was worried about herself, her husband, her mother and her half-siblings, her chief concern during 1461 would certainly have been her son. With the accession of Edward IV and Jasper Tudor's continued loyalty to the old Lancastrian regime, Henry's wardship had effectively lapsed, and when Sir William Herbert finally entered Pembroke Castle at the end of September, he found Henry Tudor there. Although he was a nephew of Henry VI, Henry Tudor was not closely related to him on the paternal line, and in 1461, with both Henry VI and his son still living, any Beaufort claim to the throne was remote. Henry Tudor therefore presented no political threat to the new king, and whilst his lands were taken away from him and given to the new king's brother George, Duke of Clarence, a blind eye was turned towards the continued use of his title as Earl of Richmond. Henry, at four years old, had caused no offence to the King, and attainders were often reversed, making it seem likely to his contemporaries that he would be restored to his lands and officially to his earldom at a later date.

Henry Tudor, both as his mother's heir and the potential heir to his father's confiscated lands, was a particularly valuable child. William Herbert took him into his custody and was later granted the boy's wardship for £1,000, a substantial sum and one that

4. Edward III from a drawing in St Stephen's Chapel. Margaret was descended from the king's third surviving son, John of Gaunt.

5. Philippa of Hainault, wife of Edward III, depicted in a drawing of a tapestry made during the reign of Edward III and which hung in St Stephens Chapel, Westminster until it was destroyed when the old Palace of Westminster burned down.

6. Richmond Palace. Henry VII built the palace to symbolise the might of the Tudor dynasty.

Left: 7. A line drawing by a French or Flemish artist of Henry VII. Margaret was only thirteen when she gave birth to Henry and they remained close in spite of his long exile in Brittany.

Opposite: 8. Plan of Westminster. Margaret spent much of her life in London and would have recognised many of the sites depicted in this near contemporary plan.

Great Hall,
by Wolsey, 15

Tennis court
G

Preaching
place

'Holbein' gate

Prevy by

King St Gate

Chamion row

Westmynster Hall (the seat of the law courts)

Starre Chamber

House of Commons
(formerly chapel of St Stephen's)
from 1547 until the fire of 1834

House of Lords

Court of Requests

The Queens bridge

Henry VII's chapel

9. A clasp from a prayer book belonging to Margaret Beaufort. Margaret was well known during her lifetime for both her piety and her love of books.

10. A youthful Margaret Beaufort.

Right: 11. Margaret Beaufort at prayer.

Below right: 12. A statue of St Nicholas from Westminster Abbey. Margaret was always devoted to St Nicholas and believed that he had directed her to divorce her first husband and marry Edmund Tudor in a vision.

Below left: 13. A statue of Henry VII in his coronation regalia from Westminster Abbey. Margaret wept at her son's coronation, terrified that some misfortune would follow her greatest triumph.

Top: 14. Edward V shown with his parents and uncle, Earl Rivers. The elder of the princes in the Tower was widely believed to have been murdered by his uncle, Richard III, shortly after he was deposed from the throne.

Left: 15. Perkin Warbeck, who claimed to be one of the missing princes in the Tower was a major threat to Henry VII's rule for a number of years.

16. Coronation of Henry VIII. Margaret made her last public appearance at her grandson's coronation.

17. The young Henry VIII. Henry was only seventeen when he succeeded to the throne and he relied on his grandmother's advice.

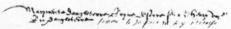

18. Margaret Tudor. Margaret's eldest granddaughter was named after her and she was always a particular favourite of hers.

19. & 20. The tombs of Henry VII and Elizabeth of York at Westminster Abbey. Margaret was devastated by the death of Henry VII, her only child, and she survived him by only a few months.

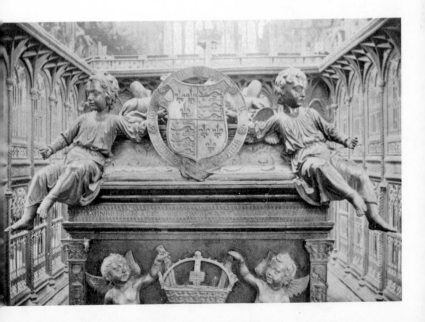

21. & 22. Henry VII's
Chapel at Westminster
Abbey. Henry VII
commissioned a fine chapel
in Westminster Abbey as his
lasting memorial.

23. Margaret Beaufort's tomb in Westminster Abbey. At her own request, Margaret was buried near her son Henry VII, in the chapel he built at Westminster.

24. Margaret Beaufort in later life. Margaret was well known for her piety and she chose to be depicted in a religious habit.

shows that Herbert was convinced of the future value of his young charge. Henry later told the chronicler Philip de Comines that 'from the time he was five years old he had been always a fugitive or a prisoner', and this certainly refers to his capture by Herbert at Pembroke Castle. If it was as a prisoner that Henry later came to see himself, it is unlikely that he was aware of this in 1461. Henry passed into the custody of Herbert's wife, Anne Devereux, who treated him as one of the family, and he was raised in a manner befitting a young nobleman. It is clear from Henry's own later conduct that he bore no grudge against his gaoler, and after he became king in 1485, Anne Devereux rushed to meet him. The meeting was obviously a success, and the King provided her with an escort for her return journey, highlighting that he must still have had some fond memories of his time with the Herberts, in spite of his later assertion that he was a prisoner. William Herbert and his wife also had a reason to invest their energies in Henry's upbringing, as they had a number of unmarried daughters. In his Will, written in 1468, Herbert stated, 'I will that Maud, my daughter, be wedded to the lord Henry of Richmond; Ann to Lord Powys; and Jane to Edmund Malafant; to Cecily, Katherine, and Mary, my daughters, MMD marks'. As a potential future son-in-law, it was in Herbert's interests to ensure that Henry was well raised regardless of the fact that, as a supporter of Edward IV who was granted Jasper Tudor's earldom of Pembroke, he was fundamentally opposed to the interests of the Tudor family. Henry was well educated, and there is some evidence that the Herberts employed two Oxford graduates, Edward Haseley and Andrew Scot, for this purpose, again suggesting that his 'imprisonment' was not as rigorous as he later implied.

Although she knew that she had permanently lost any rights in relation to her son, Margaret must have been glad that he fared no worse, especially given Jasper Tudor's continuing prominence with Margaret of Anjou and Henry VI in Scotland and the north of England. Margaret was also not barred from visiting Henry, and she and Henry Stafford kept in touch with him. They visited him at Raglan Castle in September 1467 when they were staying at their West Country estates. They made their way to the castle from Bristol and spent a week there. It is likely that the visit was the main reason for visiting the West Country, and it is clear that they were made welcome by the Herberts. Margaret apparently spent a happy week at the castle with her husband and son. The fact that the couple were able to accept William Herbert's hospitality suggests that Margaret accepted his custody of her son, even if she was not entirely happy with it. The chronicler Edward Hall later provided a description of Henry Tudor when he was in his late twenties, and during rare visits during the 1460s, Margaret would have slowly seen her son start growing into the man he would later become:

He was a man of no great stature, but so formed and decorated with all gyftes and lyniamentes of nature that he semed more an angelical creature then a terrestriall personage, his countenaunce and aspecte was cherefull and couragious, his heare yelow lyke the burnished golde, his eyes grey shynynge and quicke, prompte and ready in aunswerynge, but of suche sobrietie that it coulde neuer be iudged whyther he were more dull then quicke in speakynge (such was hys temperaunce).

Henry Tudor, like Margaret, was of a small build and their portraits in later life show a marked resemblance: both with long, thin faces and keen, searching eyes. Although Margaret had had very little contact with her son since his infancy, she always ensured that they remained in touch, and he remained her greatest focus.

Whilst Margaret was concerned about her son's welfare, she also had to ensure the welfare of her husband and herself following Edward IV's accession. Edward IV had been nearly nineteen at the time of his accession to the throne, and having seen the Wars of the Roses lead to the deaths of his father, younger brother, Edmund, Earl of Rutland, and a number of other members of his family, he was determined to be conciliatory in an attempt to bring the conflict to an end once and for all. Edward IV, whilst a shrewd ruler, was also a somewhat jovial character, inclined more to pleasure than politics. The new king had been received into London on a wave of public support, and a newsletter sent from London to Milan in April 1461 recorded that 'King Edward has become master and governor of the whole realm. Words fail me to relate how well the commons love and adore him, as if he were their God'. Edward's father, the Duke of York, had long been involved in a feud with Margaret's uncle, Edmund Beaufort, Duke of Somerset, and Edward IV was determined to prevent this continuing in the next generation, actively trying to make peace with Margaret's cousin, Henry Beaufort, Duke of Somerset. Somerset had travelled north with Henry VI and Margaret of Anjou following the Battle of Towton, but he finally surrendered to the King in 1462 and received an immediate pardon. Edward was determined to make a great show of his trust in Somerset, as demonstrated by *Gregory's Chronicle*:

[Early in 1463] the king made much of [Henry Beaufort, Duke of Somerset]; insomuch that he lodged with the king in his own bed

many nights, and sometimes rode hunting behind the king, the
king having about him no more than six horsemen at the most, and
three were men of the duke of Somerset.

Somerset's apparent support for the Yorkist cause was a major
coup for the King, and as further evidence of his determination
to honour Margaret's cousin, Edward decided to visit the north
of his kingdom in the summer of 1463 and appointed Somerset
and his men as his guards. According to *Gregory's Chronicle*, the
visit was not an entire success, and at Northampton, Somerset was
attacked by the people as a traitor to the King. It was only with
difficulty that Edward was able to save the life of his new ally, and
this incident terrified Margaret's cousin. Later that year, Somerset
secretly left the King and once again headed north to rejoin Henry
VI. He fought against the King's forces at Hedgeley Moor on 25
April 1464 and again at Hexham on 14 May 1464, where he was
defeated. Edward IV, although often kind and jovial, could be
ruthless when he was crossed, and he had Somerset summarily
executed following the battle as a warning to others that might
plan to betray him.

Although Henry Beaufort, Duke of Somerset, was the male head
of the Beaufort family at the time of Edward IV's accession, it was
well known that Margaret was the hereditary heiress, and both
she and Henry Stafford benefitted from the King's intention to
favour the Beauforts. They also soon had another link to the King
when Edward, who had announced that he had secretly married
a widow, Elizabeth Woodville, in 1464, married his sister-in-law,
Catherine Woodville to Stafford's nephew, the young Duke of
Buckingham. Although both parties were children at the time of
their marriage and it proved an unhappy union, it did serve to link

Margaret and Henry Stafford to the powerful Woodville family and to the King himself, as did the fact that Stafford was a first cousin of the new King through their mothers.

The King showed his favour towards Margaret and her husband in 1466, when he granted to them the manor at Woking in Surrey. This was a generous gift and the manor became a favourite home of the couple's. The manor had previously belonged to Henry Beaufort, Duke of Somerset, and provided a residence conveniently close to London. Unfortunately, little now remains of what was, for a time, Margaret's favourite residence, but during her lifetime, it was palatial. The large house was built around a courtyard. It was surrounded by a moat, and there were also orchards, gardens and a deer park. Margaret and Henry Stafford spent much of Edward IV's reign at the house, and the couple worked hard in managing their estates, and their household at Woking has been described as a small court, with nearly fifty servants in attendance, many of whom were gentlemen. The couple were renowned for their hospitality, and for their wedding anniversary on 31 January 1471, they feasted on curlew, plover and larks supplied by a London poulterer. It is apparent that the couple regularly celebrated their wedding anniversary, a further testament to the happy relationship between the pair.

Margaret and Henry Stafford were able to maintain a great state at Woking. They had an extensive household, as befitted their status as a couple with close links to court. On special occasions, they often sent to London for luxurious items, such as fresh lampreys and salmon. The household also consumed large amounts of white wine, with purchases recorded in their accounts. Margaret, as the mistress of the household, would have been largely responsible for organising the menus for special occasions, and many of the luxury items purchased reflected her own personal tastes. She and Henry Stafford also dressed to befit their rank. For example, their accounts show that fine velvet was purchased for a long gown for Henry Stafford to wear. Margaret always liked to appear well dressed and records of payments made in the 1470s (after Henry Stafford's death) for her clothing show her interest in rich fabrics, which, given Stafford's own interest in fine clothes, is likely to have been evident during her marriage to him and earlier. Her receiver recorded that sums were paid for furring a gown for her, an expensive process. She purchased a gown of velvet, as well as several yards of a tawny-coloured fabric for a kirtle. Margaret regularly sent to London for her clothes, the centre of fashion in England. In the accounts for the mid-1470s, it is clear that she took considerable trouble to look good, and she ordered that some cloth of velvet that she had purchased in London be sent to her at Lathom in Lancashire – a considerable distance. That she was able to do this was a mark of her status as a great lady. She further demonstrated this through the size and grandeur of her household, and she is recorded, again in the 1470s, to have purchased her New Year's gifts for the gentlewomen in her household from a London goldsmith.

For Margaret, daily life at Woking revolved around her religious observances. The funeral sermon preached for Margaret by John Fisher provides a snapshot of her life and character, which, although based on her last years, is also likely to be relevant to her earlier life. Fisher was renowned for his ascetic way of life, and this is likely to have been what attracted Margaret to him. As previously mentioned, in his sermon, Fisher spoke of the Biblical Martha, who was praised for chastising her body through abstinence, fasting, chastity and wearing 'sharp' clothes (i.e., a penitential hair shirt).

He then turned to Margaret:

> I wolde reherce somewhat of her demeanynge in this behalfe; her
> sober temperance in metes and drynkes was known to all them
> that were conversant with her, wherein she lay in as great wayte of
> her self as ony Person myghte, kepynge alway her strayte mesure,
> and offendynge as lytell as ony creature myghte: Escheqynge
> [eschewing] banketts, rersoupers, joncryes betwixt meles.

Even in her old age, Margaret was renowned for fasting, especially
in Lent, when she 'restrayned her appetyte tyl one mele and tyl one
fyshe on the day'. She also fasted on the saints' days to which she was
particularly devoted: Mary Magdalene, St Catherine and St Anthony.
Given Stafford's likely skin complaint and Margaret's concern over
his health, her fasts in honour of St Anthony almost certainly began
during their marriage, and other facets of her asceticism may also have
begun in that period, where Margaret, who always feared Fortune's
turn, must have looked continually for coming misfortune. Fisher also
related that Margaret followed her religious observance in her dress:

> As to harde clothes wearynge, she had her shertes and gyrdyls of
> heere [hair], which when she was in helthe, everi weke she fayled
> not certayn days to weare, sometyme ther one, sometyme the other,
> that full often her skynne, as I heard her say, was perced therewith.

Fisher also explained that Margaret's daily life was strictly
regulated:

> First in prayer every daye at her uprysynge, which comynly was
> not long after five of the clok, she began certain devocyons, and so

after them with one of her gentlewomen the Matynes of our Lady, which kept her to them she came into her closet, where then with her Chaplayne she said also Matyns of the Daye; and after that, dayly herde four or fyve Masses upon her knees, so continuing in her Prayers and Devocyons unto the hour of dyner, wich of the etynge [eating] day was ten of the clocke, and upon the fastynge day, eleven. After dyner full truely she wolde goe her statyons to thre aulters dayly; dayly her Dyryges and Commendacyons she wolde saye, and her Even Songs before souper, both of the day and of our Lady, besyde many other Prayers and Psalters of Davyde throughout the yeare; and at nyghte before she went to bedde she fayled not to resort unto her Chappell, and there a large quarter of an houre to occupye her [in] Devocyons.

Margaret prayed so much that she injured her knees and back. In an age where piety was expected, particularly of noblewomen, Margaret took her devotion to the extreme, and this is unlikely to be simply a trait that developed in her old age. Instead, part of her love of Woking may have been that, away from London, she was able to ignore the cares of the world and focus on her piety. Surviving representations of Margaret also attest to her piety, and she generally chose to be depicted in severe black and wearing a quasi-religious habit. One particularly famous representation of her depicts her at prayer, with an ornate Book of Hours open on the table in front of her, again demonstrating her devotion to religion. Whilst most representations of Margaret show her in her old age, one that appears to depict a younger Margaret, which is held by the National Portrait Gallery, also shows her in the dress of a religious ascetic, demonstrating that religion was likely to have taken up much of her time from her youth. Margaret appears to have been happiest in her religious devotions, and she was able to achieve a peaceful existence during the early years of Edward IV's reign. She was also able to use her piety as a means of remaining in contact with her son, and in 1465, she secured the admission of Henry Tudor to the Confraternity of the Order of the Holy Trinity near Knaresborough in Yorkshire, demonstrating that she retained an interest in his religious development.

Whilst Margaret achieved a domestic contentment in the early 1460s, she was still uncomfortably aware of the changeability of fortune. With her cousin's defection, Edward IV once again turned against the Beauforts, and Somerset's mother was stripped of her pension by the King and imprisoned. Although Edward took no active measures against Margaret and Henry Stafford, he does not appear to have entirely trusted them, and he showed Stafford little positive favour, pointedly making his younger brother, John Stafford, Earl of Wiltshire, whilst Henry Stafford remained a mere knight. The couple were, however, welcome at court, and Stafford attended a council meeting at Mortlake Palace in 1467. A letter from Sir John Paston to Margaret Paston in October 1469 also records another occasion when Stafford was with the King:

> The kynge is comyn to London, an ther came with hym, an roode ageyn hym, the Duke of Glowcestr, the Duke of Suffolke, the Erle of Aroundell, the Erle of Northumbreland, the Erle of Essex, the Lordes Harry [Stafford] and John of Bokyngham, the Lord Dakres, the Lorde Chambreleyn, the lorde Montjoye, and many other knightys and squryers, the Meyr of London, xxij Aldremen, in skarlett, and of the Crafftys men of the town to the nombre of cc., all in blewe.

They also journeyed specifically to London so that Henry Stafford could attend a parliament there on at least one occasion. Moving an aristocratic household was always a major undertaking, and

Margaret was fully involved in the preparations at Woking before their departure. In her husband's accounts, she is recorded to have purchased food for the household in readiness of their arrival. She took an interest in the minutiae and ordered that one of her gentlewomen's saddles be mended, presumably so that she could ride alongside her mistress. Margaret probably looked forward to such trips eagerly, and it is clear that she regularly accompanied her husband on his travels. On an earlier trip, the couple were ferried by boat into the city together. Margaret engaged the services of a boatman again a few days later when she went by water to visit a bishop. For Margaret, the visits to London may have been a chance to socialise; whilst they were in London for the parliament, they paid the expenses of one of their servants for waiting on 'my Lord Edwarde' on their behalf.

Margaret and Henry Stafford also received a visit from the King at Woking in December 1468, and they entertained him at their hunting lodge in a tent of purple sarsenet. Margaret purchased luxurious materials for clothes to wear for the visit, including velvet and expensive Holland and Brabant cloth, clearly intended to impress the King. She may also have found that she had something in common with the King, and they shared a love of books, with the King collecting a number of texts, such as religious works and histories, including a copy of the chronicle of Jehan Froissart, detailing the usurpation of the throne of Henry IV, which ultimately led to the Wars of the Roses. The visit was a success, and whilst Edward IV's feelings towards the couple were ambivalent, it is perhaps fair to say that Henry Stafford was not in any danger from the King, he was simply not trusted enough to be a member of his inner circle. This all changed in 1469, when, as the King's own fortunes ebbed, Margaret's actions led to both her and her husband incurring his displeasure.

6

THE FALL OF THE HOUSE OF LANCASTER: 1469-1471

During the early years of Edward IV's reign, Margaret settled down into a retired and contented life with her husband, enjoying occasional visits to her son at Sir William Herbert's residence of Raglan Castle. Everything changed in 1469 when the troubles in Edward IV's own kingship bubbled up to the surface, and for the first time in eight years, the House of Lancaster was able to mount a credible opposition to the Yorkist king.

Edward IV began his reign on a wave of public support, but within years of his accession, the situation was very different. At a council meeting in 1465, shortly after his cousin, the powerful Earl of Warwick, had returned to England after making attempts to negotiate a French marriage for the King, Edward was forced to admit that he was already secretly married. His bride was Elizabeth Woodville, the widow of a knight. Her mother, Jacquetta, the widow of Henry V's brother, John, Duke of Bedford, had caused a scandal similar to that caused by her sister-in-law, Catherine of Valois, by taking a lowly member of her household as her second husband. Elizabeth Woodville, the eldest child of Jacquetta's second marriage, was very beautiful, and after her husband was killed fighting for the Lancastrians at Towton, she decided to petition the new king, Edward IV, for the return of her lands. According to legend, Elizabeth positioned herself under an oak tree with her two young sons, knowing that Edward was due to pass that way whilst out hunting. Edward was immediately smitten with the pretty widow, although, at first, he had no intention of actually marrying her, as a contemporary, Dominic Mancini, records:

> When the king first fell in love with her beauty of person and charm of manner, he could not corrupt her virtue by gifts or menaces. The story runs that when Edward placed a dagger at her throat, to make her submit to his passion, she remained unperturbed and determined to die rather than live unchastely with the king. Whereupon Edward coveted her much the more, and he judged the lady worthy of a royal spouse, who could not be overcome in her constancy even by an infatuated king.

Elizabeth's defiance only served to increase Edward's ardour, and he rashly promised her marriage, with the couple wedding in secret on 1 May 1464.

The marriage of Edward IV and Elizabeth Woodville, although hasty, proved to be a personally very happy union, and they remained close until Edward's death nearly twenty years later. Politically, however, it was a disaster and alienated Edward both from the powerful Warwick, who would eventually be nicknamed 'The Kingmaker', and from Edward's younger brother, George, Duke of Clarence, who complained that it was beneath his brother's dignity to marry a widow. Edward's mother, Cecily Neville, was deeply offended and, damagingly, in a fit of pique, swore that Edward was the product of an adulterous affair rather than the true son of her husband, Richard, Duke of York. Edward ignored this criticism and determinedly presented Elizabeth as his queen, arranging for her to be crowned in a grand coronation and ennobling her relatives. This was personally satisfying for

Elizabeth, but it led to the deep unpopularity of the Woodvilles, who were accused of obtaining the best marriages in England. Henry Stafford's young nephew, the Duke of Buckingham, was one such target of the Queen, and he was married to her youngest sister, Catherine Woodville. Elizabeth obtained the King's niece for her eldest son Thomas Grey, Marquess of Dorset, and, scandalously, the elderly dowager Duchess of Norfolk, 'a slip of a girl of about eighty years old', for her twenty-year-old brother, John Woodville. The Woodvilles were seen as upstarts and acquisitive, which did nothing to help Edward's popularity in England.

Matters came to a head in 1469, when Warwick and Clarence came out in open rebellion against the King, issuing a proclamation jointly with Warwick's brother, the Archbishop of York, on 12 July 1469:

> The king our sovereign lord's true subjects of divers parts of this his realm of England have delivered to us certain articles [remembering] the deceitful, covetous rule and guiding of certain seditious persons, that is to say, the Lord Rivers [Elizabeth's father], the Duchess of Bedford his wife, William Herbert, Earl of Pembroke, Humphrey Stafford, Earl of Devonshire, Lord Scales [Elizabeth's eldest brother] and Audley, Sir John Woodville and his brothers, and others of this mischievous rule, opinion and assent, which have caused our sovereign lord and his realm to fall into great poverty and misery, disturbing the administration of the laws, only tending to their own promotion and enrichment.

Although, politically, Margaret Beaufort was very much opposed to William Herbert, as the guardian of her son, his mention in the proclamation would have been alarming for her.

William Herbert was one of Edward IV's staunchest supporters, and this made him an immediate target in the rebellion against the King. As well as receiving Henry Tudor's wardship, Herbert had also been rewarded with Jasper Tudor's lands and the earldom of Pembroke itself in 1468. Following his flight from Pembroke in 1461, Jasper had spent time with his half-brother Henry VI in Scotland. He was one of Margaret of Anjou's must trusted supporters and, in 1462, travelled with her to France to help negotiate an agreement with Louis XI for military aid in return for the surrender of Calais. Jasper was one of the signatories to the treaty agreed between Margaret and Louis on 28 June 1462, and he followed the Queen back to England towards the end of the year. Margaret's invasion of 1462 proved to be ineffective, and for the next few years, Jasper spent time both in Scotland and in France whilst he worked towards Henry VI's restoration. In 1465, Henry VI was finally captured at a religious house in the north of England and 'carried to London on horseback, and his leg bound to the stirrup, and so brought, through London, to the Tower, where he was kept (a) long time by two squires, and two yeomen of the crown, and their men; and every man was suffered to come and speak with him, by licence of the keepers'. Whilst the capture of Henry VI was a symbolic blow to the Lancastrian cause, in reality, it had little effect on the efforts of Margaret of Anjou, Jasper Tudor or Henry VI's other supporters, as the Lancastrian king had long ceased to have any role in the management of his cause. Jasper continued to work towards his half-brother's restoration, and in 1468, after being provided with three ships by Louis XI, he sailed to Wales. As a Welshman, Jasper was popular there, and he gathered a force of 2,000 men and carried out a number of successful raids in the principality. With such a small force, he was never going to be able to mount a full-scale invasion however, and when Edward IV sent William Herbert against him, he was once again forced to flee to France.

William Herbert was called upon by Edward IV when the King received news of Warwick and Clarence's rebellion in 1469. By the summer of that year, Henry Tudor was twelve years old and considered old enough by his guardian to receive his first taste of war. Herbert joined Edward IV at the Battle of Edgecote, near Banbury, on 26 July 1469, where the King's forces were decisively defeated, with the King being captured soon afterwards. Disastrously for Henry Tudor, who appears to have found himself in the thick of the battle, William Herbert was captured and summarily executed. The defeat and death of his guardian placed Margaret's son in a very dangerous position, and he was rescued only by the kindness of Sir Richard Corbet, a kinsman of Herbert's wife. According to Corbet's own later account to Henry, when he had become king,

> Pleaseth your Grace to call to your remembraunce the first service, that after the death of the Lord Herbert after the field of Banbury, hee [Corbet] was one of them that brought your grace out of danger of your enemyes, and conveyed your grace unto your towne of Hereford, and there delivered you in safety to your greate Uncle now Duke of Bedford [Jasper].

The young Henry Tudor evidently made an excellent impression on Corbet, and he also recorded that, when he came to England in 1485 to claim the crown, he was one of the first to join him and pledge his support.

Henry was taken first to the house of Herbert's brother-in-law at Weobley in Herefordshire, where Herbert's widow had also gone once she learned of the outcome of the battle. Margaret and

Henry Stafford were apparently taken aback at the speed of events, and they were enjoying their favourite pastime of hunting in the area around Windsor when they heard the news. Margaret did not know what had become of her son, and she must have been distraught, immediately sending a trusted servant, William Bailey, and a party of men to try to locate him. It was with relief that she heard that he was at Weobley and still in the custody of the Herberts rather than taken by the King's enemies. Henry himself does not appear to have been too troubled by all that was going on around him, and his stepfather's accounts for the period record a payment 'to my lord Richemonde at Weobley for his disportes to bie him bowes and shaftes'. Margaret and Henry Stafford moved quickly to Woking once they knew that the boy was safe, in order to consider what action to take in relation to him.

With William Herbert's death, Margaret evidently hoped to recover custody of her son and to secure the return of his lands and title. In August 1469, she resolved to take action and travelled with Henry Stafford to London. Margaret hoped to negotiate with Clarence, who had received Henry Tudor's lands from his brother and was then one of the men in authority in England, over her son's wardship. The couple carried out research into the position of Henry's wardship with Stafford's receiver, Reginald Bray, purchasing a copy of the document granting Henry Tudor to William Herbert and taking legal advice on its content. Margaret, Stafford and their advisors met with Lady Herbert, her brother and their lawyers in October 1469. No details of the agreement reached survive, but Margaret and her husband were apparently happy with its terms. In any event, the political situation was moving quickly, and Margaret's attempts to negotiate with Clarence proved to be a bad miscalculation. Whilst

Edward IV was taken prisoner after the Battle of Edgecote, Warwick and Clarence soon found that they were unable to hold him, and the King returned to London. The three men were publicly reconciled at Christmas 1469, but Edward had no intention of forgiving his cousin and brother. In early 1470, violence again erupted, and he inflicted a defeat on Warwick and Clarence at Stamford. The two men gathered up their families and fled to France. It is likely that Henry Stafford's presence with the King at Stamford can be explained by the need for him to make a conspicuous show of his loyalty to Edward IV at a time when the King was deeply suspicious of both him and his wife. He also assisted the King in April when he attempted to capture Clarence and Warwick before they fled to France.

Margaret's ill-timed attempt to negotiate with Clarence was ineffective and served only to cause the King to once again look at her with suspicion. Margaret and Henry Stafford must have spent an uncomfortable few months in the autumn and winter of 1469 whilst they waited to see what steps the King would take, and Margaret was overjoyed when Fortune once again swung away from Edward towards her brother-in-law, Henry VI.

Margaret of Anjou had settled in France following the Lancastrian defeat at the Battle of Hexham in May 1464, and she was there with her son when Warwick and Clarence arrived at the French court. Edward IV had allied himself with the Duke of Burgundy, an enemy of Margaret of Anjou's cousin, Louis XI of France. Louis immediately seized upon Warwick's arrival and offered to reconcile the earl with the Lancastrian queen. Margaret of Anjou and Warwick had always been bitter enemies, and it took a considerable amount of persuasion for Margaret to agree to meet with Warwick and hear his terms. Warwick offered to restore Henry VI to the throne on the condition that Margaret of Anjou's son, Edward of Lancaster, married his daughter, Anne. Margaret was at first reluctant to agree to this term, which she considered beneath her son, and according to a contemporary account,

> Touching the second, that is of marriage, true it is that the queen would not in any wise consent thereunto for offer shewing; or any manner of request that the king of France might make her. Some times she said that she saw neither honour nor profit for her, nor for her son the Prince. At others she (al)ledged that and (if) she would, she should find a more profitable party and of a more advantage with the king of England. And indeed, she shewed unto the king of France a letter which she said was sent her out of England the last week, by the which was offered to her son my lady the Princess [i.e., Elizabeth of York, Edward's eldest daughter]; and so the queen persevered fifteen days ere she would any thing intend to the said Treaty of Marriage, the which finally, by the means and conduct of the king of France and the councillors of the king of Sicily [Margaret of Anjou's father] being at Angiers, the said marriage was agreed and promised.

Edward's offer of his eldest daughter for Margaret's son sounds plausible, as he had earlier promised her to Warwick's nephew as a means of binding the earl to him. He later offered her to Henry Tudor in an attempt to secure his return to England, and the same tactics can be seen here. Whilst, on the face of it, the offer must have seemed tempting, in reality, Elizabeth Woodville was already pregnant with her eldest son by Edward. Edward's offer was therefore no solution to the Wars of the Roses and may simply have been intended as a trap in order to bring Edward of Lancaster to England. Whilst tempted, Margaret of Anjou, ignored Edward's offer, and on 22 July 1470, after she had kept

Warwick on his knees for over a quarter of an hour, the pair were formally reconciled. Margaret agreed to the marriage of Edward of Lancaster and Anne Neville.

With French assistance, Warwick sailed for England with an invasion fleet of sixty ships on 9 September 1470 and landed in the West Country. Jasper Tudor, as one of the most senior Lancastrians, sailed with him, and in landing, the two men separated, with Jasper moving towards Wales to raise troops. Warwick, in accordance with his agreement with Margaret of Anjou, marched directly to London. Edward IV, who did not have a standing army, knew that he did not have the military strength to defeat Warwick, and he fled to Flanders, leaving his wife and family to take sanctuary at Westminster. For the oblivious Henry VI, who was, by 1470, merely a cipher, this meant another turn of Fortune's Wheel and, according to *Warkworth's Chronicle*,

> Here is to know, that in the beginning of the month of October, the year of our Lord 1470, the Bishop of Winchester, by the assent of the Duke of Clarence, and the Earl of Warwick, went to the Tower of London, where King Harry was in prison, (by King Edward's commandment,) and there took him from his keepers, which was not worshipfully arrayed as a prince, and not so cleanly kept, as should (be-)seem such a Prince. They had him out, and new arrayed him, and did to him great reverence, and brought him to the palace of Westminster, and so he was restored to the crown again.

Henry VI was lodged in the rooms prepared for Elizabeth Woodville's lying in, and shortly after entering the sanctuary, she gave birth to her eldest son by Edward, who was named after his father. The following month, as a further statement of Henry VI's reinstatement, he called a parliament. At the parliament, Jasper

Tudor, Margaret's cousin, Edmund, fourth Duke of Somerset, and a number of other Lancastrian lords who had returned from exile with Warwick had their lands and titles restored to them.

On hearing of Jasper Tudor's return to Wales, Sir Richard Corbet, who was married to a niece of Lady Herbert and remained close to Weobley, where his wife's aunt was staying with Henry Tudor, took the boy to Hereford and handed him over to his uncle. This was the first time that Jasper and Henry had met since 1461, and it was to be the beginning of a long association between the pair. Jasper immediately took care to safeguard his half-brother's position in Wales and then, by the end of the October, moved to London with his nephew. It is clear that Margaret and Henry Stafford had been watching events anxiously, and on 28 October, Jasper and Henry Stafford dined together at Stafford's house in London. The meeting was a success, and Jasper temporarily handed over custody of his nephew to Margaret. According to the historian Polydore Vergil, who was employed by Henry VII to write a history of the period, Margaret took him to meet his uncle, Henry VI, for the first time:

> When the king saw the chylde, beholding within himself without speache a prety space the hautie disposition therof, he ys reportyd to have sayd to the noble men ther present, 'This trewly, this is he unto whom both we and our adversaryes must yeald and geave of over the dominion'.

> Thus the holy man shewyd yt woold coome to passe that Henry showld in time enjoy the kingdom.

Although Henry VI was aware of Henry's position, after Margaret, as the senior Beaufort heir of John of Gaunt, it is very unlikely that, in 1470, with both himself and his son still alive, he would have predicted that Henry Tudor would one day wear the crown. Henry Tudor was always immensely proud of his status as the nephew of Henry VI, and whilst this was only through the Lancastrian King's mother rather than also through his father, Henry V, he was determined to honour his uncle and later attempted to have him canonised. It is likely that Henry VI's 'prophecy' is a later elaboration of the meeting. In spite of this, both Margaret and her son may well have recalled later to Vergil that the meeting itself was a success and that Henry VI showed a great deal of affection and honour to the son of his deceased half-brother. It is also possible that Henry VI, anxious to reward Jasper's loyalty, may have made a tacit acknowledgement of Henry Tudor's position in the succession after his own descendants.

After the successful meeting with Henry VI, Margaret, Henry Stafford and Henry Tudor travelled to Woking. Margaret and her son spent a week together at her favourite residence, and it appears that this was treated as a holiday by them and a chance to get to know each other again. For Margaret, who had already spent a considerable time apart from her only child, such moments would have been precious, and after leaving Woking, the pair travelled slowly with Henry Stafford to Maidenhead and Henley-on-Thames before Margaret once again passed her son over to the control of his uncle. By 1471, Henry Tudor was rapidly approaching adulthood: he was already older than Margaret had been when she gave birth to him. Although it must have been a wrench for Margaret to part from her child once again, she recognised that it was time for the boy to make his way in the world and that his uncle, who had shown himself to have they boy's best interests at heart, was, for the time being at least, the man best suited to be his guardian. It is likely that Margaret also remembered that Henry VI had previously granted Henry's wardship to Jasper, and whilst this had been annulled by Edward IV, it was likely to be reaffirmed under the new Lancastrian regime.

By meeting with both Henry VI and Jasper Tudor, Margaret made a clear demonstration of her Lancastrian support during Henry VI's restoration. She, along with everyone else in her party, hoped that the dynasty was firmly replanted on the throne, but it soon became apparent that the restoration was nothing more than a brief Indian summer. By March 1471, rumours had begun to reach England that Edward IV was ready in Flanders with an invasion force, and that month, Margaret received a visit at Woking from her cousin, Edmund Beaufort, Duke of Somerset, whilst he tried to persuade Henry Stafford to join the Lancastrian army. Stafford, who was in ill health by 1471, was undecided, and whilst his marriage to Margaret and affection for both her and her son naturally predisposed him to support the Lancastrians, his young nephew, the Duke of Buckingham, who was the head of his family, was firmly a member of the Yorkist camp. Margaret's sympathies were wholly Lancastrian, but it is unclear whether she attempted to persuade her husband to join Henry VI's army. If she did, she was unsuccessful, and Stafford was in London when Edward IV entered the city unopposed on 12 April. Perhaps bowing to the inevitable, he joined Edward's army. Edward IV had always been popular with the Londoners, and he had entered the city after receiving word from his wife and other supporters that it would be safe to do so. He was promptly re-proclaimed as king, immediately ordering Henry VI to be returned to the Tower and removing his family from the sanctuary. For Margaret Beaufort, this must have seemed a disaster and worse was to come. On 18 April 1471, Edward rode out of the city with Henry Stafford as a member of his train and met the Earl of Warwick in battle at Barnet. The outcome of the battle was decisive, and Warwick was killed, allowing Edward to return in triumph once again to his capital. Margaret spent an anxious day waiting for news, and she was devastated to hear that her husband, who was always a somewhat reluctant soldier, was wounded. The nature of Stafford's wounds is not clear, but as he was allowed to return home rather than play any further role in Edward's campaign, it appears that they were serious.

On the very day that Edward won his victory at Barnet, Margaret of Anjou, who had been delayed by bad weather in France, finally landed in the West Country. According to Polydore Vergil, news of Warwick's death and defeat was immediately brought to her:

> When she heard these things the miserable woman swooned for fear, she was distraught, dismayed and tormented with sorrow; she lamented the calamity of the time, the adversity of fortune, her own toil and misery; she bewailed the unhappy end of King Henry, which she believed assuredly to be at hand, and, to be short, she behaved as one more desirous to die than live.

Margaret of Anjou had no choice but to press on, and she began gathering soldiers for the inevitable confrontation with Edward IV. On 4 May 1471, she and her daughter-in-law, Anne Neville, retired to a religious house whilst the Lancastrian and Yorkist armies met in battle at Tewkesbury. Fortune was once more against the Lancastrian cause, and the battle proved to be another decisive victory for Edward IV, with Edward of Lancaster, the only child of Henry VI, killed either during the battle or executed soon afterwards. Margaret Beaufort's cousin, Edmund Beaufort, Duke of Somerset, was also captured and executed. Margaret of Anjou was brought back to London as a prisoner by the triumphant Yorkist king. The very night that she was taken to the Tower, Henry VI was quietly murdered, bringing to an end the direct line of the House of Lancaster.

Jasper Tudor was in South Wales when Margaret of Anjou landed, and he had been unable to reach her in time. He and Henry Tudor were at Chepstow when they learned of the disaster, and aware that the Lancastrian cause was lost, Jasper immediately decided to flee. Henry VII's earliest biographer, Bernard Andreas, later claimed that it was Margaret Beaufort herself who, recognising the danger that her son was in, persuaded Jasper to take Henry Tudor into exile. With the deaths of Henry VI and his son, Margaret and, through her, Henry Tudor suddenly had the best claim to be the heirs of the house of Lancaster. In the late fifteenth century, the idea that a woman could successfully hold the crown was laughable, and it would have been apparent to everyone that Henry Tudor had the potential to emerge as the leading Lancastrian claimant. This meant that, for the first time, Henry's life was in danger at the hands of Edward IV, who viewed him as a potential rival. There is no evidence that Margaret saw her son after he left her to rejoin Jasper Tudor, but she was certainly in touch with him and approved when he and Jasper sailed from Tenby to go into exile in France.

As well as her worries about her son, Margaret was also deeply concerned about her husband. Henry Stafford had been badly wounded at Barnet, and he returned to Margaret at Woking. Although the cause of his death is not recorded, it is likely to have been due to the wounds he suffered. On 2 October 1471, aware that his death was imminent, he made his Will and died two days later on 4 October 1471. For Margaret, the loss of her husband, coming in addition to the exile of her son, must have been devastating. She also found herself under the suspicion of the King, and aware that, with her husband's death, she was vulnerable, she was unable to give herself the luxury of time to mourn, instead immediately looking around for a new protector.

7

A FOURTH HUSBAND: 1471-1483

During Henry VI's brief restoration to the throne, Margaret had clearly shown that her loyalties remained with the House of Lancaster, and with the return of the Yorkist king Edward IV, she found herself once again under suspicion. The death of Henry Stafford, who, although mistrusted by the King, had at least made a show of loyalty by fighting for Edward at Barnet, further increased Margaret's isolation, and within months of her husband's death, she began to cast her eye around for a further powerful male protector.

In June 1472, only eight months after the death of her third husband, Margaret married her fourth: Thomas, Lord Stanley. None of Margaret's previous marriages had started as love matches, and her fourth was no exception. Stanley was around eight years older than Margaret and approaching his forties at the time of the marriage. He was a widower and had previously been married to Eleanor Neville, a daughter of the Earl of Salisbury and a sister of the Earl of Warwick. He was, therefore, a cousin by marriage to both Edward IV and to Margaret's third husband, Henry Stafford, and it is possible that he and Margaret met through the Stafford family. Stanley also had strong connections with the family of Elizabeth Woodville, as his eldest son, George, had married the Queen's niece, the heiress of Lord Strange.

Although he had a strong Yorkist pedigree, Stanley was adept at keeping himself out of the Wars of the Roses as much as possible. He was a major landowner in Lancashire, and both the House of Lancaster and the House of York had sought his support on various occasions. In September 1459, for example, Stanley's two kinsmen, his uncle by marriage, the Duke of York, and his father-in-law, the Earl of Salisbury, requested his aid when they came to face the Lancastrian army at Blore Heath. Stanley's younger brother, Sir William Stanley, to whom he was close and who was looking to make a name for himself, rushed to aid the Yorkist cause, but Stanley, who never lightly committed either his person or his men to battle, moved towards the engagement only slowly, finally stopping at Newcastle-under-Lyme, six miles away. Stanley had no intention of joining either side, and when word reached him of Salisbury's victory, he simply sent a letter congratulating him and his apologies that he had been unable to reach the field in time. Stanley's policy of keeping his distance from any fighting paid off, and when, in November 1459, Henry VI's parliament considered attainting him for treason for his lack of aid to the King at Blore Heath, the matter was quietly allowed to drop. Stanley was somewhat remarkable as a major landowner in the late fifteenth century in that he never once led his troops into battle in any of the disputes that made up the Wars of the Roses. On Edward IV's accession, he immediately moved to support the King, receiving the office of Justice of Chester. He blotted this record somewhat by showing support for Henry VI at his restoration, but he refused to aid either side at Barnet and Tewkesbury and soon found himself back in royal favour, once again taking up a seat on the royal council in 1471 and receiving the important office of Lord Steward of the Household, a role that kept him close to the King.

Lord Stanley was prominent at court at the time of his marriage to Margaret, and whilst Edward IV, who could rely on the loyalty of so few of his nobility, may not have entirely trusted him, he was cautious enough to keep any suspicions to himself. The Stanley family were one of the leading families in the North West, and it was widely acknowledged that no king could govern the area without their support. In 1471, with the deaths of Henry VI and his son, there was no credible rival to the throne, and it appeared to everyone that the Yorkist dynasty, represented by the King and his children, was the future of England. For Margaret, therefore, Stanley offered her a role in the Yorkist regime and protection for her lands and position. It is also likely that she hoped, at a later date, to use his influence to secure the rehabilitation of her son. At the time of the marriage, Margaret was widely considered to be infertile, and Stanley, who already had a large family of children, had no dynastic need of a wife. For him, the advantage of marriage to Margaret was her prestigious family name, her royal descent and, also, her wealth. There is evidence that the couple approached their marriage as something of a business arrangement, and when, in 1485, their marriage contract was restated by parliament, it recorded, in an Act addressed to Henry Tudor, who was then king,

That where certeine appointments and agreements were late made by youre said Moder [Margaret] and her said Husband [Stanley], that is to say, that the said Erle shuld cause a sufficiaunt and lawfull Estate of Lordshipps, Mannors, Lands and Tenements of his inheritaunce, to the yerely value of v c . [500] Marcs over all charges, to be made to youre said Moder, or to certeine Feoffees to her use, for terme of her lyfe, in full recompense of all her Joyntures and Dower, hereafter in eny wise to be claymed or had by youre said Moder, in any Lordshipps, Mannors, Lands and Tenements, the which the said Erle, or any other to hys use, hath or hereafter shall have; and that the said Erle shuld be made sure, for the terme of hys lyfe, of such parte of th'enheritaunce of yowre said Moder, as shulde amounte to the yerely value of viii c. [800] Marks over all charges.

In order to ensure that both could rely on the life interests promised in the other's property, Margaret and Stanley made leases of a number of their manors to a group of protectors. Whilst Stanley, with his promise of only 500 marks to Margaret, appears to have had the stronger hand in the negotiations, receiving back 800 marks from Margaret, it is clear that she was fully involved in all arrangements, and the protectors chosen, who included Margaret's friend, John Morton, Bishop of Ely and Reginald Bray, a prominent member of Henry Stafford's household who had remained with Margaret following her husband's death, demonstrate that she was also able to insist upon her own interests being safeguarded.

Whilst Margaret and Stanley's relationship began as a business arrangement, the development of their feelings for each other is less easy to determine. In his Will dated 28 July 1504, written after over thirty years of marriage, Stanley directed that he be buried in Buscough Priory with his executors 'having provided a tomb to be there placed, with the personages of myself and both my wives, for a perpetual remembrance to be prayed for'. This suggests that a space for Margaret to be buried with Stanley was available, if she wished, and may perhaps show some evidence of feeling. However, this must be countered by the fact that Stanley had already paid for similar tombs to be made in the same priory for his parents, grandfather and great-grandfather, and it may be that he simply desired to create a Stanley family mausoleum with

Margaret, as the most prominent member of the family by that time, included only for the sake of completeness and prestige. In the same document, Stanley also made a bequest to the canons of the priory in order that they would 'say mass in the said chapel for my soul, and for the soul of my lady now my wife, after her decease, and for the soul of Eleanor late my wife, and for the souls of my father, mother, ancestors, children, brethren, and sisters, and for the soul of William late Marquess Berkeley'. Again, there is a sense that Stanley fully considered Margaret to be a member of his family, but she was not singled out for any particular display of affection. He left no bequests to Margaret in his Will, although he did declare that 'I will that my lady my wife shall peaceably enjoy all the lordships, manors, &c. assigned for her jointure, as by act of parliament'. Following her son's accession in 1485, Margaret distanced herself from Stanley somewhat, receiving a declaration from parliament that her actions would be as valid as those of a widow (rather than a wife, who, by law, was under her husband's control) and also making, with his consent, a vow of chastity. The couple were both in their fifties by the time the vow was made however, and it may be that any physical relationship between them had simply come to an end. They remained associated with each other until Stanley's death in 1504, with the couple jointly welcoming Henry VII and his wife, Elizabeth of York, on a visit to Stanley's home at Lathom in 1494. Margaret was not, however, above using her superior influence with the King after her son's accession to her own advantage. In one letter to her son from his reign, she asked him to help her actively deceive her husband:

My good king, I have now sent a servant of mine into Kendall, to receive such annuities as be yet hanging upon the account of Sir

William Wall, my lord's chaplain, whom I have clearly discharged; and if it will please your majesty's own heart, at your leisure, to send me a letter, and command me that I suffer none of my tenants be retained with no man, but that they be kept for my lord of York, your fair sweet son, for whom they be most meet, it shall be a good excuse for me to my lord and husband; and then I may well, and without displeasure, cause them all to be sworn, the which shall not after be long undone.

By asking for Henry to give royal authority to what was, in fact, her personal wish, it is at least possible that Margaret acted to spare her husband's feelings, as he would not have been aware that his wife was acting alone in defiance of him. The couple were happy to live largely separate lives in their last few years, and this suggests that there was no great passion in their relationship. However, there is no evidence of an estrangement, and the fact that they were often associated with each other suggests that they were fond of each other and that some affection developed in the marriage.

It is therefore likely that Margaret found some contentment with Stanley during the early years of their marriage. As Edward IV's reign progressed, Stanley was shown greater trust and given more authority by the King, and both he and Margaret were frequently at court. In 1475, Stanley accompanied Edward IV on his invasion of France, and he was one of the lords selected to negotiate a peace treaty with Louis XI. In 1482, he was also chosen to assist the King's youngest brother, Richard, Duke of Gloucester, in an invasion of Scotland. This proved to be a largely unsuccessful campaign, and it was Stanley who provided the only glimpse of success, capturing Berwick with a force of 4,000 men. It was later suggested by the Elizabethan poet Robert Glover that this success led to some jealousy between Stanley and the King's brother, and he claimed that, when the pair quarrelled, Stanley responded by capturing the duke's standard. Whether this actually occurred can no longer be verified, but it does provide a hint of earlier tension between Stanley and Gloucester, which may account for something of the conduct of the two men towards each other after Edward IV's death.

Another motivation for Margaret in her choice of Stanley may have been her hope that, through becoming reconciled with Edward IV herself, she could secure Henry Tudor's return to England. Jasper and Henry had intended to travel to France when they sailed from Tenby in 1471, where, due to their descent from Catherine of Valois, they could claim kinship with the French king, Louis XI. Unfortunately, the weather was against them, and they were forced to land in Brittany, an independent duchy ruled by Duke Francis II. Henry later told the chronicler Philip de Comines that 'he had endured an imprisonment of fifteen years or thereabouts in Bretagne, by the command of the late Duke Francis, into whose hands he fell by extremity of weather'. According to Polydore Vergil, as soon as the pair had landed, Jasper went to Francis II and submitted both himself and Henry to the duke's protection. They received a favourable response, and 'the duke receavyd them willingly, and with suche honor, curtesy, and favor intertaynyd them as thowgh they had bene his broothers, promysing them uppon his honor that within his domynyon they showld be from thenceforth far from injury and passe and ther pleasure to and fro withowt danger'. This was encouraging for the pair, and Comines, who was at the Breton court at the time of their arrival, also confirmed that 'the duke treated them very handsomely for prisoners'. Whilst Francis II attempted to keep his 'guests' content and entertained them well, it was soon apparent to both Jasper and Henry that they were, as Comines asserted, prisoners, and Francis had no intention of allowing the pair to leave Brittany.

In spite of the violent manner in which he had come to the throne, Edward IV was always a remarkably popular figure in England, and as the sixteenth-century historian Thomas More related,

> At such time as he died, the displeasure of those that bore him grudges – for King Henry's sake (the sixth), whom he deposed – was wel assuaged, and in effect quenched, in that mony of them were dead in more than twenty years of his reign, and a great part of a long life. And many of them in the mean season grown unto his favour, of which he was never strange.

With Henry VI and his son's deaths, the Lancastrian cause in England seemed to be dead, and most prominent Lancastrians, including Margaret Beaufort, were prepared to accept the Yorkist king. The idea of a Lancastrian revival with Henry Tudor at its head in 1471 would have seemed laughable, and whilst, by strict heredity, Margaret and her son were the heirs to the House of Lancaster if the legitimation of the Beauforts was considered valid, in reality, they were so far from the main Lancastrian line and Henry such an obscure figure that it is doubtful that he could have mustered any Lancastrian support for an attempt on the crown. Henry and Jasper's value as prisoners was therefore limited in 1471, but as prominent Lancastrians and rivals to Edward IV, even ignoring Henry's potential claim to the throne, they were of some interest. Louis XI, who was always anxious for a means to attack Edward IV, demanded that Francis II hand the two Tudors over to him, declaring that Jasper, who he had taken into his household during the 1460s and was his cousin, should be returned to France. After strenuous efforts, all of which were ignored, Louis finally demanded that, at the very least, Francis keep the pair under guard to ensure that Edward IV did not kidnap them.

Edward was also anxious that the pair be kept under guard if he, like Louis, could not secure their extradition. According to Polydore Vergil, after 1471, Edward felt secure on his throne,

> but yeat because he might have soomwhat to think uppon, and that he showld not lyve altogethers in perfyte securytie, he had intelligence at the same time that therles of Pembrowgh and Richemond were transportyd into Bryteyn, and of the duke ther curtesly receavyd and intertaynd; which matter indede he tooke very grevously, and thowgh hys mynd gave him that soome evell wold coome therby, which to prevent he sent in all hast secret messengers to the duke, promysing to geave great rewardes so that he wold make delyvey of both therles. The duke herd wilingly king Edwardes ambassage, and whan he understoode that therles were so riche a pray he determynyd not to let them go, but to kepe them more warely than befoor, making awnswer to thambassadors that he might not delyver them to the king, bye reason of his promyse and fydelyte geaven to the contrary; but he wold for his cause kepe them so sure as ther should be none occasion for him to suspect that they should ever procure his harme any maner of way.

Edward was forced to be content with the duke's promise to keep the two men as prisoners, and in order to ensure that Francis complied, he sent him gifts of money and promises of aid against the aggression of France. Jasper and Henry do not appear to have been mistreated in Brittany, but they were certainly made aware that they were not permitted to leave. Francis kept the pair separately and removed their English servants from them, instead permitting them contact only with Bretons of his own choosing.

Whilst, in 1471, Edward had to settle for this promise, in 1475, when he finally made peace with France, he was once again able to put pressure on the duke, throwing up the possibility of an aggressive Anglo-French alliance against the duchy. Edward sent ambassadors to Francis with promises of great rewards if he would only hand over Henry, of whom, as Polydore Vergil claimed, the King 'lyvyd, as yt wer, in perpetuall feare'. Francis appears to have been somewhat attached to Henry, and Edward, anxious to ensure that he would be returned, instructed his ambassadors to inform the duke that he only required Henry's return so that he could arrange a marriage between him and his eldest daughter, Elizabeth of York. This was the same tactic employed by the King in 1470, when he attempted to stop Margaret of Anjou forming an alliance with Warwick by offering his daughter to her son in marriage. Such a match had its advantages, and whilst Edward had sons of his own to continue his dynasty on the throne, the marriage would have bound Henry Tudor to him and, in all likelihood, secured his loyalty. However, in 1475, it is certain that, for Edward, it was merely a ploy to obtain the return of his enemy and that, as Vergil claimed, when Francis agreed to deliver Henry to Edward, 'he had commyttyd the sheepe to the woolffe' rather than 'the soone to the father'.

Once he had made his agreement with Edward, Francis handed Henry over to the English ambassadors. It appears that Margaret had, through her connections at court, learned something of the trick that was intended by the offer of marriage, and according to Bernard Andreas, she had already sent a message to Henry warning him to be wary of any promised match with Elizabeth of York. Henry had also received warnings from other sources, and when he and the ambassadors reached St Malo, he feigned illness in order to slip his guard and flee to the sanctuary of a church there. The English ambassadors immediately tried to remove Henry from the church forcibly, and Margaret's son found himself defended by the townsmen furious at the violation of church law. This was just the delay that Henry needed, and when Jean de Quelenec, a leading member of Francis's council who was also favourable to Henry, returned to court, he remonstrated with the duke for breaking his promise. It appears that Francis, whose decision to hand Henry over had been guided by his treasurer, Pierre Landais, was already having second thoughts, and he immediately sent to St Malo to secure Henry's return to his custody. Henry was invited to the Breton court, and whilst still a prisoner in Brittany, he had cause to be thankful. As Vergil commented tartly, 'thus derely dyd the king of England bye the custody of his enemy for three days'.

Margaret's intervention was the first of many in support of her son, and although she did not see Henry at all between 1471 and 1485, she kept in contact with him through messengers. She also worked tirelessly to secure his rehabilitation in England. Margaret gradually came into favour at court, and in 1476, she was prominent in her attendance on Elizabeth Woodville and her daughters at the ceremonial reburial of Edward's father, Richard, Duke of York. At the christening of Edward's youngest child, Bridget, in 1482, she was given the honour of holding the infant. She gradually set about persuading Edward of the advantages of her son returning to England, and this appears to have had some effect. In June 1482, Edward agreed that Henry could receive a share of Margaret's lands worth £400 a year, on the condition that he return to England. Edward also discussed with Margaret, Stanley, John Morton, Bishop of Ely, and the Bishop of Worcester, the possibility of Henry marrying Elizabeth of York, and it appears that, on this occasion, the King was genuine in his desire to make Henry his son-in-law. Negotiations advanced well, and Edward, who was as tired as everyone in England of the years of civil war, was finally persuaded by Margaret and her supporters of the value of bringing her son into the Yorkist camp. A draft pardon from Edward for Henry exists, and this demonstrates that matters were considerably far advanced and that both Margaret and Henry would have been confident that they would soon be reunited in England. Margaret must therefore have been devastated when, on 9 April 1483, Edward died suddenly, leaving the pardon incomplete and his twelve-year-old son, Edward V, as his heir.

8

MOTHER TO THE KING'S GREAT REBEL & TRAITOR: APRIL 1483-DECEMBER 1483

Edward IV's death ushered in a new period of uncertainty in England. With an underage king, it was clear that some kind of regency would have to be declared. Edward IV had brought a stability to the English crown that it had not known since the 1440s, but his dynasty survived him by a period of only just over two years. As one historian has commented, Margaret played a major role in presenting her son, for the first time, as a credible candidate for the throne. She can be considered the second great kingmaker of the Wars of the Roses, after the famous 'Warwick the Kingmaker'.

Edward IV's death was unexpected and his heir, the twelve-year-old Edward V was staying at Ludlow. The new king's mother, Elizabeth Woodville, met with the royal council shortly after his accession, and it was agreed that he would make his way to London as soon as possible. Given the unpopularity of Edward V's Woodville kin, who had played a prominent part in his upbringing, Elizabeth also agreed that her son would travel with a retinue of no more than 2,000 men, a concession that she would later come to regret bitterly.

Edward V set out accompanied by his maternal uncle, Earl Rivers, and half-brother, Sir Richard Grey. At a similar time, Edward IV's youngest and last surviving brother, Richard, Duke of Gloucester, and his friend, Margaret's nephew, the Duke of Buckingham, set out to meet him, arriving at Northampton as the King reached Stony Stratford. In order to pay their respects to the two dukes, the King's uncle and half-brother, who were, in any event, related to Buckingham through his marriage to Catherine Woodville, Rivers's sister and Grey's aunt, went to Northampton to greet them. The four men spent a convivial evening together, feasting and drinking, and due to the late hour, Rivers and Grey agreed to spend the night at Northampton. They noticed nothing amiss and were stunned to find, on waking in the morning, that they had been placed under guard. The two dukes rode to Stony Stratford, where they took custody of the protesting King, riding with him to London.

News of Gloucester and Buckingham's coup reached Elizabeth Woodville the following day, and she and her eldest son by her first marriage, the Marquess of Dorset, attempted to raise an army in order to wrest back custody of the King. Unfortunately for them, 'when they exhorted certain nobles who had come to the city, and others, to take up arms, they perceived that men's minds were not only irresolute, but altogether hostile to themselves'. Without Edward IV to protect them, the nobility and people of London were free to give vent to their dislike of the Woodvilles, and there was nothing that the Queen could do but gather up her youngest son, Richard, Duke of York, and her daughters and hurry with Dorset to the sanctuary at Westminster. Many of Elizabeth's contemporaries thought that she was overreacting, and the Archbishop of York, who was Chancellor of England, made a great show of bringing the great seal of England to her in the sanctuary. He was soon, however, forced to ask for its return. Shortly after he arrived in London with the young king, Gloucester demanded that the Queen hand over her youngest son, and when the sanctuary was surrounded by soldiers, she was forced to comply. Margaret played no role in the political events immediately after Edward IV's death, but she would have been aware of all that was happening. Her husband, Lord Stanley, was dangerously exposed.

On the night that Elizabeth Woodville entered sanctuary, the Archbishop of York assured her 'be you of good cheer. For I assure you if they crown any other king than your son, whom they now have with them, we shall on the morrow crown his brother whom you have here with you'. On 22 June, only six days after the Queen surrendered her youngest son, a sermon was preached at Paul's Cross in London, claiming that Edward IV had been the product of an adulterous affair and that his marriage to Elizabeth Woodville was invalid. Any reference to Edward IV's supposed illegitimacy was quickly dropped, perhaps due to the anger of Edward and Gloucester's mother, Cecily Neville. However, the assertion that Edward IV and Elizabeth Woodville had not been truly married, thus making their children illegitimate, was soon elaborated upon. According to the chronicler Philip de Comines, the Bishop of Bath informed Gloucester

> that his brother King Edward having been formerly in love with a beautiful young lady, promised her marriage, upon condition he might lie with her, the lady consented, and as the bishop affirmed, he married them when nobody was present but they two and himself. His fortune depending upon the court, he did not discover it, and persuaded the lady likewise to conceal it, which she did, and it remained a secret to that very day.

The lady in question was Eleanor Butler, a noblewoman who had conveniently died several years before. Edward IV had married

Elizabeth Woodville secretly when she refused to become his mistress, and it is not impossible that he earlier acted in the same way when confronted with another lady intent on maintaining her virtue. He did, however, acknowledge his secret marriage to Elizabeth, which suggests that, whatever occurred between him and Eleanor Butler, it was not a full marriage. It is possible that the couple entered into a precontract, which, when consummated, could be considered as valid as a full marriage. However, there was little evidence even for this, and most people in England, Margaret Beaufort included, considered Edward IV's family by Elizabeth Woodville to be his legitimate one.

Once he had possession of the two sons of Edward IV, Gloucester showed his intentions more openly. His greatest supporter was Buckingham, who had always resented his forced marriage to a Woodville, and it is likely that both men were primarily motivated by their fear of the Woodvilles, who had succeeded in winning the young king's trust. Certainly, in May 1483, Elizabeth Woodville's brother, Sir Edward Woodville, fled to Brittany. Gloucester also took steps to eliminate other potential supporters of Edward V, and at a council meeting at the Tower of London on 13 June, he had the powerful Lord Hastings seized and executed. According to the later writer Thomas More, Margaret's husband, Lord Stanley, had tried to warn Hastings to no avail. Gloucester was concerned about Stanley's loyalty, and at the same meeting, he and John Morton, Bishop of Ely, were arrested and imprisoned. More was a protégé of Morton's, and his account of Stanley's conduct, although biased against Gloucester, may well be accurate. Morton was committed to Buckingham's custody at Brecon Castle. Stanley, however, who always avoided danger wherever he could, agreed to support Gloucester and was soon released unharmed. Stanley, upon whom Gloucester relied for support, was undoubtedly in as grave danger as Hastings had been, and both he and Margaret were relieved that he survived with his offices at court intact. Soon afterwards, Gloucester was declared king by parliament as Richard III, with Edward IV's children declared illegitimate and the children of Richard's other elder brother, George, Duke of Clarence, declared to be barred from the throne due to the their father's attainder for treason.

No king of England has a more controversial reputation than Richard III, and he was later slandered by the Tudor dynasty, with one writer fancifully recording that 'this tyrant King Richard, who was born at Fotheringhay in the country of Northampton, retained for two years in his mother's womb and issuing forth with teeth and hair down to his shoulders'. He was also described as a hunchback and the murderer of Henry VI, his brother's two sons and his own wife. Much of what has been written about the King is inaccurate, and it is clear that Margaret was, at least at first, content to make a show of support for the new king.

Both Margaret and her husband were prominent figures at the coronation of Richard III and his wife, Anne Neville, the widow of Edward of Lancaster, the Lancastrian Prince of Wales, on 6 July 1483. The new king liked to dress well to show his kingly rank. A letter from Richard to the keeper of his wardrobe survives:

We will and charge you to deliver to the bringers hereof for us the parcels following: that is to say, one doublet of purple satin lined with Holland cloth and interlined with busk. One doublet of tawny satin lined in likewise; two short gowns of crimson cloth of gold, the one with drips [tassels], and the other with nets lined with green velvet; one stomacher of purple satin, and one stomacher of tawny satin; one cloak with a cape of velvet ingrained, the bow lined with black velvet.

The list continued, and it is likely that Richard required these items for his coronation, which he intended to be a spectacular affair. Margaret also appeared at the coronation magnificently dressed, and she received ten yards of scarlet cloth from the King, the same amount granted to the other countesses in attendance on the Queen. According to the King's Wardrobe Account, a further grant was also made for Margaret's clothes:

> To the Countesse of Richemonde, a longe gowne made of vj [6] yerds of crymysym velvet and purfiled with vj yerds of white cloth of gold; and a long gowne made of vj yerds of white cloth of gold; and a longe gowne made of vj yerds di' of blue velvett, and purfiled with vj yerds di' of crymysyn cloth of gold.

Margaret looked magnificent in her finery at the coronation, and she was given a position of great honour, being appointed to bear the Queen's train. During the ceremony, as a mark of her high rank, she was permitted to sit to the left of the Queen. Margaret watched Stanley take an equally prominent role as he carried the mace before Richard III as he entered Westminster Abbey. At the coronation banquet, Margaret sat at the same table as the Duchess of Norfolk, close to the Queen. Richard was grateful for Stanley's support, and he was determined to reward both him and Margaret. There is, however, evidence that, even by the time of Richard's coronation, Margaret had begun to plot against him.

The sixteenth-century historian John Stow, who had access to documents now lost, recorded that, soon after Richard's coronation, four men were arrested for treason against the king:

> Robert Russe sergeant of London, William Dauy pardoner of
> Hounslow, Iohn Smith groome of King Edwardes stirrop, and
> Stephen Ireland wardrober in the Tower, with many other, that
> they should haue sent writings to the earles of Richmond and of
> Pembroke, and the other lords: and how they were purposed to
> haue set fire on diuers partes of London, which fire, whilest men
> had beene staunching, they woulde haue stolen out of the Tower,
> the prince Edward [Edward V], & his brother the Duke of Yorke.

Few details of this conspiracy survive, but the decision to contact
both Henry and Jasper Tudor in Brittany is interesting. Some recent
historians have suggested that Margaret was involved in the plot
to rescue the princes in the Tower, whose bid for the throne would
then be supported by Henry and Jasper commanding a force from
Brittany. This was also suggested by Richard's earliest biographer,
George Buck, who, whilst often unreliable, had access to a number
of now lost sources. He claimed that Margaret was only dissembling
when she attempted to open negotiations with the new king in an
attempt to bring her son home and that she was a 'cunning countess',
suggesting that she was already plotting with Richard's enemies.
Margaret's involvement is possible, and whilst she attempted to keep
on good terms with Richard, she was already also beginning to plot
with some of his leading opponents. The attempt to rescue the princes
was small in scale and disorganised, and its leaders were executed.
It was around this time that the princes were last seen alive at the
Tower. Whether the princes were murdered and on whose orders
is still passionately debated. However, regardless of what the truth
was, they were certainly soon believed to have been murdered on

the orders of their uncle by most of their contemporaries, Margaret Beaufort included.

With the likely murder of Edward IV's sons, Margaret's actions on behalf of her own son changed from an attempt to secure his safe return to England towards an active bid for him to be recognised as the heir to the House of Lancaster and acknowledged as King of England. Richard III's actions, in snatching the throne, had demonstrated once again that, in many respects, a king in the late fifteenth century was the man who could successfully win and hold the throne rather than, necessarily, the man with the best hereditary title. One person who came to realise this in the summer of 1483 was Richard's great supporter, Margaret's nephew, the Duke of Buckingham.

As well as being a descendant of Edward III through his youngest son, Buckingham was also the son of another Margaret Beaufort, the daughter of Margaret's uncle, Edmund Beaufort, 4th Earl, and 2nd Duke, of Somerset. Edmund Beaufort's three sons had all been killed during the Wars of the Roses, leaving no children of their own and his line therefore descended to his daughters. Buckingham, as the most prominent grandson of Edmund Beaufort, was in the strongest position to claim to be his heir and, effectively, in the eyes of some, the male heir to the Beaufort claim to the throne. Buckingham himself was fully aware of this.

On the surface, Richard III and Buckingham parted in friendship after the coronation, but in reality, the duke had already decided to oppose the new king. A number of contemporary and near-contemporary sources speculated that Buckingham's opposition to Richard was due to the King's refusal to grant him the earldom of Hertford, which he had demanded, or to allow his daughter to marry the new Prince of Wales. The chronicler Edward Hall claimed that Richard spoke harshly to the duke about the matter before the coronation and that Buckingham was so furious that he feigned illness and had to be compelled to attend the ceremony. That this was the sole cause of Buckingham's discontent is debateable, and in fact, Richard did grant him the lands of the earldom of Hertford soon after his accession. More likely, Buckingham's decision to rebel against Richard was motivated by jealousy, and 'the duke of Buckyngham was a highe mynded man, and euill coulde beare the glory of another, so that I have heard of some that saw it, that he at such tyme as the crowne was set vpon the protectours hed, his eye could neuer abyde the sight therof, but wryed his hed another way'.

Buckingham returned home to Brecon Castle soon after the coronation, where he was holding John Morton, Bishop of Ely, on Richard's orders. Morton had been renowned for his loyalty to Henry VI and only turned to support Edward IV when it became clear that the Lancastrian cause was lost. He became equally attached to Edward and refused absolutely to support Richard III, vowing loyalty to Edward IV's two sons. On his arrival at the castle, Buckingham sought out the Bishop, and the pair spoke about Richard, with Morton flattering the duke by declaring that he wished God would give the king 'some suche other excellente vertues mete for the rule of the realme, as our lord hath planted in the person of your grace' . Buckingham listened intently and, emboldened, Morton continued, speaking of Richard's tyranny, before stating, 'But nowe my lorde to conclude what I meane towarde your noble persone, I saye and affirme, yf you love God, your lynage, or youre natyue contrye, you muste yower selfe take vpon you the Crowne and diadem of thys noble empire.'

Buckingham took a day to think about all that Morton had

said before returning to the bishop. He stated that he had indeed thought of taking the crown:

> I sodainly remembred that lord Edmond duke of Somersett my grandfather was with kynge Henrye the sixte in the ii and iii degrees from Ihon duke of Lancaster [John of Gaunt] lawefully begotten: so that I thought sure my mother being eldest doughter to duke Edmunde, that I was nexte heyre to kyng Henry the sixte of the house of Lancaster.

He had been considering this as he journeyed towards Brecon, and as he travelled along the road from Worcester to Bridgnorth, he happened to come across Margaret Beaufort, which reminded him of her own superior claim. He and Margaret spoke for some time about Henry Tudor before they parted, with Margaret travelling on to the residence of the Countess of Worcester.

Margaret's meeting with Buckingham is interesting, and it is very unlikely that the pair met by chance. In the early weeks of Richard's accession, Margaret was still hopeful that the King would ratify the agreement that she had made with Edward IV to allow her son to return from exile. Buckingham, who was believed to be Richard's greatest supporter and was also Margaret's nephew by marriage, would have seemed an excellent choice for an intercessor between her and the King. Buckingham apparently informed Morton that

> the countess of Richemonde in my returne from the newe named kyng metyng me in the high way, praied me fyrste for kinred sake, secondarily for the loue that I bare my grandfather duke Humphrey, whiche was sworne brother to her father, to moue the kynge to be good to her sonne Henry erle of Richemond, and to

licence him with his fauor to returne again into England: and yf it were his pleasure so to do, she promised that the erle her sonne shoud mary one of kyng Edwardes daughters at the appoinctement of the kyng, without any thing to be taken or demaunded for the saide espousals, but onely the kynges fauour, whiche request I sone ouer passed and gaue her fayre wordes & so departed.

It was this meeting that persuaded Buckingham to admit both Margaret and her son into his conspiracy, and it is likely that, when Margaret realised that her nephew was opposed to the King, she spoke to him of a separate conspiracy in which she was already involved.

Morton encouraged Buckingham to link his own rebellion to Henry Tudor's cause, and the duke wrote to Margaret's trusted retainer, Reginald Bray, who was with Margaret and Stanley in Lancashire. Bray went immediately to Brecon, where Buckingham asked him to convince Margaret to involve Elizabeth Woodville in the plot and to contact her son in Brittany. Bray hurried back to his mistress to tell her what he had learned, to Margaret's joy.

It appears that Margaret had already made contact with Elizabeth Woodville, who was still lodged with her daughters in the sanctuary at Westminster, and the two women and their supporters had been planning a rebellion of their own when Buckingham declared his discontent with the King. Richard's earliest biographer, George Buck, claimed that Margaret was the instigator of the conspiracy, 'for she was entered far into them, and none better plunged in them and deeply acquainted with them. And she was a politic and subtle lady'. Margaret and Elizabeth shared a physician, a Welshman named Lewis Caerleon, and Margaret brought him into her confidence when she was in London, declaring 'that the tyme was come that her sonne shoulde be ioyned in mariage with lady Elizabeth daughter and heyre to king Edward, and that King Richard being taken & reputed of all men for the common enemye of the realme, shoulde out of all honour and estate be deiected, and of his rule and kyngedome be clerely spoyled & expulsed'. Lewis went at once to the Queen Dowager and, pretending that the idea for an alliance was his, broached the subject with her. Elizabeth Woodville had, by then, been in the sanctuary for some months and was at the lowest ebb of her fortunes. On hearing the message, she was overjoyed and promised that she would give her daughter in marriage to Henry if he could win the crown from Richard. She also promised to use her efforts to persuade Edward IV's supporters to turn their allegiance to Henry and, as a gesture of her good faith, she allowed her eldest son by her first marriage, the Marquess of Dorset, to become deeply involved in the conspiracy. Caerleon took Elizabeth's response to Margaret, and she immediately set to work with Reginald Bray, rousing their supporters. She sent a trusted agent, Hugh Conway, to Brittany with a message for Henry, telling him to be ready to sail to claim the throne. In order to ensure that the message reached Henry, a second messenger, Thomas Rame, was sent separately with a large sum of money, and the pair, by coincidence, arrived in Brittany at the same time. Henry was overjoyed when he received his mother's message, and he went to the Duke of Brittany to request his support. Francis II, Duke of Brittany, had already been offered money by Richard's ambassador to ensure that Henry remained a prisoner, but ignoring this, he promised the earl aid. Henry then sent a message to England to declare that he would come and began to make his preparations.

Buckingham's rebellion initially developed separately to that envisaged by Margaret and Elizabeth Woodville, and it was only through Morton, and Margaret's own meeting with the duke, that the two conspiracies were joined together. Margaret, by involving herself in the conspiracy to rescue the princes from the Tower, had already proved that she was ready to bring down the King, and as people came to suspect the princes were dead, she persuaded many disaffected people in England to accept her son as a plausible alternative candidate. In this, the key was the agreement of Elizabeth Woodville to Henry marrying her eldest daughter, who was widely regarded as the heir of Edward IV. Henry Tudor had, by 1483, spent nearly half his life in Brittany, and he was an unknown quantity in England. For Margaret to have secured Elizabeth Woodville's support for her son was a major coup, and for the first time, he began to look like a credible claimant for the throne. It is unlikely that Buckingham saw him as such, and whilst he agreed to join his rebellion to Margaret's, asking Henry to join him, he did not specifically invite him to claim the throne. It is possible that Buckingham duped Margaret by suggesting that he would support Henry when he really intended to claim the crown himself. Alternatively, the trickery may well have come from Margaret, with her remaining silent on her ambitions for her son in order to secure such influential support.

Richard III, who was already wary of Buckingham, soon learned of the conspiracy through his spies and set about raising an army. The rebellion, when it happened, came quickly, and the Marquess of Dorset suddenly left the sanctuary at Westminster, where he was staying with his mother, the Queen Dowager, and half-sisters. He went to Yorkshire and began raising men whilst other Yorkist supporters, Sir Edward Courteney and his brother, the Bishop of Exeter, raised men in the West Country. A further rising in Kent was led by Richard Guildford. The rebellions, which began on 18 October 1483, were intended to happen simultaneously, with Buckingham, who led his own men from Wales, intending to join the main force. Unfortunately, the weather that autumn was terrible, and flooding made it impossible to cross the Severn and left many roads impassable. Buckingham, who found himself cut off, discovered that his Welsh tenants, who he had pressed into his army, disliked him and began to desert. He also found that he could rely on less support than he had hoped, and likely to Margaret's chagrin, Lord Stanley refused to join the conspiracy, remaining conspicuously loyal to Richard. Although the rebels had been confident of widespread support, the only peer to join the revolt, apart from Buckingham and Henry Tudor, was Elizabeth Woodville's son, Dorset. In the pouring rain, as his troops began to desert, Buckingham finally gave up, hiding at the home of an old servant of his near Shrewsbury.

When his allies heard of Buckingham's failure, they fled to Brittany, with Dorset and Margaret's younger half-brother, John, Lord Welles, prominent amongst them. Morton went into hiding and eventually travelled to exile in Flanders. Richard, who had acted decisively to save the situation, quickly issued a reward for Buckingham's capture, and as the final indignity, Buckingham's servant promptly betrayed him, leading to the duke being beheaded in the market place at Salisbury on 2 November. Amongst the only people not to be aware of what had happened was Henry Tudor, who sailed from Brittany on 12 October with a fleet of forty ships and an army of 5,000 Breton mercenaries. To add to the rebellion's poor fortune, his fleet was scattered by storms with many forced to turn back and land in Normandy. Henry himself made it to the Dorset coast from where he saw the shore covered with armed men. The men on the bank attempted to persuade Margaret's son that they were Buckingham's army, but unconvinced, he immediately turned round. On his return to Brittany, he found a substantial group of English exiles awaiting him, and in order to ensure that they were bound closely to him, at Christmas 1483, he made a solemn vow in church to marry Elizabeth of York as soon as he was king.

With Buckingham dead, Richard soon turned his attention to the other main conspirators. Henry, Dorset, Morton and Elizabeth Woodville were out of his reach in either exile or sanctuary, but Margaret, unprotected in England, was a focus of his wrath. Richard immediately called a parliament at which Henry and other members of the conspiracy were attainted for high treason. According to *Hall's Chronicle*, Stanley was expected by many to be amongst those condemned and 'in this troubleous ceason, nothinge was more merueled at then that the lord Stanley had not bene taken and reputed as an enemy to the king, considerynge the workynge of the ladye Margarete his wife mother to the earle of Richemond'. Stanley, who was usually supremely cautious, must have been furious with Margaret, and it is likely that he felt some regret at having married such a politically controversial bride. In spite of this, he proved to be her protector, and Richard, anxious to maintain the powerful magnate's support, was forced to be lenient towards his wife. Margaret, like the rest of her son's supporters, was attainted for treason by parliament at the end of 1483, with the act beginning,

> Forasmuch as Margaret Contesse of Richmond, Mother to the kyngs great Rebell and Traytour, Henry Erle of Richemond, hath of late conspired, confedered, and comitted high Treason ayenst oure soveraigne lorde the king Richard the Third, in dyvers and sundry wyses, and in especiall in sendyng messages, writyngs and tokens to the said Henry, desiryng, procuryng and stirryng hym by the same, to come into this Roialme, and make Werre ayenst oure said Soveraigne Lorde.

Richard was fully apprised of Margaret's role, and she was also accused of sending large sums of money to Henry for use in the rebellion. The Act is full of frustrated indignation against Margaret and continued, stating,

> Yet neverthelesse, oure said Soveraigne lorde, of his grace especiall, remembryng the good and faithfull service that Thomas lord Stanley hath doon, and entendeth to doo to oure said Soveraigne lorde, and for the good love and trust that the kyng hath in hym, and for his sake, remitteth and woll forbere the greate punyshement of atteynder of the said countesse, that she or any other so doeyng hath deserved.

Stanley's loyalty to Richard III saved Margaret's life, and her sentence was commuted to life imprisonment rather than the usual death for treason. Even this was lenient, and whilst Margaret's goods and lands were confiscated, the Act declared that they would, instead, pass to Lord Stanley for the term of his life, ensuring that Margaret, in effect, lost nothing as long as her husband lived. Her imprisonment was also not particularly onerous, and the King commanded that she be kept closely confined by Stanley at one of his residences for the remainder of her life: house arrest.

Margaret appears to have spent her 'imprisonment' at Stanley's residences of Lathom and Knowsley, and whilst she was officially cut off from the world, her husband allowed her a great deal of leeway, ensuring that she remained in contact with her son. There is also some evidence that Stanley, in spite of his conspicuous show of loyalty to the King, was in contact with Henry Tudor and actively supported his wife in her attempts to win the crown for her son.

9

BOSWORTH FIELD: JANUARY 1484-AUGUST 1485

For Margaret, the year 1483 saw her fortunes change. She went from being a respected noblewoman with a position at court to an attainted traitor, condemned to life imprisonment, and she began 1484 at her lowest ebb. As ever with her life, Fortune's Wheel continued to turn, and within eighteen months, she found herself at the height of her power and prestige.

With the failure of Buckingham's rebellion, the future must have looked bleak to Margaret. Henry Parker, who served in her household during the last decade of her life, provided the only evidence for Margaret's own feelings on her imprisonment when he recorded that 'neither prosperitye made her proude, nor aduersytye overthrewe her constant mynde, ffor albeyt that in king richards daies, she was often in jeopardy off her lyfe, yet she bare patiently all trouble in such wyse, that it ys wonder to thinke it'.

Margaret looked forward to a day when she could secure her release. Although a prisoner, she continued to support Henry, and the pair remained in contact. Henry had built a court of English exiles around him in Brittany, who addressed him as though he were king already. From his exile, he began to try to gather support in England, and he sent over a circular letter to leading figures in the kingdom, adopting a regal style and asking for their support:

Right trusty, worshipful, and honourable good friends, I greet you well.

Being given to understand your good devoir and entreaty to advance me to the furtherance of my rightful claim, due and lineal inheritance of that crown, and for the just depriving of that homicide and unnatural tyrant, which now unjustly bears dominion over you, I give you to understand that no Christian heart can be more full of joy and gladness than the heart of me your poor exiled friend, who will, upon the instant of your sure advertising what power you will make ready, and what captains and leaders you get to conduct, be prepared to pass over the sea with such force as my friends here are preparing for me.

And if I have such good speed and success as I wish according to your desire, I shall ever be most forward to remember and wholly to requite this your great and most loving kindness in my just quarrel.

Given under our signet. H.R.

It is unclear what response Henry received to his letters, but Richard was sufficiently concerned to once again make efforts to secure Henry's extradition from Brittany. He sent ambassadors to Francis II, promising him the confiscated revenues of Henry and the other exiled noblemen. He also offered the Bretons the support of 1,000 English archers in the event of an attack from France. Francis II was in ill health, and the ambassadors spoke to his treasurer, Pierre Landais, who disliked Henry and agreed to hand him over in late 1484. It appears that Lord Stanley, who was one of Richard III's councillors, heard of the plot at a council meeting and informed Margaret. She immediately sent her chaplain, Christopher Urswick, whom she trusted implicitly, to Bishop Morton in Flanders. The two men conferred, and Urswick then travelled to the French court to obtain a safe-conduct for Henry. With this safely received, Margaret's chaplain hurried to her son in Brittany to warn him of the danger that he was in. Henry was apparently oblivious to what was happening and, after nearly thirteen years in the duchy, may have considered himself safe. With no time to lose, he donned a disguise and slipped out of his house in the city of Vannes accompanied by only five servants, without even waiting to inform his English supporters. The danger that Henry was in was very real, and he rode hard, crossing the border into Anjou only an hour ahead of Breton soldiers, who had been sent in pursuit. Margaret must have felt a sense of dread as she waited to hear whether her message had had an effect, and she was no doubt quickly informed that Henry was well received by his kinsman, the fourteen-year-old King Charles VIII of France. When Francis II of Brittany recovered from his illness, he was furious to learn of how his guest had been treated and paid for all the English exiles in Brittany to join Henry's new court in exile in Paris. Henry was safe, but he remained uncomfortably aware of the changeability of fortune. Shortly after arriving in France, he had to forcibly prevent the Marquess of Dorset from returning to England after the peer received a message from his mother, Queen Elizabeth Woodville, urging him to abandon Henry and make terms with Richard.

The future seemed bleak to Elizabeth Woodville following the failure of Buckingham's rebellion, and during the first half of 1484, she remained in the sanctuary at Westminster with her daughters. With parliament's declaration that her marriage was invalid, she had been stripped of her title of queen and was referred to in all official documents as simply 'Dame Elizabeth Grey', by reference to her first marriage. She also lost the dower granted to her by Edward, and with her five daughters remaining with her, the sanctuary must have seemed impossibly crowded. Elizabeth was aware that, whilst they remained in sanctuary, the future of her daughters was uncertain, and ever a pragmatist, she slowly began to respond to Richard III's overtures of friendship. The fact that Elizabeth was prepared to make terms with Richard has, on occasion, been used to support the belief that she did not consider him to have been responsible for the murder of her sons, the princes in the Tower. However, this position is impossible to substantiate, and Elizabeth was already well aware that the King had ordered the execution of her second son by her first marriage, Sir Richard Grey, as well as her brother, Earl Rivers, following his coup at Stony Stratford in 1483. Elizabeth Woodville appears to have set aside personal feeling in her agreement with Richard, and it is clear that this was done, in the main, to ensure that both she and her daughters had some kind of future in England. She took steps to ensure her daughters' safety against the man who had murdered their half-brother, uncle and, in all likelihood, their two brothers. On 1 March 1484, Richard made a written agreement with Elizabeth, declaring that

I Richard by the Grace of God King of England and of Fraunce, and Lord of Irland, in the presens of you my Lords spirituell and temporell, and you Mair and Aldermen of my Cite of London, promisse and swere verbo regio upon these holy Evangelies of God by me personelly touched, that if the doughters of dame Elizabeth Gray late calling her selff Quene of England, that is to wit Elizabeth, Cecill, Anne, Kateryn, and Brigitte, woll come unto me out of the Sanctwarie of Westminster and be guyded, ruled, and demeaned after me, than I shall see that they shalbe in suertie of their lyffs, and also not suffre any manner hurt by any maner persone or persones to them or any of theim or their bodies and persones, to be done by way of ravissement or defouling contrarie their willes, nor them or any of theim emprisone within the Toure of London or other prisonne; but that I shall put them in honest places of good name and fame, and theim honestly and curtesly shall see to be founden and entreated, and to have all things requisite and necessary for their exibicion and findings as my kynneswomen.

The fact that Richard was required to swear that he would not imprison his nieces in the Tower suggests a great deal about what was believed to have happened to their brothers. For Richard, obtaining the princesses was a major coup, and he placed Elizabeth, the eldest, with his own wife at court.

Elizabeth of York turned eighteen in February 1484, and as the eldest daughter of Edward IV, she was, politically, of great interest. To many people in England, she was the heiress of the house of York and had the best hereditary claim to the throne of England. This had not been lost on Margaret when she promoted the match for Elizabeth with her son, and Richard III was also aware of her value. Although, legally, Elizabeth was illegitimate, this was not how she was viewed by most people, and in securing her person, Richard hoped to frustrate Henry's pretensions.

By 1484, Richard had been married to the youngest daughter of Warwick the Kingmaker, Anne Neville, for around twelve years. Anne was always sickly and bore her husband only one child, a son who was named as Prince of Wales on his father's accession to the throne. In April 1484, soon after Edward IV's daughters emerged from the sanctuary, Richard's son died suddenly, leaving the King without an heir and with a wife who, although still only in her twenties, was recognised as being incapable of further childbearing. By the end of 1484, rumours had emerged that Richard intended either to kill or discard his wife so that he could marry his niece, Elizabeth of York, and as if to fuel this speculation, it was noted that, at Christmas,

25. Margaret Beaufort. Margaret had a reputation for piety and, in later life, followed an ascetic lifestyle.

26. Statue of Margaret Beaufort from Christ's College, Cambridge *c.* 1510. Margaret oversaw the foundation of Christ's personally and her statue is proudly displayed over the gate of the college.

EDWARDVS . III .

27. Edward III. The rivalry between the descendants of Edward's sons led to the Wars of the Roses.

28. John of Gaunt. Margaret was the great granddaughter of the third surviving son of Edward III through his relationship with Katherine Swynford.

29. Henry IV and Joan of Navarre from their tomb at Canterbury Cathedral. Henry IV's usurpation of the crown caused the turbulent Wars of the Roses through which Margaret lived.

Above left: 30. Catherine of Valois - Margaret Beaufort's mother in law - giving birth to the future Henry VI. She shocked contemporaries by marrying Owen Tudor around 1430 (her second husband), her first husband was Henry V. From the *Beauchamp Pageant*.

Above right: 31. Henry VI depicted as a saint. Margaret later claimed that the Lancastrian king had prophesied that her son would rule England and he was widely regarded as a saint.

Above: 32, 33, & *Opposite page top*: 34. Pembroke Castle. Margaret took refuge in the castle following the death of her husband, Edmund Tudor, and it was there that she bore her only child. The interior images show life as it would have been in the castle during Margaret's residence there.

36. Elizabeth of York. Margaret entirely overshadowed her daughter-in-law and she took to signing her letters as 'Margaret R' to emphasise her queenly role.

Opposite: 35. Henry VII and Henry VIII portrayed together in an attempt to show the might of the Tudor dynasty. Henry VII, Margaret's son was the focus of all her ambition and she referred to him as her 'worldly joy'.

Above left: 37. Elizabeth Woodville. Edward IV's widow plotted with Margaret to bring Henry Tudor to the throne as the husband of her daughter, Elizabeth of York.

Above right: 38. Edward IV. The first Yorkist king was suspicious of Margaret and her son and he made strenuous efforts to secure Henry Tudor's return from Brittany.

Right: 39. Richard III stripped Margaret of all her possessions and placed her in her husband's custody as a punishment for her involvement in Buckingham's plot.

Far left: 40. Margaret of York, duchess of Burgundy. The sister of Edward IV and Richard III was determined to depose Henry VII and assisted pretenders to the throne.

Left: 43. Richmond Palace gatehouse. Little survives of Henry VII's finest palace today.

Top of page and above: 41. & 42. Greenwich Palace was a favourite residence of Henry VII and Margaret was a regular visitor there.

44. The tomb of Sir David Owen at Easeborne in West Sussex. Henry VII's generosity to the illegitimate son of Owen Tudor demonstrates his affection for his father's family and he was proud of his Tudor blood.

45. William Warham, Archbishop of Canterbury was appointed by Henry VII and was known to Margaret personally.

46. & 47. Christ's College, Cambridge. Margaret initially intended to patronise both Oxford and Cambridge Universities, but she was persuaded by her chaplain, John Fisher, to focus her energies on Cambridge.

Above & laft: 48. & 49. St John's College, Cambridge. Margaret did not live to see St John's College and it was left to her friend, John Fisher, to oversee the foundation.

Above left & right: 50. & 51. Henry VIII at Trinity College, Cambridge and King's College, Cambridge. Margaret's grandson followed her interest in education through his patronage of the University of Cambridge.

Right: 52. Henry VIII in later life. Margaret selected her grandson's first councillors but died before she could have much influence over his rule. Margaret's grandson resembled his Yorkist mother's family rather than his Beaufort or Tudor paternal family and he was proud of being the grandson of Edward IV.

KATHERINA VXOR HENRICI · · VII

Opposite page centre: 53. View of Westminster.

Opposite page bottom: 54. Great Tournament Roll of Westminster. Margaret's grandson, Henry VIII, was only seventeen when he became king and Margaret took control of affairs, appointing the new king's council for him.

Centre: 55. Catherine of Aragon. Margaret attended the marriage of Catherine of Aragon to Prince Arthur and she later witnessed the princess marry Arthur's younger brother, Henry VIII.

This page and opposite top spread: 56. London Bridge was one of the major landmarks of London during Margaret's time. Margaret was given a London residence by Henry VII and she spent a large proportion of her time in the capital.

Right: 57. Westminster Abbey. Margaret plotted to make her son king and she attended his coronation in the Abbey.

Above: 59. The Tower of London. Margaret's brother-in-law, Henry VI was imprisoned in the Tower following his deposition and he was murdered there soon after the Battle of Tewkesbury.

Left: 58. The Jewel Tower at Westminster Palace. Very little now remains of the medieval palace in which Henry VI prophesied to Margaret that her son would one day become king of England.

60. The Tower of London in around 1485, only two years after the mysterious disappearance of the princes in the Tower.

61. St Paul's Cathedral. Margaret's great-grandfather, John of Gaunt, chose to be buried in the cathedral and it was an important landmark in the London that Margaret knew.

62. Mary I was England's first effective reigning queen, something that would have been unthinkable in the late fifteenth century when Henry VII took Margaret's place in the succession.

63. Elizabeth I. Margaret's great-granddaughter drew on her as a model of a powerful and political woman.

Elizabeth appeared wearing the same dress as the Queen. From a dynastic point of view, a marriage to Elizabeth did indeed make perfect sense for Richard, and it would have served both to ensure that his children had the best possible claim to the throne and to frustrate Henry Tudor's claims once and for all. The fact that the potential couple were uncle and niece was not insurmountable, and the Pope had the power to grant a dispensation for such a union. There is also some evidence that Elizabeth herself desired the marriage, and the early seventeenth-century historian George Buck paraphrased a now lost letter supposedly written by Elizabeth in February 1485:

> When the midst and last of February was past, the lady Elizabeth, being more impatient and jealous of the success than every one knew or conceived, writes a letter to the Duke of Norfolk, intimating first, that he was the man in whom she most affied, in respect of that love her father had ever bore him, &c. Then she congratulates his many courtesies, in continuation of which, she desires him to be a mediator for her to the king, in behalf of the marriage propounded between them, who, as she wrote, was her only joy and maker in this world, and that she was his in heart and thought; with all insinuating that the better part of February was past, and that she feared the queen would never die.

Buck has been described as a 'faithless writer', and the fact that the letter no longer exists and was mentioned by no other writer must cast doubt on its truth. However, it is interesting in that the forceful character that it shows Elizabeth to have had is echoed in another, more reliable source, the ballad *Ladye Bessiye*, which also deals with the period. It is possible that Elizabeth of York, who so desired to be the queen of Henry Tudor, may first have sought to marry her uncle in order to achieve her ambitions. Even the *Crowland Chronicle Continuations* suggest that Elizabeth of York may not have been as placid as she is often portrayed, with the chronicler claiming that Richard's councillors were concerned at the prospect of the match 'for fear lest, if the said Elizabeth should attain the rank of queen, it might be in her power to avenge upon them the death of her uncle, earl Anthony [Rivers], and her brother Richard [Grey]'. Henry Tudor in Brittany was concerned enough about the rumours to look around for an alternative bride, seeking to marry a daughter of his old guardian, Sir William Herbert, in an attempt to win that family's support. This scheme progressed as far as messengers being sent to the lady's brother, Sir Walter Herbert, and her brother-in-law, the Earl of Northumberland.

Queen Anne Neville died on 16 March 1485, amidst rumours that the King had poisoned her in order to free himself to marry Elizabeth. This is unlikely, and Anne almost certainly died of the illness that had plagued her for much of her life. However, it demonstrates just how unpopular Richard had become in a reign that was still less than two years old. The idea that he might marry his niece, whilst possible with a dispensation, was against custom in England and caused disgust. Finally, amidst mutterings of discontent, the King was forced to make a public denial that any marriage was planned:

Whereas as there have been long discussions and much uninformed talk among the people by evil-disposed persons, who have ... sown these rumours to the very great displeasure of the king, showing how the queen was poisoned by consent and will of the king, so that he might marry and have to wife the Lady Elizabeth, eldest daughter of his brother, late King of England, deceased, whom God pardon ... the king sent for and had before him at St John's Day, yesterday, the mayor and aldermen. And in the great hall in the presence of many of his lords and many other people he shewed his grief and displeasure, and said it never came into his thought or mind to marry in such manner, nor was he pleased or glad at the death of his queen but as sorry and heavy in heart as a man could be ... And he then admonished and charged every person to cease from such untrue talking, on peril of his indignation.

For a king to have to take such a humiliating and unprecedented step demonstrates that Richard's rule was in trouble, and this would not have been lost on Margaret, who, whilst under house arrest, was allowed a great deal of contact with the outside world.

For Margaret, Richard's increasing unpopularity once again raised the possibility of her son succeeding to the throne. The execution of Buckingham, although a disaster for his rebellion in 1483, proved to be fortuitous for Henry Tudor, as it removed a dangerous rival to the Lancastrian succession. Although Margaret was unable to take any direct action during her imprisonment, she persuaded her husband to look more favourably on her son's cause, and there is some evidence that the ever-cautious Stanley began to commit himself secretly to Henry Tudor. The only detailed contemporary source for the activities of Elizabeth of York and Lord Stanley between March and August 1485 is the ballad *Ladye Bessiye*, which was composed by a member of Stanley's household, Humphrey Brereton, during the reign of Margaret's son. The ballad only survives in later copies, but even allowing for poetic licence, it is likely to contain much that is factual.

According to *Ladye Bessiye*, after the Queen's death, Richard placed Elizabeth of York in Stanley's London house, remembering that Edward IV, on his deathbed, had asked Margaret's husband to watch over his daughters. Margaret was certainly not allowed to live in London in 1485, and it is likely that she remained in Lancashire during the events described in the ballad. As Stanley's wife, it is inconceivable that she would have been oblivious to what was going on in her husband's house, and it is possible that she was able to make contact with Elizabeth of York, as she had previously done with Elizabeth Woodville. According to the ballad, Elizabeth hated Richard and blamed him for the murder of her brothers. She summoned Stanley to her and begged him to help Henry:

> For & he were King, I shold be Queene;
> I doe him loue, & neuer him see
> Thinke on Edward, my father, that late was King,
> Vpon his deathe-bed where he did lye:

> Of a litle child he put me to thee,
> For to gouerne and to guide;
> Unto your keeping hee put mee,
> & left me a booke of prophecye;-

> I haue itt in keeping in this citye;-
> He knew that yea might make me a Queene,
> Father, if thy will itt be;
> For Richard is no righteous kinge.

Although certainly romanticised, the idea that Elizabeth of York was determined to be a queen does agree with the supposed letter that she wrote to the Duke of Norfolk and suggests that she, like her mother and Margaret, may have been involved in the plot against Richard. Elizabeth was remarkably well informed of Stanley's strength, pointing out that his brother, Sir William Stanley, could muster 500 men and that his son, Lord Strange, could bring another 1,000. Stanley's younger son, Edward, could provide a further 300 and his nephew, Sir John Savage, 1,500. Stanley, at first, refused to listen, declaring that they would both be undone if Richard heard of what was said. Elizabeth berated him and threw her headdress to the ground, weeping and declaring that she would never be queen. Trying desperately to silence her, Stanley promised to meet with her again that night and finally agreed to send Brereton to fetch Sir William Stanley and Lord Strange. The Stanleys arrived in London on 3 May, and it was agreed to send a message to Henry in Brittany, with Elizabeth personally sending £10,000 (a figure which is likely to be grossly exaggerated). Once again, Brereton was sent as messenger, and when he reached Henry, he gave him a letter from Elizabeth, as well as her money and a ring, which Henry kissed three times. After thinking of what was proposed for some time, Henry said to Brereton,

> Comend me to Bessye, that Countesse cheere,-
> & yett I did neuer her see,-
> I trust in god shee shall be my Queene,
> for her I will trauell the sea.
> Comend me to my ffather Stanley,-
> My owne mother marryed hath hee.

If accurate, the ballad suggests that Henry was already assured of the support of the Stanleys before he sailed for England, and this was almost certainly down to Margaret's persuasions as much as Elizabeth's. According to the ballad, when Henry landed and met with Stanley, his stepfather declared that 'thou hast thy mothers blessing by mee', a further indication that Margaret was fully aware, and involved, in all that was happening. For Stanley too, the prospect of becoming the stepfather of the king must have been an enticing one and overpowered his usual caution to some extent.

Margaret remained active in her support of her son, and in the early months of 1485, her servant, Reginald Bray, set about collecting a large sum of money for the payment of Henry's mercenaries, presumably at Margaret's request. Bray also sent messages urging Henry to mount his invasion, and by the middle of 1485, Richard's fortunes appeared at their lowest ebb. The King was worried enough about the threat posed by Henry to issue a proclamation attacking Jasper Tudor, the Bishop of Exeter, the Earl of Oxford, Sir Edward Woodville and others who were with him in France, referring to them as 'his Rebels and Traitors, disabled and attainted by the authority of the High Court of Parliament' and accusing them of forsaking 'their natural country'. He then moved on to attack Henry's claims to the throne, declaring,

The said Rebels and Traitors have chosen to be their Captain one Henry Tydder, son of Owen Tydder, which of his ambitions and insatiable covetise encroacheth and usurpeth upon him, the name and title of Royal Estate of this realm of England; whereunto he hath no manner of interest, right, title, or colour, as every man well knoweth; for he is descended of bastard blood, both of father's side, and of mother's side; for the said Owen the Grandfather, was bastard born; and his mother was daughter unto John, Earl of Somerset, son unto Dame Katherine Swynford, and of their indouble avowtry gotten; whereby it evidently appeareth, that no title can nor may vest in him.

Richard had a point in demonstrating the dubious nature of Henry's claim to the throne, and the incumbent king undoubtedly had a better hereditary claim to the throne than the pretender. The difficulty for Richard was, however, that most people in England considered that Elizabeth of York had the best claim of all. Richard was unable to neutralise her claim by marrying her himself, and he therefore did the next best thing, sending Elizabeth and her cousin, the Earl of Warwick, who was the son of Richard's elder brother, the Duke of Clarence, to Sheriff Hutton Castle in Yorkshire under guard, in order to ensure that the pair did not fall into Henry Tudor's hands.

Henry had continued to be treated with favour at the French court, and he secured Charles VIII's agreement to granting him funds for 3,000 to 4,000 men and arms. As surety for his debts, he left the untrustworthy Marquess of Dorset behind at the French court before sailing from Harfleur in August 1485 and landing, after some days at sea, at Milford Haven. Margaret was soon aware of the landing, and Henry immediately wrote to her to ask for her support. He sent similar letters to Lord Stanley and his brother, Sir William Stanley, as well as other friends. It appears that, by the middle of 1485, Stanley had decided to commit himself to his stepson's cause, and in July, he informed the King that he intended to visit his home and family in Lancashire. Richard was suspicious, and whilst he reluctantly gave his permission, he insisted that Stanley's eldest son, George, Lord Strange, remain at court as a hostage to ensure his father's loyalty. This was a major blow to Stanley and caused him to distance himself from Henry's cause. According to the *Ballad of Bosworth Ffeild*, a contemporary ballad written by a follower of the Stanleys, when news of Henry's landing reached the King, he ordered Lord Strange to be imprisoned, before sending a message to his father to declare that

You must raise those that vnder you bee,

& all the power that you may bringe,

Or else the Lord Strange you must neuer see,

Which is in danger of our king.

Richard also ordered Stanley to come to him at Nottingham 'for the king was afraid lest that, as it really turned out, the mother of the said Earl of Richmond, whom the Lord Stanley had married, might induce her husband to go over to the party of her son'. Stanley refused to attend, feigning illness, but this was as far as he dared to go in his defiance of the King. Fear for his son's safety stalled Stanley, and far from openly supporting Henry on his landing, he remained at a cautious distance, something that must have discomfited Margaret.

Although Lord Stanley was not prepared to openly show his support for Margaret's son, his brother, Sir William Stanley, who had ignored a summons to court from Richard, declared his hand. After landing, Henry began the march through Wales to confront the King. Due to Jasper Tudor's presence with his forces, the town of Pembroke immediately sent word that it would support him. He also managed to persuade a leading Welshman, Rhys ap Thomas, to support him, in return for a promise to make him governor of Wales. When Henry arrived at Shrewsbury, he was concerned to find that the city gates were closed against him. This was evidence of Henry's relative obscurity in England, and it was only when the townsmen received a message from Sir William Stanley that they agreed to open the gates. In spite of this, they still refused to let him spend a single night in the town, and Margaret's son was forced to move on, travelling to Stafford, where he met with Sir William Stanley for the first time. Sir William had two battalions of men at his command, and his support was essential to Henry. More importantly for the

pretender, he knew that whatever was said between him and Lord
Stanley's brother would be related to his stepfather, and Henry was
still anxious to secure Stanley's aid, with the *Ballad of Bosworth
Ffielde* claiming that, on landing, he declared,

> Send me the loue of the lord Stanley!
>
> He marryed my mother, a lady bright;
>
> That is long sith I saw her with sight;
>
> I trust in Iesu [Jesus] wee shall meete with winne,
>
> & I shall maintaine her honor right
>
> Ouer all England when I am Kinge.

Although still undecided about what action to take, Lord Stanley
left Lathom on 15 August, where it is likely that he took his leave
of Margaret. Margaret had seen her third husband leave for battle
and return seriously wounded, and she must have been apprehensive
about the safety of her fourth husband. She would have recognised
how torn Stanley was by the danger that his son was in, although,
for Margaret, her focus was always on her own son, and it is likely
that she took the opportunity to once again try to persuade Stanley
to go to Henry's aid. On 20 August, Henry reached Lichfield, where
he heard that, only three days earlier, Lord Stanley had arrived with
a force of 5,000 men. Sir William Stanley arrived the same day and
once again had a conference with Henry. The following day, Henry,
who commanded a force considerably smaller than the King's and
was anxious to make use of his stepfather's men, went in person
to meet with the two Stanleys. It appears that the meeting was
largely satisfactory, and whilst Stanley refused to commit himself, he
undertook not to support the King. Further evidence of his sympathy
for his stepson was shown when he sent four knights and their men

to reinforce Henry's vanguard. This was the best that Henry could hope for, and he returned to his troops to prepare for battle.

Richard had been at Nottingham when he heard of Henry's landing, and gathering his forces, he moved to cut off the pretender's route to the capital. He soon arrived at Leicester and, on 21 August, moved to a field near Atherstone that had been chosen as the site of the battle, which would later be called the Battle of Bosworth Field. Richard had a larger army than Henry, but his camp was disorganised, and when he woke from a night of bad dreams on the morning of 22 August, he found that no breakfast had been prepared for him and there was no priest available for him to hear Mass.

Henry's army included Margaret's half-brother, John, Lord Welles, as well as Jasper Tudor, the Earl of Oxford, Sir Edward Woodville and the Bishop of Exeter, and the group must have been apprehensive as they prepared to face Richard in battle on the morning of 22 August. Henry himself apparently showed no fear, and according to *Hall's Chronicle*, he rode up and down his line, encouraging his troops and urging them forward. As Richard watched the display, he commanded that Lord Strange, who was imprisoned in his camp, be brought to him. He then ordered the young man's execution as a warning to his father, and it was only through luck that, at that moment, the battle commenced, and Lord Strange was granted a temporary reprieve, being ordered back to the camp under guard.

The battle itself is very poorly documented, but it appears that it was Henry's force that moved first, after coming under fire from Richard's archers. The centre of the army, which was commanded by Henry himself, made straight for Richard, whilst the Earl of Oxford moved to attack the wing of the King's army commanded by the Duke of Norfolk. To Henry's dismay, neither of the Stanleys moved to join him, and both stood by with their forces, perhaps intending to claim loyalty to whoever emerged the victor. Richard himself showed great personal courage, and when the battle began to turn against him, he refused the offer of a horse to allow him to flee. Instead, the King went straight towards Henry and killed his standard bearer, Sir William Brandon. Richard's actions were heroic, and he deliberately placed himself in danger in an attempt to finally bring to an end the danger represented by Henry to his throne. Unfortunately for Richard, it was at that moment that Sir William Stanley finally intervened, and he came to Henry's aid with his men, driving the King backwards. Overwhelmed, Richard fell in battle, along with many of his supporters.

According to tradition, the crown that Richard had worn in battle was found lying under a hawthorn bush. It was brought to Lord Stanley, and Henry's stepfather, who had maintained his record of failing to serve in any of the battles of the Wars of the Roses, ceremonially placed it on Henry's head, declaring him to be King Henry VII. For Henry, who had defeated a rival with a considerably better claim to the throne than his own, it was his moment of greatest glory. For Margaret, in Lancashire, it was also a triumph, and Henry's success owed a great deal to her belief in him and her promotion of his interests. As the King headed south, Margaret, liberated from her imprisonment with one stroke of the sword, moved to London to take up her new position as 'the King's Mother' and to be finally reunited with her son.

10

THE KING'S MOTHER:
AUGUST 1485-JANUARY 1486

When news reached Margaret of her son's victory at Bosworth and his proclamation as King Henry VII, she was immediately struck by the turn of Fortune's Wheel, and as her friend John Fisher observed, she wept at Henry's coronation for fear of the reversal of fortune that had always, in the past, followed triumph. Margaret made her way south to share in her son's victory, and 1485 marks the beginning of the second phase of her life as the most powerful woman in England: My Lady, the King's Mother. It also marks a watershed in Margaret's life, and from 1485 onwards, her life became one of the most well documented of any woman of her time.

Margaret's house arrest ended the moment that news arrived of Henry's victory, and it is likely that she moved south at once, intending to meet up with both her husband and son, who had travelled to Leicester together. Henry entered the city in great style, carrying Richard III's body trussed to the side of a horse as a trophy of victory. The new king spent only two days in the city but took the time to order that all Richard's badges be removed. He also sent Sir Robert Willoughby to Sheriff Hutton to secure control of both Elizabeth of York and her cousin, the Earl of Warwick. Elizabeth, who was Henry's betrothed bride, was placed in the custody of her mother in London. Warwick, who, as the only surviving male member of the House of York, was a danger to the King, was placed in Margaret's custody soon after the arrival of her son in London: a clear sign of the trust that the new king had in her. Margaret's custody of the boy proved to be brief, and he was soon lodged in the Tower, remaining there as the most high-profile state prisoner for the remainder of his short life. It is unlikely that Margaret would have reached Leicester in time to join her son and Stanley there, but she may have met them on the road to London. If not, her first meeting with Henry in over fourteen years was in the capital of his new kingdom: for mother and son, it must have been emotional.

Although fourteen years had passed since they had last met, the bond between mother and son remained as strong as ever. Almost as soon as he became king, Henry set about rewarding those who had supported him and punishing those who had not. On 16 September 1485, for example, Sir Edward Woodville, the brother of the Queen Dowager, who had spent over two years in exile with Henry, received a grant of the castle and lordship of Carisbrook Castle on the Isle of Wight, as well as being appointed the keeper of the castle and town of Portchester in Hampshire. Sir William Stanley, whose intervention at Bosworth had proved so useful, received on the same day a grant of a manor in Hertfordshire. Margaret's brother-in-law was also appointed one of the chamberlains of the exchequer a few days later, and her stepson, James Stanley, who had taken holy orders, received an appointment as a dean of the King's royal chapel of St Martin the Great in London. Christopher Urswick and Reginald Bray, Margaret's two most trusted servants, received generous grants. The greatest rewards were given to Jasper Tudor, who was created Duke of Bedford by his grateful nephew, and Margaret's own husband, who was referred to in one grant as the King's 'righte entierly beloved fader' and was made Earl of Derby. Stanley also received substantial grants of property 'in consideration of the good and praiseworthy services performed by him before now with great personal exertions and costs, in many ways and on divers occasions, and now lately in the king's conflict within the realm of England, and which services he ceases not to continue'. The Stanley family received an immediate boon when they were permitted to take away the rich hangings found in Richard III's tent at Bosworth.

Margaret became Countess of Richmond and Derby when her husband was granted his earldom. On her son's accession, she also became entitled to a much more prestigious title, and throughout the reign, she was commonly referred to as 'the king's mother'. The only recent precedent for such a role had been Cecily Neville, Duchess of York, the mother of Edward IV and Richard III. Cecily, who was still living in 1485, had taken on a semi-regal status during her sons' reigns, and it is likely that Margaret based her own conduct on this. She was certainly personally rewarded by her son. On 11 October, the King's 'most derrest moder, Margaret, countesse of Richmond' received the power to appoint the officers of the lordship of Ware in Hertfordshire, something that could be lucrative. Margaret's confiscated estates were returned and the attainder against her was reversed. In order to ensure that she was provided for, she had her marriage contract with Stanley confirmed by parliament. In August 1486, Henry granted Margaret the wardships of the two sons of her nephew, the executed Duke of Buckingham, a grant that gave her access to the boys' vast revenues. Margaret was able to use this to benefit her own kin, and even before the grant was finalised, Henry made her half-brother, John Welles, a grant out of the Buckingham estates, something that was likely to have been done at Margaret's request. She also appears to have been fond of the young duke, being recorded to have received at least one visit from him to her household at Collyweston after he was an adult, when she gave him a gift of a jewel worth one hundred pounds, a generous gesture. Shortly after the accession, she was able to arrange royal marriages for two of her kinsmen, persuading her son to allow John Welles to marry Cecily, the second surviving daughter of Edward IV, and for her nephew, Richard Pole, who was a son of her half-sister, Edith St John, to marry Margaret of Clarence, the sister of the Earl of Warwick.

Although Henry had pledged to marry Elizabeth of York before mounting his invasion of England, the couple were too closely related to marry without a papal dispensation, which did not arrive until early 1486. In spite of this, Henry was determined to formalise his kingship as soon as possible, and he arranged his coronation for 30 October 1485. Henry's early biographer, Sir Francis Bacon, stated that the King claimed the throne through three separate titles: marriage, descent and conquest:

The first of these was fairest, and most like to give contentment to the people, who by two and twenty years reign of King Edward the fourth had been fully made capable of the clearness of the title of the white rose or house of York; and, by the mild and plausible reign of the same king toward his latter time, were become affectionate to that line. But then it lay plain before his eyes, that if he relied upon that title, he could be but a king at courtesy, and have rather a matrimonial than a regal power; the right remaining in his queen, upon whose decease, either with issue, or without issue, he was to give place and be removed. And though he should obtain by parliament to be continued, yet he knew there was a very great difference between a king that holdeth his crown by a civil act of estates, and one that holdeth it originally by the law of nature and descent of blood.

A claim by conquest was fraught with danger, and it opened up the possibility of a rival claimant vanquishing the King in battle in his turn. Henry therefore always chose to prioritise his claim as the heir to the House of Lancaster, making good use of Margaret's Beaufort portcullis badge and the Lancastrian symbol of the red rose (which he particularly appears to have adopted as a contrast to the more common Yorkist white rose). He also stressed his links to Henry VI, referring to his murdered uncle's saintliness in a number of documents.

As a further demonstration of his claims, Henry planned a magnificent coronation. In August 1485, Margaret's son was virtually unknown in England, and it is likely that he had only previously visited London on one occasion, during the restoration of Henry VI. Henry's kingdom in 1485 was, after years of civil war, impoverished, and whilst one contemporary Italian visitor in 1497 was able to praise the position of Henry's capital city, noting that 'it would be hard to find one more convenient and attractive', the infrastructure of London itself was in a poor state:

All the streets are so badly paved that they get wet at the slightest quantity of water, and this happens very frequently owing to the large numbers of cattle carrying water, as well as on account of the rain, of which there is a great deal in this island. Then a vast amount of evil-smelling mud is formed, which does not disappear quickly but lasts a long time, in fact nearly the whole year round. The citizens, therefore, in order to remove this mud and filth from their boots, are accustomed to spread fresh rushes on the floors of all houses, on which they clean the soles of their shoes when they come in. This system is widely practised not only by Londoners but also by all the rest of the islands' inhabitants, who, it seems, suffer from similar troubles from mud.

Henry's rather unsophisticated subjects were renowned for their fierce tempers and dislike of foreigners, something that further drove the new king, who could claim English blood only through his mother, to emphasise his claims to be the heir to Henry VI. Henry was able to impress at his coronation, which Margaret attended, and he required so much scarlet cloth that his officers were forced to scour the city for supplies. The King spared no expense in his own wardrobe for the ceremony, purchasing powdered ermine and also black furs to augment his black velvet jacket. He ordered a surcoat of fine blue cloth and crimson cloth of gold for a long gown. Further robes of crimson velvet and crimson satin were also made, as well as fine Holland cloth used to line the King's doublets. The Abbey itself was decorated with red Lancastrian roses, red dragons to emphasise Henry's claim of descent from the mythical ancient kings of Britain, and 105 portcullis badges made of silver and gilt. Without a queen to share his coronation, the role of women at the ceremony was naturally limited, but as John Fisher recalled, Margaret was prominent in the congregation and wept at her moment of greatest triumph, fearful of another sudden turn of Fortune's Wheel.

Henry VII has a somewhat poor personal reputation and is remembered both as a miser and for his suspicious and joyless reign. This is, however, in many respects, very far from the truth, for Margaret's son, whilst he was determined to replenish the depleted English coffers, was also ready to spend money. At the time of his accession, Henry had still not reached thirty, and he was a tall and striking young man. His privy purse expenses, which survive for the years between 1492 and 1505, show a lively and pleasure-loving king. In January 1492, for example, the King lost £5 at 'pley at cards'. A further £4 were expended in July of that year 'to the king which he lost at cardes'. Henry appears from his expenses to have been an enthusiastic, if often unsuccessful, gambler. In January 1494, he lost £2 at cards, with further sums lost in August 1494 and March 1495. He upped the stakes in May 1496 when payments were recorded 'to the kinges grace to play at the cardes, in gold, £20, in grotts, 100s. in grotts, £19, and in grotes, 60s.' By 1502, he had started to gamble, and lose, at dice. Henry employed a number of fools, making grants to Patch the fool in February 1492, Diego, the Spanish fool, in October 1492 and Dick the fool in January 1494. He loved music and rewarded minstrels belonging to Cecily Neville, the old Duchess of York, as well as, in February 1494, making a payment to Margaret's own troupe. His expenses for 14 August 1494 at Windsor record that he gave £2 'to my Lady the Kinges moder for the wages of Sir John Bracy, singing before our Lady of the pewe for a quarter wages'. On a more personal level, he purchased a lute for his youngest daughter, Mary, in 1505. He made a payment to a troupe of morris dancers in 1494 and a number of rewards paid to players testify to his love of the theatre. On 3 December 1497, he paid over £3 'to my Lady the kinges moder poete', demonstrating, once again, Margaret's own love of literature. Payments for 'disguisings' demonstrate that Henry's court saw lavish entertainments, with masques staged at important occasions. He loved finery and purchased a gold ring from his brother-in-law, the Marquess of Dorset, in July 1492, as well as making gifts of gold wire, furs and a quantity of jewels to Elizabeth of York and using his privy purse to purchase a further three gold rings and a diamond. March 1504 saw the payment of the vast sum of £30,000 'for diverse precious stones and other juells that com from beyonde the see'. Henry was very far from the joyless character of popular repute, at least in the first two decades of his reign, and he shared many of his interests with his mother. Henry's expenses record a number of visits made to Margaret's household, and it is clear that, when she was not at court, she and Henry remained in regular and close contact.

Although Margaret was happy to pass her claim to the throne to her son and actively supported him in his kingship, she was not prepared to be simply a background figure and expected a great degree of prominence. As a married woman, Margaret would ordinarily be able to do very little legally without her husband's consent, for example, in relation to the management of her property. Wives were not legally allowed to leave a Will at their death and were generally considered to be subservient to their husbands. Whilst Henry was prepared to follow convention and address Stanley as his father and was grateful for what his stepfather had done in helping him win the throne, it is clear that he did not have the personal relationship with him that he had had with his first stepfather, Henry Stafford, who had left him a personal bequest in his Will. As the mother of the King, Margaret outranked Stanley, and whilst it is likely that there was some affection in the marriage, her main interests were firmly focused on her son. Shortly after he came to the throne, Henry passed a remarkable Act of Parliament that was made in consultation with Margaret and was likely to have been made at her request:

And furthermore hit be ordeined, enacted and stablisshed by the same auctoritee, that the same countesse, in her name sole, by the name of Margaret countesse of Richmond, modre of the most Christian prince King Herrie the VIIth, King of England and of France, maie fro' henceforth terme of her lyfe sue all manner of actions reals and personalls and also all actions mixtes, and plede and be ympleded for all manner of causes in all manner of courts spirituells and temporells, ayenst all persons, as any other persone or persones may or shall more doe, in as good, large and beneficiall manner, as any other sole persone not wyfe ne covert of any husband, att anie tyme might or maie do. And that she, as well onely, as with other persones, att her pleasure may from henceforth, dueringe her lyfe, as well make, as take and receive, all manner of feoffments, states, leases, releases, confirmations, presentations, bargains, sales, yefts, deeds, wills and writeings, as well of landes and tennements and all manner of hereditaments, as of all manner goods, cattells and other thinges, to her owne use oonly, or to the use of such as shall please her.

The Act made Margaret a 'sole person' and effectively gave her the autonomy to act as a widow, in spite of the fact that her husband was still alive. This was an unprecedented position for a married woman to be in and demonstrates the superior position in which Henry's accession to the throne placed his mother. As a further testament to her autonomy, during Stanley's lifetime, Margaret secured his consent to her taking a vow of chastity, which she later restated once she was widowed:

In the presence of my Lord God Jesu Christ & his blessed Mother the glorious Virgin St Mary & of all the whole company of Heaven & of you also my Ghostly Father I Margaret of Richmond with full Purpose & good Deliberation for the Weale of my sinfull Soule with all my Hearte promise from henceforth the Chastity of my Bodye. That is never to use my Bodye having actuall knowledge of manne after the common usuage in Matrimonye the which Thing I had before purposed in my Lord my Husbands Dayes then being my Ghostly father the Byshop of Rochester Mr Richard Fitz James & now eftsence I fully confirm it as far as in me lyeth beseeching my Lord God that He will this my poor wyll accept to the Remedye of my wretched Lyfe & Relief of my sinfull soule and that He will give me his Grace to perform the same. And also for my more Meryte & quietness of my Soule in doubtful things perteyning to the same I avowe to you my Lord of Rochester to whom I am & have been sence the first time I see you admitted verely determined (as to my chiefe trusty Councellour) to owe my Obedience in all things concerning the weale and profyte of my Soule.

Stanley's consent was probably easily obtained, and whilst he remained in high favour with the King, Margaret had the superior influence. She both legally and spiritually obtained her independence from her husband, but it is clear that she retained a fondness for him and did not cut her ties from him completely, retaining rooms for him at her residences and visiting him at his own houses. However, the accession of Henry VII meant that, for the first time in her life, Margaret was able to act entirely independently of any kind of male control.

Shortly after his accession, Henry provided Margaret with a fine London residence, Coldharbour. Coldharbour was palatial and commanded fine views over the River Thames. This easy access to the river, when the main travel around the city was by boat, was essential and allowed Margaret direct contact with her son even when she was not with him. During Henry's reign, she acquired a house at Collyweston in Bedfordshire, which was to become her favourite home. Collyweston had been built in the fifteenth century by Lord Cromwell, and whilst it was already a substantial house, Margaret set about turning it into a palace. By the time of her death, the house had a chapel, library, counting-house, great parlour, guest chambers and a jewel house. Perhaps as an indication of what Margaret felt her true status to be, the main room was called the 'Queen's Chamber'. Margaret ensured that her house was furnished as befitted her rank and wealth. She had a bed with a counterpane and curtains of fine white damask, as well as a chair upholstered in red velvet and another of russet cloth of gold with a blue fringe. One tablecloth was decorated with Tudor roses and Margaret's own Beaufort portcullis badge. She had cushions of silk, velvet and cloth of gold. It is likely that much of Margaret's collection of gold plate was kept there, some of which was used to augment her chapel. For Margaret, part of the attraction of Collyweston may have been that, with the exception of Coldharbour, it was the only house that she had been able to build and use totally independently of any of her husbands.

During Henry's reign, Margaret was often at court. When she was in her own home, however, she was able to follow an orderly and homely routine, with, as had always been the case for her, her daily activities focusing on her religious devotions. Henry Parker, who would later become Lord Morley, arrived in Margaret's household towards the end of the fifteenth century to serve her as her carver or cupbearer, and more than forty years after his employer's death, he set down an account of her household for her great-granddaughter, Mary I. This provides a brief view of Margaret's daily life at Collyweston, or Coldharbour, or any of the other residences in which she stayed during the reign of her son:

Thus did she use her life, her grace was every mornyng in the chapple betwixt five and sevyn of the clock, and dayly sayde matyns off the day with one off her chaplyns, and that sayde from sevyn tyll yt was eleven off the clocke, as sone as one preist had sayd masse in her syght another beganne, one tyme in a day she was confessyd, then going to her dynner how honorably she was seruyd I think fewe kings better, her condityon alwaies of the begynnyng of her dyner was to be joyous, and to heare those tales that were honest to make her mery, the myddes of her dynner either her amner or I redde some vertuous tale vnto her of the life of chryst, or such like, the latter ende off hir dinner agayne she was disposed to talk with the bishop [John Fisher, her chaplain] or with her chauncelour which satt at her bordis ende of some goldly matter.

Margaret usually dined with her household, and Parker's anecdote demonstrates that she enjoyed a joke, as well as insisting on strict religious adherence in her household.

As the mother of the King, Margaret was able to live in some style when she was not at court. Parker recorded an anecdote of one Christmas period at Margaret's residence when he was aged around fifteen. This information, coupled with the fact that Margaret's half-brother, Lord Welles, who was present, died in 1499, suggests a date of Christmas 1498 or, perhaps, a year before. According to Parker, Margaret lived in luxury and was able to entertain on a lavish scale:

In Cristmas tyme she kept so honorable a house, that upon one newe yeares day I being her carver off the age of fyftene yeares, had fyve & twentye knights folowing me of whom myne owne father was one, and sytting at her table the erle of derby her husband, the vicount Wellys, the olde Lord Hastings, the Byshoppe of Lincolne, and by her person under her clothe of estate the lady cecyle king Edwardes doughter your [Queen Mary I's] awnte. In her hall from nyne of the clock tyll it was sevyn off the clock at night as fast as one table was up another was sett, no pore man was denayed [denied] at that sayde feast of cristmas if he were of any honestye, but that he might come to the Buttrye, or to the cellar to drinke att his pleasure, her liberalytie was such that ther came no man of honour or worship to her as ther came many of the greatest of the realme.

Parker claimed that Margaret employed a household of 440 people, including ladies, gentlemen, yeomen and officers and that she surprised everyone by knowing the names of all her attendants. The size of Margaret's household might be an exaggeration, and it is very unlikely that she employed such a high number of people on a daily basis. It is, however, clear that she lived in a royal manner as befitted the mother of the King.

Although few of either Margaret's or Henry's letters survive, it is evident from those that do that the pair enjoyed a warm relationship throughout Henry's reign, and they are amongst the most personal documents of the pair to survive. Margaret's first surviving letter to her son, which dates to 1501, demonstrates the familiar way in which they coupled affection with a businesslike manner:

My own sweet and most dear King, and all my worldly joy.

In as humble manner as I can think, I recommend me to your grace, and most heartily beseech our Lord to bless you. And my good heart, where that you say that the French King hath at this time given me courteous answer, and written letter of favour to his Court of Parliament, for the brief expedition of my matter, which so long hath hanged; the which I well know he doth especially for your sake, for the which my ......ly beseech your Grace it ...... to give him your favourable ...... thanks, and to desire him to continue his ...... in......e...... me. And, if it so might like your Grace, to do the same to the cardinal; which, as I understood, is your faithful, true, and loving servant. I wish my very joy, as I oft have shewed, and I fortune to get this, or any part thereof, there shall neither be that or any good I have, but it shall be your's, and at your commandment, as surely and with as good a will, as any ye have in your coffers; and would God ye could know it, as verily as I think it. But, my dear heart, I will no more encumber your Grace with further writing in this matter, for I am sure your chaplain and servant, Dr. Whytston, hath shewed your highness the circumstances of the same; and if it so may please your Grace, I humbly beseech the same, to give further credence also to this bearer. And our Lord give you as long good life, health, and joy, as your most noble heart can desire, with as hearty blessings as our Lord hath given me power to give you.

Margaret's 'French matter' concerned a ransom due to her family from the family of the Duke of Orléans, who had become King of France as Louis XII in 1498. In 1412, the stepfather of Margaret's father, Thomas, Duke of Clarence, had made a treaty with the then Duke of Orléans at which it was promised that in order to stop Clarence from attacking France with his army, a large sum of money would be paid. As a pledge, Orléans' younger brother Jean, Count of Angoulême, and six others were surrendered as hostages to Clarence. On Clarence's death, custody of the hostages and the entitlement to the debt passed to his widow, Margaret's grandmother, and was in turn inherited by Margaret's father. On his death, Margaret's mother, Margaret Beauchamp, inherited the entitlement, and she arranged to release Angoulême in return for a promise to pay the sums outstanding by instalments. The payments quickly fell into arrears, and on her mother's death, Margaret took up the cause, taking the matter to court in France in 1482, where it was adjourned indefinitely. During Richard III's reign, Margaret and Stanley approached the King personally for his assistance in obtaining what was, by then, a vast sum outstanding, but with Margaret's disgrace following Buckingham's rebellion, the matter had once again become dormant. With Henry's accession, Margaret pressed for her matter to be settled, and Henry, as her heir, enthusiastically supported her. By the early sixteenth century, with the heir to Clarence's claim represented by the King of England and the heir to the Orléans debt represented by the King of France, the matter had taken on a new political dimension, of which both Margaret and Henry were aware. The old English claim that their King was also King of France had never been abandoned, and both Margaret and Henry, in their correspondence, show that they were aware of the leverage the claim gave them if they chose to press it. In 1504, Margaret formally surrendered her interest to Henry.

A letter of Henry's from July 1504 survives, demonstrating again the closeness that existed between mother and son and the pair's joint political awareness:

Madam, my most entirely well-beloved lady and mother.

I recommend me unto you in the most humble and lowly wise that I can, beseeching you of your daily and continual blessings. By your confessor the bearer, I have received your good and most loving writing, and by the same, have heard at good leisure such credence as he would shew unto me on your behalf, and thereupon have sped him in every behalf without delay, according to your noble petition and desire which resteth in two principal points; the one for a general pardon for all manner causes; the other is for to alter and change part of a licence which I had given unto you before, for to be put into mortmain at Westminster, and now to be converted unto the University of Cambridge for your soul's health, etc. All which things according to your desire and pleasure, I have with all my heart and good-will given and granted unto you. And my Dame, not only in this but in all other things that I may know should be to your honour and pleasure, and weal of your soul, I shall be as glad to please you as your heart can desire it, and I know well that I am as much bounden so to do as any creature living, for the great and singular motherly love and affection that it hath pleased you at all times to bear towards me. Wherefore, my own most loving mother, in my most hearty manner I thank you, beseeching you of your good continuance in the same. And, Madam, your said confessor, hath moreover shewn unto me on your behalf, that ye of our goodness and kind disposition, have given and granted unto me such title and interest as ye have or ought to have in such debts and duties which is owing and due unto you in France, by the French king and others; wherefore, Madam, in my most hearty and humble wise I thank you. Howbeit, I verily think it will be right hard to recover it without it be driven by compulsion and force, rather than by any true justice, which is not yet as we think any convenient time to be put in execution.

Nevertheless it hath pleased you to give us a good interest mean, if they will not conform them to reason and good justice, to defend or offend at a convenient time when the case shall so require hereafter. For such a chance may fall that this your grant might stand in great stead for a recovery of our right, and to make us free, whereas we be now bound, etc. And verily, Madam, and I might recover it at this time or any other, ye be sure ye should have your pleasure therein, as I and all that God has given me, is and shall ever be at your will and commandment, as I have instructed Master Fisher [Margaret's confessor] more largely herein, as I doubt not but he will declare unto you. And I beseech you to send me your mind and pleasure in the same, which I shall be full glad to follow with God's grace, which send and give unto you the full accomplishment of all your noble and virtuous desires.

Henry signed his letter 'with the hand of your most humble and loving son' and it is clear that he both sought Margaret's advice and discussed his own political actions with her. By the time that his letter was written, he had already invaded France in 1492 both as part of England's ancient claim to the country and in support of Brittany, and whilst he had quickly accepted the peace terms offered by Charles VIII of France, Margaret's claim did provide him with a useful excuse to make war again if he ever chose to. As it happened, Henry never did press the claims, and it was left to his successor, Henry VIII, to finally receive payment of the funds, a century after they had first become due.

The extent of Margaret's influence over Henry VII is debateable, and his early biographer Bacon claimed that he listened only to his own mind and that 'his mother he reverenced much, heard little'. This may have been true in some instances, but it is clear from his correspondence that Henry did indeed actively seek his mother's advice. He also allowed Margaret to adopt the status of a queen, and her more formal letters adopted a quasi-regal tone, with an early letter to the Bishop of Exeter, for example, declaring,

Right reuerend Fader in God and oure right welbiloued. In our harty wise, we commaund vs vnto you, and for asmoche as John Dalkyn, receiuor of oure Lordshippe of Holdernes belonging vnto oure cousin of Bukes hath not commen vp and made his accompt as he ought to doo by raison of his said office, but hath sodenly departed from hous othrewise than according to the trust that was put in hym: We therefore desire and herty pray you to send us by this bringer a pryve seill for the said John after the tenure of this bille whiche we send you herein closed, as our specialle trust is in you and as we may doo for you at your desires hereafter, whereunto we shalbe always redy by Goddes grace who send you right good lif and long.

Yeuen vndre our signet at oure place of Colde Harborowe, the 21st day of Marche. My lord y pray you y may her of your newes of Flaundyrse.

This letter was signed 'M. Rychemound', a usual signature for a member of the nobility, where the first name was commonly abbreviated and the title written in full. After only a few short years, however, Margaret adapted her signature to the more regal 'Margaret R', which, whilst it could stand for 'Margaret Richmond', could equally be read as 'Margaret *Regina*', an ambiguity that she undoubtedly intended. Henry made no protest to this, and it was clearly done with his tacit approval, again suggesting that he was aware of his mother's ambitions and supported them. In many respects, mother and son can be seen as a partnership, and the assessment of the Spanish ambassador in 1498 may therefore be correct when he wrote 'the king is much influenced by his mother and his followers in affairs of personal interest and in others. The queen, as is generally the case, does not like it'. Within months of Henry VII's accession to the throne, Margaret had established herself as an independent and regal political force beside the King, and she was reluctant to give up any of her position when Henry finally married Elizabeth of York in January 1486.

11

MARGARET R: JANUARY 1486-JULY 1504

Margaret Beaufort has a reputation as a somewhat difficult and formidable mother-in-law, and to a certain extent, this is justified. In most areas, she was able to overshadow her daughter-in-law, Elizabeth of York. Margaret, who was used to being the dominant female force in her only child's life, was reluctant to cede her position to his wife.

Although Henry was determined to be seen to claim the throne as the heir to the House of Lancaster, most people in England considered the real heiress to be Elizabeth of York, who had been declared to be legitimate by him in his first parliament. Elizabeth spent the months following Henry's accession with her mother, Elizabeth Woodville, in London, although, from the date of birth of her first child, it is possible that she and Henry had begun to cohabit some weeks before their marriage on 18 January 1486, soon after the papal dispensation had been received. Although, during the reign of her uncle, Richard III, there is some evidence that Elizabeth of York had an ambitious character, once she became queen, there is little information on her thoughts and personality, and she was, from the first, dominated by Margaret and by her own mother, the Queen Dowager. Elizabeth fell pregnant either shortly before her marriage or immediately afterwards. Henry, who was anxious to stress the links of his dynasty to the mythical ancient kings of Britain, insisted that she enter her confinement at Winchester, the ancient capital of the Anglo-Saxons and a city that was believed to have been linked to King Arthur. The birth of an heir to continue the Tudor dynasty was of great importance to both Henry and his mother, and Margaret threw herself into ensuring that everything was just right for the birth.

In preparation for the birth of her first grandchild, Margaret prepared a remarkable set of ordinances, which set out the correct protocol for the Queen's confinement, the christening of the child and arrangements to be made for the royal nursery. The ordinances are a testament both to Margaret's determination to express the grandeur of her son's dynasty and her eye for detail. She began by setting out the furnishings and decorations to be prepared in the Queen's chamber:

> Her Highnes Pleasure beinge understoode in what Chamber she will be delivered in, the same must be hanged with riche Clothe of Arras, Sydes, rowffe, Windowes and all, excepte one Windowe, which must be hanged so as she may have light when it pleasethe her. Then must there be set a Royall Bedde, and the Flore layed all over and over with Carpets, and a Cupboard covered with the same Suyte that the Chamber is hanged withall. Also there must be ordayned a faier Pallet, and all Things appertayninge therunto, and a riche Sparner hanginge over the same. And that Daye that the Queene (in good Tyme) will take her Chamber, the Chappell where her Highnes will receave and heare Devine Service, must be well and worshipfully arrayed. Also the greate Chamber must be hanged with riche Arras, with a Clothe and Chaire of Estate, and Quishins [cushions] thereto belonginge, the Place under and aboute the same beinge well encarped. Where the Queene (comminge from

the Chappell with her Lords and Ladyes of Estate) may, either standinge or sittinge, at her Pleasure, receave spices and wyne. And the next Chamber betwixt the greate Chamber and the Queenes Chamber to be well and worshipfully hanged; which done, Two of the greatest Estats shall leade her to her Chamber, where they shall take their leave of her. Then all the Ladyes and Gentilwomen to goe in with her, and none to come unto the greate Chamber but Women; and Women to be made all Manner of Officers, as Butlers, Panters, sewers, &c. and all Manner of Officers shall bringe them all neadfull Thinges unto the greate Chamber Dore, and the Women Officers shall receave it there of them.

Margaret decreed that the Queen, a month before the birth, should retire to an entirely female and candlelit world. Although no account survives of the birth of her first grandchild, it is certain that the ordinances were followed and that both Margaret and the Queen's mother, Elizabeth Woodville, would have been present, in all likelihood, vying for influence. Elizabeth of York herself may have felt somewhat lost in the well-ordered world, and Margaret's specifications extended even so far as the materials to be used in making the bed sheets and their exact sizes. She also specified the stuffing for the mattresses and the colour of the cushions. It is possible that, as she grew older and more experienced, Elizabeth found ways to rebel, and her accounts for July 1502, a few months into her last pregnancy, record payments made for twenty-seven cushions 'vi with blewe cloth of gold with cheverons the oon half of the said quysshons of satyn figure the other six with crymysn velvet and six of crymsyn dammaske and six of satyn figure two of purple velvet and oon quysshon of cloth of gold'. The Queen, perhaps, intended to pre-empt her overbearing mother-in-law by at least choosing her own cushions to be used in her confinement. An account of the birth of Elizabeth's second child in 1489 also shows that the Queen, on occasion, was able to rebel against the confines of Margaret's protocol. According to a contemporary manuscript, after Elizabeth had taken to her chamber,

> Thier came a great Ambassade oute of Frannce, among the whiche ther was a kynsman of the Quenes called Francois Monsieur de Luxemburg, the Prior of Saint Mattelyns, and Sir William de Zaintes, Bailly of Senlis, and Montjoie, King of Armes of Frenshemen, whiche desired to se the Quene, and so they dide, and in her awne Chambre. Ther was with her hir Moder Quene Elisabeth, and my Lady the Kinges Moder; but ther entred no more then ben affore rehersed, savyng my Lord the Quenes Chamberlayn, and Garter Principal King of Armes.

Margaret's thoughts on Elizabeth's breach of protocol in admitting men to her presence is not recorded, but given that the ambassador was kin to Elizabeth through her mother, Elizabeth Woodville's own maternal family, it is possible that Margaret blamed the Queen Dowager. Margaret undoubtedly meant well in the care that she took over her ordinances, and she looked towards her daughter-in-law's comfort, but to Elizabeth, the attention may well have seemed overbearing. Margaret also laid down specifications for the decoration of the church for the christening of her grandson, Prince Arthur, who was born in September 1486. It cannot have pleased her that the baby's maternal grandmother, Elizabeth Woodville, who outranked her, was named the prince's godmother, although, as a compliment to his mother, Henry appointed Lord Stanley as Arthur's godfather. Margaret was given a great deal of input into the prince's upbringing, and her ordinances decreed the furnishings for the nursery, what servants should be appointed and the precautions to be taken in the appointment and management of the wet nurse, who was to be observed by a doctor at every meal to ensure that 'she geveth the Childe seasonable Meate and Drinke'. Margaret was present at the birth of her second grandchild in November 1489, a girl who was named Margaret in her honour, and she was named godmother to the princess, making her a gift at her christening of 'a chest of silver and gilt, full of gold'. Elizabeth of York would eventually bear eight children, and they provided a common interest between the pair, as they found themselves almost constantly in each other's company.

Henry VII's early biographer Francis Bacon claimed that the relationship between the King and his wife was poor. Bacon suggested that, whilst Elizabeth had greatly desired the marriage, Henry had preferred to marry Anne of Brittany, the heiress of his former protector, Duke Francis II. These rumours 'bred some doubt and suspicion amongst divers that he was not sincere; or at least not fixed in going on with the match of England so much desired: which conceit also, though it were but talk and discourse, did much afflict the poor Lady Elizabeth herself'. Elizabeth may well have spent an anxious few months before her marriage with her mother, but Henry would always have been aware that a marriage with the Yorkist heiress was in his best interests, and as Bacon also pointed out, whilst his 'victory [at Bosworth] gave him the knee [of his subjects], so his purpose of marriage with the Lady Elizabeth gave him the heart; so that both knee and heart did truly bow before him'. The limited evidence that survives for the relationship between Henry and Elizabeth suggests that the marriage was happy and that the couple, who would only have met for the first time in the autumn of 1485, were fond of each other. Henry's grief at Elizabeth's early death, which 'was heveye and dolorous to the kings heighness', certainly devastated Margaret's son, and even before her funeral, he 'departed to a solitary place to passe his sorrows and would no man should resort to him but such his grace appointed'. The couple's shared grief at the loss of their eldest son is also a testament to the affection in the marriage, and whilst it appears that, by 1502, they had ceased to consummate their marriage, this was quickly resumed when they desired a further child to replace their son, with Elizabeth almost immediately falling pregnant for an eighth time. Henry gave regular gifts to Elizabeth and made payments for her debts. The couple were often together, although the relationship may well have been coloured, in its early days, by the position of their respective mothers.

On Henry's accession, Margaret took on something of the role of Queen Dowager, and this led to friction with the actual Queen Dowager, Elizabeth Woodville, the Queen's mother. Henry had restored Elizabeth Woodville to her titles and possessions, and the christening of Prince Arthur was intended to glorify the Woodville and Yorkist families and demonstrate their close links to the Tudor dynasty, with Elizabeth Woodville, her daughters and her eldest son, the Marquess of Dorset, playing prominent roles. Margaret had had links with the Woodville family during the reigns of Edward IV and Richard III, and it is clear that she had no indiscriminate dislike of the Queen's family. Her brother-in-law, Jasper Tudor, with whom she had always been associated, was married to Elizabeth Woodville's sister, Catherine, the widow of Margaret's own nephew by marriage, the Duke of Buckingham. Margaret also had a particular liking for Elizabeth Woodville's second surviving daughter, Cecily of York, who had become Margaret's sister-in-law through her marriage to John Welles. Cecily had been lodged with Margaret shortly after Henry's victory at Bosworth as a means of ensuring that she did not fall into the hands of the King's enemies, and Margaret became fond of her. When John Welles, who was considerably older than Cecily, died in 1499, leaving his widow childless, Margaret ensured that Cecily retained a large portion of his estates rather than allowing them to pass to her half-brother's paternal kin. At the same time, Margaret also received a special dispensation permitting the Yorkist princess to worship regularly in her household, and it is likely that the pair were often together. Three years later, when Cecily secretly married Thomas Kyme, a man considerably below her in rank, Margaret helped to protect her from the King's anger. Cecily and her husband were forced to retire to the Isle of Wight, but Margaret remained in contact with her sister-in-law and, in 1506, reserved a room for her use at her manor in Croydon. She met some of her funeral expenses in August 1507, something that again attests to Margaret's fondness for her sister-in-law and Elizabeth of York's sister.

With, essentially, two competing Queen Dowagers at court, as well as a Queen Consort, there was always going to be friction, and Henry, who naturally favoured his own mother, first attempted to solve the problem of Elizabeth Woodville by suggesting that she marry James III of Scotland and that two of her younger daughters marry the Scottish king's sons. Elizabeth Woodville's own thoughts on such a scheme are not recorded, but in any event, the proposed marriages came to nothing. From the first, Henry's reign was plagued by rebellions and pretenders. The most important early pretender was a boy named Lambert Simnel, who emerged in 1487, claiming to be Edward IV's nephew, the Earl of Warwick. According to Francis Bacon, Simnel had been well-schooled:

So that it cannot be, but that some great person that knew particularly and familiarly Edward Plantagenet [Warwick], had a hand in the business, from whom the priest might take his aim. That which is most probable, out of precedent and subsequent acts, is, that it was the Queen Dowager, from whom this action had the principal source and motion. For certain it is, she was a busy negotiating woman, and in her withdrawing-chamber had the fortunate conspiracy for the king against King Richard the third been hatched; which the king knew, and remembered perhaps but too well; and was at this time extremely discontent with the king, thinking her daughter, as the king handled the matter, not advanced but displeased: and none could hold the book so well to prompt and instruct this stage-play as she could.

Although no action was officially taken against Elizabeth Woodville for any part in the Simnel plot, the timing of Henry's attack on her is telling, and it is indeed possible that the Queen Dowager, resentful of her marginalisation at court, sought to depose her son-in-law, perhaps intending to replace him with her grandson, Prince Arthur. Henry VII seized Elizabeth Woodville's goods and forced her to retire to Bermondsey Abbey from where, apart from a visit to court in 1489 to witness the birth of her second grandchild, it appears she did not emerge again. By her Will, dated 10 April 1492, Elizabeth Woodville rather pointedly made no mention of her son-in-law, the King, and referred to her lack of goods to bequeath:

Whereas I have no worldly goods to do the Queen's Grace, my dearest daughter, a pleasure with, neither to reward any of my

children according to my heart and mind, I beseech Almighty God
to bless her Grace, with all her noble issue; and, with as good heart
and mind as is to me possible, I give her Grace my blessing, and all
the aforesaid my children.

Elizabeth Woodville died at Bermondsey Abbey on 8 June 1492,
although, for the previous five years, with the Queen Dowager's
forced retirement, Margaret had already been able to emerge as the
dominant female force at court.

The relationship between Margaret and Elizabeth of York was
a complex one, as the pair were often thrown into each other's
company. Throughout Elizabeth of York's marriage, Margaret was
a near-constant presence at her side by virtue of her position as
the King's mother. She remained with Elizabeth after the birth of
Prince Arthur and attended her churching before travelling with
the King and Queen and the court to Greenwich, where they kept
the feast of All Hallows in 1486. Henry required that his court was
magnificent, and a contemporary document records that he wore
a furred gown of cloth of gold. The court remained at Greenwich
until after Christmas, with Margaret remaining with her son and
daughter-in-law. By May 1487, Henry had left his wife and mother
and was staying at Kenilworth Castle when word reached him
that Lambert Simnel, who was supported by Edward IV's sister,
Margaret of York, Dowager Duchess of Burgundy, and his nephew,
John de la Pole, Earl of Lincoln, (the son of Margaret Beaufort's
divorced first husband by Elizabeth, the sister of Edward IV) had
landed with an army in England. Touchingly, Henry's first thought
was for the safety of his wife and mother, who had remained in
each other's company, and he wrote to Elizabeth's chamberlain, the
Earl of Ormond, on 13 May:

Right trusty and right well-beloved cousin, we greet you well, and have tidings that our rebels landed the fifth day of this month in our land of Ireland. Wherefore, and forasmuch as we have sent for our dearest wife and for our dearest mother to come unto us, and that we would have your advice and counsel also in such matters as we have to do for the subduing of our said rebels, we pray you that, giving your due attendance upon our said dearest wife and lady mother, ye come with them unto us, not failing hereof as ye purpose to do us pleasure.

Margaret and Elizabeth moved to Kenilworth, doubtless anxious to be with the King as he faced the first great crisis of his reign. Henry, as Richard III had done before him, decided to lead his troops personally, and he travelled on to Coventry, sending the Bishop of Winchester to Elizabeth and Prince Arthur, who was left in nominal control of affairs. The King continued to move, gathering men, and no doubt to Margaret's gratification, at Loughborough, he was joined by her stepson, Lord Strange, with an army of both his and his father's men. Henry's army met the pretender's army in battle at Stoke on 16 June 1487, where the King won a decisive victory. The Earl of Lincoln, who had almost certainly intended to dispose of the Yorkist pretender if the battle was won, was killed in the field, and Simnel, who was recognised by everyone as a mere puppet, was mockingly put to work by Henry in the royal kitchens. For both Margaret and Elizabeth, news of the victory must have been a great relief, and they quickly rejoined Henry.

A number of disaffected Yorkists had joined Simnel's ranks and one of their complaints was that the king did not show enough honour to his wife by arranging for her to be crowned. Henry's own coronation had taken place before his marriage, and Elizabeth had therefore not been able to share it. It was, however, unusual for a queen not to be crowned before she bore an heir and the delay seemed, to contemporaries, striking. It may be that Henry had simply not got round to arranging the coronation or baulked at the expense, but given his love of pageantry and his determination to stress the power and prestige of his dynasty, this is unlikely. It may, therefore, be that he was concerned about elevating Elizabeth too much due to the danger that it would appear that he only possessed the crown through marriage. From Margaret's point of view, the fact that there was no crowned queen in England (with the exception of the disgraced Elizabeth Woodville) may also have been pleasing and further bolstered her position as one of the leading ladies in the land. In 1487, however, with the concern that Henry's Yorkist supporters were beginning to fall away, both the King and his mother recognised the importance of stressing Elizabeth's role, and in November, Henry finally consented to having his wife crowned.

In October 1487, Henry and Elizabeth set out from Warwick for London, spending All Hallows Day at St Albans. Margaret's presence is not specifically mentioned, but it would be unusual for her not to have been with her son and daughter-in-law at such an important moment, and she probably travelled with them. Alternatively, she certainly joined the couple once they reached London. It was the first time that Henry had entered his capital since his victory at Stoke, and he was determined to make a show of his power. According to a contemporary manuscript,

Against his coming into his Citie of London, all the streets that his Grace should rid through with his royal company, were clensed;

and, upon both sides of the streets, the sitizens of every craft that rod not, were set in rowe, every crafte in dewe Order in their Livereys well besene, from Bisshops Gate unto Powles.

The grand entrance was intended to be Henry's moment and Margaret and Elizabeth had slipped into the city earlier.

All the Houses, Wyndowes, and streetes wheras he passed by, were hugely replenished with people in passing great Numbre, that made great Joye and Exultacion to beholde his most royall person so prosperously and princely coming into his Citie after his late Triumphe and Victorie against his Enimies. And so to beholde the fayre and goodlie sight of his comyng, the Quenes Grace, and my ladie the Kings Mother, and many other great Estates, both lordes and Ladyes, richely besene, were secretely in a Howse beside St Mary Spittle, without Bisshops Gate; and when the sight was passed, thei went from thence to Grenewich to their Beddes.

The scene must have reminded Margaret of Henry's great triumph in winning the crown only two years earlier, and she was proud of all her son had achieved, with her assistance. Once the procession was over, the moment belonged to Elizabeth of York, attended, as ever, by Margaret. On 24 November, Elizabeth appeared wearing a dress of white cloth of gold and damask and a furred mantle, fastened with gold and silk lace. She was generally regarded as a beauty and her blond hair hung loose over her shoulders, adorned by a circlet of gold studded with precious stones. Elizabeth's sister, Cecily, bore her train, and she was attended by most of the nobility as she processed through the streets. The following day, Elizabeth was crowned in Westminster Abbey. As she would have expected,

Margaret was granted a prominent place to watch the proceedings, and 'in the aforesaid church, on the right side, betwene the Pulpit and the High Aulter, was ordeyned a goodly stage, coverid and well besene with Clothe of Arras, and well latised, wherin was the Kings Grace, my Ladie his Mother, and a goodlie sight of Ladies and Gentlewomen attending upon her; as my Ladie Margaret Pole, daughter to the Duke of Clarence, and many other'. Margaret returned with the assembled company to Westminster Abbey in order to attend Elizabeth's coronation feast. She sat privately with her son on a hidden stage in order to observe the festivities, and both she and Henry must have been pleased with the success of the coronation, which once again had demonstrated the might of their Tudor dynasty. The banquet itself was splendid, and Margaret and Henry, dining in private, shared some of the twenty-three dishes in the first course, which included such exotic and expensive fare as pheasant, swan, capons, lamphreys, crane, pike, carp, perch, richly garnished mutton, custard and tarts. The second course was equally lavish, and its twenty-nine dishes included peacock, pheasant, cocks, partridge, sturgeon, rabbit, quails, larks, baked quince and, as a final flourish, 'castles of jelie in Temple wysely made'. Margaret went to bed that night well satisfied with the show her son had put on for his wife, and whilst she was naturally forced to yield somewhat to the Queen at Elizabeth's coronation, she remained prominent, with the same contemporary manuscript recording,

On the Morow the king heard Masse in St Stevens Chappell; and the Queene, my Ladie the Kings Mother also, greatly and nobly accompanyed with Duchesses, Countesses, Viscountesses, Baronnesses, and other Ladies and Gentlewomen, to the Number of lxxx [eighty] largely. And the Queene kept her Estate in the Parliament Chambre; and my ladie the Kings Mother sat on her Right Hande, and my ladie of Bedforde and my Ladie Cecyll sat at the Bourds Ende on the left Hande.

Margaret remained with the court after the coronation, and she dined with Elizabeth in the Queen's Chamber at Greenwich on Christmas Day. She was still at court on New Year's Day when she made gifts of largesse to members of her household. The triple nature of the monarchy continued on Twelfth Night, when Henry and Elizabeth appeared crowned and in company with Margaret, who wore a rich coronet as the three walked in procession before Matins. As an emphasis of her regal rank, Margaret wore the same mantle and surcoat as the Queen, and the two women were followed by the other leading ladies of the court:

And when the High Masse was done, the king went to his Chambre, and from thence to the Hall, and there kept his Estate as enseweth, crowned with a riche crown of Golde set with Perle and pretious stones, and under marveilous riche Clothe of Estate, and the Archebusshop of Canturburye on his Right Hande; and the Queene, also crowned, under a Clothe of Estate hanging somwhat lower than the Kings, on his left hande, and my ladie the Kings Mother, with a rich coronell on her Heade, on her Left Hande, with all foure Estates, were servid coverid.

At Easter, both Margaret and Stanley were prominent at Henry's St George's Day celebrations, and unusually for women, in an effort to emphasise their ranks, both Elizabeth and Margaret 'were in Gownes of the Garter of the same as the king and the lordes ware'.

Once again, Elizabeth and Margaret's clothes were identical, and they had been given as a gift from the King from his great wardrobe in good time for the celebrations, as the accounts record:

> To Elizabeth queen of England, as a gift from the king, for her robe made of sanguine cloth in grain, furred with the wombs of menever pure, garter with letters of gold. To the Countess of Richmond, the king's mother, as a gift from the king, for her robe made of sanguine cloth in grain, furred with pure menever, garter with letters of gold.

When Elizabeth had appeared wearing the same dress as her predecessor as queen, Anne Neville, at court at Christmas 1484, it had caused comment, and the symbolism of the Queen and her mother-in-law wearing the same clothes would not have been lost on their contemporaries in 1488. Whilst Margaret, who was some years older than the beautiful Elizabeth, could not possibly have hoped to compete with her in the matter of appearances, by wearing identical clothes, she emphasised that she was of the same (or very close to the same) rank as the Queen, something that can also be seen in her adoption of the signature 'Margaret R'. Margaret's anomalous position was recognised by her contemporaries. For example, in February 1487, the constable of the town of Farnham in Surrey was granted a licence to found a perpetual chantry in the town, tellingly 'for the good estate of the king, Elizabeth queen of England, prince Arthur, and the king's mother the countess of Richmond'.

As Margaret and Elizabeth were constantly in each other's company, there is no doubt that there would have been friction between them as they vied for status and position. However, whilst Margaret was determined to be the dominant party, it is clear that there was some affection between the two women. There are a number of recorded examples of them working together, and they shared some interests. On 21 December 1487, for example, Elizabeth, Margaret, the Archbishop of Canterbury, Bishop of Exeter, and Reginald Bray were granted the next presentation to the deanery of the college or free chapel of St Stephen in the Palace of Westminster. An earlier document, made on 6 February 1486, only a few weeks after Elizabeth's marriage, granted the two women, with a number of their other associates, including Reginald Bray, a licence to found a perpetual chantry in the parish church at Guildford, close to Margaret's residence at Woking. Both women shared an interest in religion and were active patrons of the Church. A greater common interest between them was in relation to Elizabeth's children, Margaret's only grandchildren.

Elizabeth's second child, Margaret, was followed by a son, Henry, in 1491, Elizabeth in 1492, Mary in 1496, Edmund in 1499 and Katherine in 1503. There was also a further unnamed son who died at birth. Margaret always had a particular fondness for her eldest granddaughter, Margaret, and her youngest grandson, Edmund, who was created Duke of Somerset by his father and for whom she stood godmother. Elizabeth, Edmund and Katherine sadly died young, but Margaret was very involved in the upbringing of the remaining children. Henry VII was able to secure a major diplomatic coup when he succeeded in betrothing his eldest son, Prince Arthur, to Catherine, the daughter of King Ferdinand of Aragon and his wife Isabella, Queen of Castile. From the first, both Elizabeth and Margaret took an active interest in the prestigious marriage. In 1498, for example, the Spanish ambassador was able to report to Catherine's parents that he had enjoyed an interview with the King that lasted for four hours. Elizabeth and Margaret were both present and 'to hear what they spoke of your Highnesses and of the Princess of Wales [Catherine] was like hearing the praise of God'. At that meeting, the ambassador gave Elizabeth two letters from Catherine's parents and two from the princess herself. This caused the only recorded quarrel between the royal couple, and 'the king had a dispute with the queen because he wanted to have one of the said letters to carry continually about him, but the queen did not like to part with hers, having sent the other to the Prince of Wales'. Only two days later, Elizabeth and Margaret jointly sought out the ambassador to ask that Catherine should make a point of always speaking French with her sister-in-law, Margaret of Austria, who had been raised in France, so that she would be able to converse with the court in England. They also asked that Catherine accustom herself to drinking wine, concerned that the water in England was not drinkable. Both women actively made a point of involving themselves in the future Princess of Wales' life and upbringing, although it was Elizabeth who took the greater interest, writing personally to Isabella of Castile and her daughter and also enquiring as to her future daughter-in-law's progress in French. Margaret and Elizabeth collaborated together again in 1498 when a marriage was suggested between the nine-year-old Princess Margaret and the already adult James IV of Scotland. In an interview with the Spanish ambassador, Henry informed him that

> I am really sorry that I have not a daughter or a sister for him [James]; for I have loved him most sincerely since the conclusion of the peace; not to mention that he is my relative. He has behaved very well towards me. I wish to see him as prosperous as myself. But I have already told you, more than once, that a marriage

between him and my daughter has many inconveniences. She has not yet completed the ninth year of her age, and is so delicate and weak that she must be married much later than other young ladies. Thus it would be necessary to wait at least another nine years. Beside my own doubts, the queen and my mother are very much against this marriage. They say if the marriage were concluded we should be obliged to send the Princess directly to Scotland, in which case they fear the King of Scots would not wait, but injure her, and endanger her health.

The idea that her namesake and favourite granddaughter should be exposed to the perils of early marriage that she herself had gone through was too much for Margaret, and it is likely that, in this case, it was she who enlisted Elizabeth's support, warning her of the dangers to the princess of risking childbirth at too young an age.

Margaret also played a role in the upbringing of her younger grandchildren and, in particular, her precocious second grandson, Henry, whom his father was considering making Archbishop of Canterbury. She is known to have helped superintend his education. The famous scholar Erasmus was granted an audience with Henry and Elizabeth's younger children in 1499, and he recorded one of the few impressions of the family in childhood:

I was staying at Lord Mountjoy's country house when Thomas More came to see me, and took me out with him for a walk as far as the next village, where all the king's children, except Prince Arthur, who was then the eldest son, were being educated. When we came into the great hall, the attendants not only of the palace but also of Mountjoy's household were all assembled. In the midst stood

Prince Henry, then nine years old, and having already something of royalty in his demeanour, in which there was a certain dignity combined with singular courtesy. On his right was Margaret, about eleven years of age, afterwards married to James, King of Scots, and on his left played Mary, a child of four. Edmund was an infant in arms. More, with his companion Arnold, after paying his respect to the boy Henry, presented him with some writing. For my part, not having expected anything of the sort, I had nothing to offer, but promised that on another occasion I would in some way declare my duty towards him. Meantime I was angry with More for not having warned me, especially as the boy sent me a little note, while we were at dinner, to challenge something from my pen. I went home, and in the Muses' spite, from whom I have been so long divorced, finished the poem within three days.

Margaret's second grandson, Henry, resembled his maternal grandfather, Edward IV, in both stature and appearance and proved just as charming. Margaret was again prominent at the ceremonies that surrounded his creation as Duke of York in 1494, when, at the jousts that were held in celebration at Westminster, the challengers appeared wearing her livery of blue and white on the third day of the tournament.

Margaret may have been consulted by her son on his decision to create his second son Duke of York. There were sound political reasons for creating a new Duke of York as the previous holder was Elizabeth of York's brother, the younger of the princes in the Tower, Richard, Duke of York. In 1490, a new pretender emerged at the ducal court at Burgundy, claiming to be Richard. This second great pretender of Henry's reign was considerably more convincing than Lambert Simnel, and he quickly gathered international support with Margaret of York, Dowager Duchess of Burgundy, proving particularly influential when she formally recognised the pretender as her nephew and persuaded the husband of her stepdaughter, the Archduke Maximilian, who ruled Burgundy in right of his deceased wife, to do likewise. Henry was alarmed by the pretender's emergence and made some enquiries, quickly declaring that he was one Perkin Warbeck from Tournai. In spite of this, he was very effectively coached by his 'aunt', whose identification of him was suspect, given that she had seen the real Richard only once during her brief visit to England in 1480. Margaret of York, who apparently hated Henry for the death of her brother, Richard III, had no compunction about trying to bring about the ruin of her niece's husband, and both Margaret Beaufort and Henry viewed her as a particular threat. In a letter that illuminates Margaret Beaufort's character, she made a subtle dig at the Dowager Duchess of Burgundy, writing to the Earl of Ormond in 1496 to thank him for a gift he sent her from Flanders: 'I thank you heartily that ye list so soon remember me with my gloves, the which were right good, save they were too much for my hand. I think the ladies in that parts be great ladies all, and according to their great estate they have great personages'. The greatest of the 'great' ladies in Flanders was, of course, Margaret of York, and it appears that the tiny and abstinent Margaret Beaufort intended to make a comment about her rival's weight problem.

In an attempt to deflect the danger of the new pretender, Henry VII proclaimed his own second son as the legitimate Duke of York, but the shadow of Perkin Warbeck hung over his reign for some years. In 1495, Warbeck went to Scotland, where he was duly recognised by James IV and married to Catherine Gordon, a kinswoman of the King of Scots. Something that also touched Margaret, her husband,

Lord Stanley and the King personally regarding the rebellion was that, early in 1495, her brother-in-law, the hitherto loyal Sir William Stanley was found to have been in contact with Warbeck and was executed for 'certeyn treasons, ymagened and compassed traiterously, to the destruccion of the moost roiall persone of the King oure Sovereign Lorde'. Sir William's execution was a blow for Henry, and his accounts show that he contributed towards his former supporter's funeral. Margaret may well have attempted to smooth matters over between her son and her husband following the execution, and it does not appear that the execution caused any breach with Stanley, who remained loyal to the King until his death. Warbeck was finally captured in 1497 when he attempted to mount a full-scale invasion of England, only to lose his nerve when he found limited support for his cause, surrendering to the King. As with Lambert Simnel, Henry at first dealt leniently with the pretender, but when Warbeck was captured trying to escape from house arrest at court in 1498, he was executed at a similar time to the genuine Earl of Warwick in 1499.

Elizabeth of York's own thoughts on the pretenders who claimed to be her kinsmen cannot be known, but it is unlikely that she would have believed them. As she aged, Elizabeth appears to have come to assert herself more and more against the dominant, if well-meaning, force of her mother-in-law, and by 1502, she was primarily responsible for purchasing clothes for her two daughters, Margaret and Mary, something that suggests that she was increasingly able to demonstrate her authority in relation to her children. At the betrothal of her eldest daughter, Margaret, to the King of Scots in January 1502, which took place in Elizabeth's chamber at Richmond Palace, it was very much the Queen who was in control, and contemporary sources do not even mention if

Margaret was present. It was Elizabeth, as the princess's mother, who was asked for her consent to the match, and following the ceremony, 'the Queene tooke her Daughter the Queen of Scotts by the Hand, and dyned both at one Messe covered'.

Margaret played only a limited role in the marriage of her eldest grandchild, Prince Arthur. Arthur's betrothed bride, Catherine of Aragon, landed at Plymouth in late 1501 and Henry and Arthur immediately rushed to meet her. She made a good impression on the King, and on his return to Richmond, 'he was mett by the Queene's Grace, whom he ascertained and made privye to the Acts and Demeanor betweene himselfe, the Prince, and the Princesse, and howe he liked her Person and Behaviour'. Securing a daughter of the famous Ferdinand and Isabella for their son was a major coup, and Henry was determined to show the world that he was equal to the famous 'Catholic Kings of Spain', putting on a great tournament in his new daughter-in-law's honour. Margaret was present with Elizabeth of York, Catherine and her two granddaughters, Princesses Margaret and Mary, sitting on a specially prepared stage to watch the jousting, in which Margaret's former ward, the Duke of Buckingham, took part. That night, the same company watched a masque at court, as well as a number of fine pageants. The younger company then danced, with Arthur partnering his aunt, Cecily of York, and Prince Henry dancing with his sister Margaret. Although it was Arthur's wedding, it was Prince Henry that shone, and 'he pereceiving himselfe to be accombred with his Clothes, sodainly cast off his Gowne, and daunced in his Jackett with the said Ladye Margarett'. The evening finished with a banquet, with a further feast the next day at which Elizabeth was flanked by Margaret and the Spanish ambassador, whilst the king sat with Catherine of Aragon. Further masques and tournaments followed before the couple were finally married on 14 November 1501.

For Margaret and Henry, the marriage of Prince Arthur to a princess of Spain was a major achievement and symbolised the prestige and stability of the Tudor dynasty that they had founded together. Soon after the wedding, Arthur and his bride set out for Ludlow Castle to enable the young couple to rule their principality. Whilst they were there, both Arthur and Catherine fell ill with sweating sickness, a mysterious and often deadly illness that had arrived on the ships that carried Henry to England in 1485. Catherine survived the attack, but Arthur, to everyone's horror, died suddenly on 2 April 1502 at the age of only fifteen. Margaret, who would have been as shocked as everyone else to hear the news, does not appear to have been at court when word of it reached Henry, and a contemporary manuscript, which details their reaction, demonstrates just how close Henry and Elizabeth had become, in spite of Margaret's near-constant presence in their marriage. When the news of the death reached court, it was given to Henry's chaplain who immediately took the news to the king:

When his Grace understood that sorrowful heavy Tydings, he sent for the Queene, saying, that he and his Queen would take the paineful sorrowes together. After that she was come and sawe the king her Lord, and that naturall and painefull Sorrowe, as I have heard saye, she with full great and constant comfortable words besought his Grace, that he would first after God, remember the Weale of his owne noble Person, the Comfort of his Realme, and of her. She then saied, that my Ladye his Mother had never no more Children but him onely, and, that God by his Grace had ever preserved him, and brought him where that he was. Over that, howe that God had left him yet a fayre Prince, Two fayre Princesses, and that God is, where he was, and we are both young ynoughe: And that the Prudence and Wisdome of his Grace spronge over all Christendome, so that it should please him to take this accordingly thereunto. Then the king thannked her of her good Comfort. After that she was departed and come to her owne Chamber, naturall and motherly Remembraunce of that great Losse smote her so sorrowfull to the Hart, that those that were about her were faine to send for the king to comfort her. Then his Grace of true gentle and faithfull love, in good Hart came and relieved her, and showed her howe wise Counsell she had given him before; and he for his Parte would thanke God for his sonn, and would she should doe in like wise.

The grief of Arthur's parents was genuine and heart-felt and something that Margaret, although fond of the prince as his grandmother, could not share. It was Elizabeth who kindly thought to send for Arthur's widow, bringing her back to London in 'a lytture of blake velvet with blake cloth'. Elizabeth was also correct that she and Henry were young enough to have another child, and she conceived soon after Arthur's death. Elizabeth's last child had been Edmund, who was born in 1499 when she was thirty-three. According to a report of the Spanish ambassador, 'there had been much fear that the life of the queen would be in danger, but the delivery, contrary to expectation, has been easy'. Given the speed at which Elizabeth conceived in 1502 and the three-year gap between her final two children, it appears that the couple had made a decision to cease having children after Edmund's birth, and this may have been due to Elizabeth's ill health. Henry and Elizabeth took a risk in trying to replace Arthur with another son, and the Queen's last pregnancy did not go smoothly. She was delivered, prematurely, of a daughter on 2 February 1503 at the Tower of London. The baby, who was christened Katherine, died soon afterwards. Her mother also failed to recover from the birth, and she died on 11 February 1503, the day of her thirty-seventh birthday.

Henry was devastated by Elizabeth's death and immediately shut himself away to grieve. It is likely that Margaret, who was always such a dominant force in his life, sought to comfort him. She also grieved for the daughter-in-law she had spent so much time with. In spite of her grief, Margaret kept herself busy, and she produced a set of ordinances for mourning, dealing with the 'apparell for princesses and great estatis and other ladies and gentilwomen for the tyme of mornyng'. Margaret put as much thought into these as she had her earlier ordinances in relation to royal births. Intending that the ordinances be used for all future royal deaths, she set out the mourning clothes for a queen to wear, which included a surcoat with a train both in front and behind. A mantle with a train was also to be worn, and it was necessary to ensure that the queen, as the 'grettest estat', had the longest train. Immediately after the death, the queen was to wear a plain hood over her hair. After three months, if she wished, a queen could wear a mantle lined with black satin or fine sarcenet. Alternatively, it could be lined with fur of powdered ermine. Margaret then set out what other ladies should wear, beginning with 'my ladie the kinges modir', then the King's daughters and married sisters, duchesses, countesses, duke's daughters, lord's daughters and knight's wives, the gentlewomen of the Queen, the King's mother and the King's daughters. She even considered the apparel for the gentlewomen of assembled duchesses and countesses. Tellingly, Margaret, although only a countess, eschewed the plain surcoat and mantle assigned to that rank, instead declaring that the King's mother is 'to werre in every thinge lyke to the quene'. Even with Elizabeth's death, Margaret could not bring herself to abandon the rivalry that had dominated her daughter-in-law's marriage. As the author of the ordinances, Margaret would have ensured that she complied with them and appeared at court with the longest train and a black dress of the finest fabrics. She would only just have put her mourning for Elizabeth away when she was forced to don it once again.

The following year, on 29 July 1504, Margaret was widowed herself, and whilst she had been effectively separated from Stanley for some time, his loss may still have been a personal blow. The couple had been married for over thirty years, and he had protected her at her time of greatest danger, also assisting, albeit cautiously, her son in his path to the throne. Stanley left a gold cup to the King in his Will, along with a request that he be a good lord to his son. To Margaret, he left nothing, save a request that she be accorded all the rights set out in their marriage contract. Margaret was, by 1504, a very wealthy woman, and Stanley may have realised that she needed nothing further from him. The Stanley arms were later included on the adornments to Margaret's tomb, suggesting that the death may have saddened her.

In June 1503, Margaret had taken Elizabeth of York's role in seeing off Princess Margaret when she left to marry the King of Scots, hosting both the King and court at her residence at Collyweston. With the deaths of Elizabeth of York, Thomas Stanley and Prince Arthur and the departure of Princess Margaret to Scotland, the royal family was substantially reduced and Margaret, who had for so long vied with the Queen for prominence, became, officially, the first lady in the land and the person on whom the King relied the most.

12

A PATRONESS OF LEARNING:
JULY 1504-APRIL 1509

In the early years of the sixteenth century, the royal family had been significantly reduced, allowing Margaret to finally establish herself as the first woman in the land. By 1504, Margaret had passed her sixtieth birthday, old by the standards of her time. In spite of this, she remained active and it was in the last few years of her life that she created her own lasting memorial. Margaret had always been interested in education, and even in the early years of her son's reign, she had begun to look with interest on the universities of Oxford and Cambridge, the centres of learning in England at the time. Henry visited Cambridge as part of his first progress following his accession, and he was well received by both the university and the town. This sparked the interest of both Henry and his mother in the university, although, at first, Margaret decided to split her patronage between both ancient institutions.

Oxford University first came to Margaret's attention in 1493 when it wrote to Reginald Bray, who had remained associated with her, to offer him the office of steward of the university. He accepted the post and gave the university a donation of 40 marks to be used towards a church in the city. His interest in Oxford brought it to Margaret's attention, and in 1497, the university was able to write to her in the most fulsome terms, praising her generosity:

Those most respected kings, prelates, and generals, and men of almost every rank of society have been solicitous for our welfare and the progress of education; but it has remained for one princess, of rank most exalted and of character divine, to do that which none have done before. Nothing can be nobler than to provide, as you have done, unasked, for the teaching of theology. This is the subject we value, relish, and love above all others; and we cannot but reckon you among the founders of our University, and deserving at our hands the same thanks, and the same prayers.

The letter refers to a lectureship in theology that Margaret founded at Oxford through letters patent granted in December 1496. At the same time, she also founded a similar lectureship at Cambridge.

Around 1495, Margaret met a cleric, John Fisher, who was visiting the court at Greenwich. Fisher had been born in 1459 in Yorkshire and came from a family of reasonably well off merchants. From his early childhood, it was recognised that he was intellectually able, and his mother, who was widowed whilst her son was young, ensured that he was well educated. As he grew, his mother continued to support his academic career, and seeing that he was 'naturally indowed with a sober and deep witt, a perfect and stedfast memorie, and a will prompt & forward to lerne', she decided to send him to Cambridge University. He was an all-rounder and one of the best-educated men of his day, with one early *Life of Fisher* declaring that 'in fewe yeres he became singulerly well learned, as well in humanitie, as in logicke; philosophie and other sciences: not ignorant, but well acquainted, with the greeke and hebrew tonges which were then verie straungers in this land'. He took his degree in 1488 and completed a Masters degree the following year. He remained for some years at Cambridge, taking holy orders, as well as becoming a doctor of divinity. Around the time that Fisher became a Proctor of the University, his reputation came to Margaret's attention, and she specifically sought him out when he visited court, as the *Life of Fisher* comments:

At length his name grewe so famous, that, passinge the bondes of the vniversitie, it spred over all the Realme, in so much as the noble and vertuous ladie, Margaret, Countesse of Richmond and Darbie, mother to the wise and sage prince Kinge Henrie the viith, hearinge of his great vertue and learninge, ceased not till she had procured him out of the vniversitie to her service, by meane wherof he resigned the maistership of Michaell house [a Cambridge college that was dissolved in 1546] and lefte the vniversitie for that time. After he had a space remayned with this noble ladie, she perceived his vertue and good lyfe farr to exceed the fame that before she heard of him, and thervpon soone after made him her ghostly father: wherin after he was a while established, he ordered himselfe so discretly, so temperatly and so wysely, that both she and all her familie [i.e., household] were governed by his high wisdome and discretion.

Margaret's meeting with Fisher marked the start of a long-standing association in which the two worked closely together. She had always had a deep and sincere interest in religion, and Fisher, who was both highly educated and had a reputation for asceticism, was the perfect candidate for her chaplain. Once established as a member of her household, Fisher persuaded Margaret that her charitable works, which were already extensive and included repairing bridges and roads, making payments to poor women to allow them to marry, and paying the fines of prisoners, would be better directed towards his own chief interest: Cambridge University.

A surviving letter from Oxford University to 'the Lady Margaret' dating from 1498 survives. No further details of the intended recipient are given, but Margaret was certainly the most prominent lady of her name in England and this, coupled with the fact that the addressee was a patron of the university, suggests that it was intended for Margaret. The letter is interesting, as it demonstrates that the university were concerned about losing Margaret's favour. It begins 'that a report should have been made to you, calculated to diminish that generous favour you have hitherto shown us, is a bitter vexation; the more so that it is without foundation'. The report that had reached Margaret was made by one John Roys, an 'inveterate enemy' of the university, and concerned a scandal over the imprisonment of a prostitute in the city. The fact that the university felt the need to write to Margaret to explain itself suggests that they were aware that she no longer looked quite as favourably on them as before, something that may well have been due to Fisher's influence.

In spite of this, the university continued to correspond with Margaret and petition her for support for some time. In 1500, for example, her lectureship in theology fell vacant, and the university wrote to inform her of the name of the new holder. The selected candidate pleased Margaret, no doubt to the university's relief, and she wrote back to them:

And this present day have recevyd your right kinde lettres and lovinge tokins by our welbeloved Thomas Pantre, oon of your bedells; for the whiche we thank you in owre harty wise; Wherby we perceyve ye have electe and chosen oon m. Rooper, doctor of divinite, to rede owre lecture there; whereof we be right gladde, and trust with godd's mercy it shalbe to the greate honour and weal of your said Universite; aswele to thyncrease of vertu as lernyng off Students with in the same, whiche we right specially tender, and shalbe gladde to further at altymes to the best we can.

Margaret was also not above asking for favours, and in that same year, she wrote to the university, requesting an appointment there for one Richard Wootton, who had been recommended to her by Richard Fitzjames, Bishop of Rochester, a former vice-chancellor of the university:

Trusty and welbelovyd, we grete you wele; and understonde the Rowme of gentilmen bedell in divinite within youre universite is now voide by deceasse of your late office in the same; wherunto ye in breve tyme intende to electe soome honest and hable person. We specially tendering thonnoure and thincrease of lernyng in divinite, and be credybly enformed by the right reverent fader in god, the bysschopp of Rochestre, and certain other whiche be verray lovers of the said faculte, that one Rychard Wotton is a right hable and convenient person for the said office, Desire therfore and pray you so to owe youre good favores unto hym as rather for oure sake he may be proferryd to the said Rome. Wherby ye schall not oonly do a thing for the grete honowre and weale of youre said universite but also unto us full Singuler plesur. Yeven under signet at the manour of Buckdoone, the xxiii day of Auguste.

Anxious to please Margaret, the university was only too happy to oblige, responding quickly to tell her that 'on receipt of your letter, we almost unanimously elected the candidate you recommended for the office of bedell in Divinity'. They once again made a plea for her aid, pointedly adding that, by making the appointment requested, 'we have reason to fear that we have incurred the displeasure of the bishop of Lincoln, our Chancellor; we entreat you, therefore, to defend us if any trouble comes, for to support his anger will be beyond our strength'. Margaret's response to this does not survive. Another letter of hers to the university is extant, in which she asked that the university dispense with its residency requirements for one of its students, Maurice Westbury, of whom she was a patron. As an incentive, the King's mother added that 'and ye thus doing shal have us youre good lady in any thing reasonable that ye shal desire of us, concernyng the weal of you or the saide Universite hereafter'. With Fisher's increasing influence over Margaret changing her focus to Cambridge, Oxford was fighting a losing battle in trying to secure her patronage, although a letter survives as late as 1502 that was a clear attempt to secure further funding, through blatant flattery, from the King's mother:

> How great and unremitting has been your benevolent and watchful solicitude for our advancement, it were difficult to express; and if our former benefactors are constantly commemorated, surely never-ceasing thanks are due to you for your promise to endow a theological lecture here, and the fulfilment of that promise.

Margaret had originally intended to continue benefitting both universities and, in the latter years of the fifteenth century, she began to fund lecturers at both universities as part of her personal expenses. However, when, in 1505, she decided to support a preachership at a university, requiring the holder to preach six sermons a year, she directed her generosity at Cambridge alone.

Margaret's growing Cambridge bias increased in 1501, when Fisher was elected as vice-chancellor of the university. He was appointed chancellor in 1504, remaining in office throughout the rest of Margaret's life and securing an appointment of the office for life in 1514.

As well as providing funds for lectureships and a preachership, Margaret turned her attentions towards the Cambridge colleges themselves. Her ancestress, Philippa of Hainault, the queen of Edward III, had begun a lasting association between queenship and learning when she had founded Queen's College at Oxford in the fourteenth century. This was followed, in the mid-fifteenth century, by Margaret of Anjou, the queen of Henry VI, founding Queen's College at Cambridge. Margaret Beaufort's sometime co-conspirator and rival, Elizabeth Woodville, had taken a great interest in Margaret of Anjou's college, and in 1465, she had been granted a licence by her husband to patronise the college. Elizabeth's support had been so generous that the college flatteringly referred to her as its true founder in a number of documents. It seems likely that Elizabeth, whose marriage had caused such a scandal and who had always been at pains to demonstrate her queenship, had sought to use her patronage of the college as a way of enforcing and legitimising her position. Margaret Beaufort's own interest in the college, which began after Elizabeth of York's death when Margaret was the highest-ranking woman in England and, in many respects, a queen in all but name, may have been for a similar reason: seeking to demonstrate her queenly rank to the world.

After Elizabeth's death, Margaret fulfilled the function of the queen towards Queen's College, Cambridge, and she interested herself in its management. She was also responsible, in 1505, for persuading her great-nephew and former ward, the Duke of

Buckingham, to make a grant to the college. By an indenture, he 'bestowed on the college, (for his safe state while living, and for the good of the souls of his ancestors and of his own soul after his death,) at the instance of the most excellent princess Margaret, countess of Richmond and Derby, the king's mother, 31 acres of meadow land in Essex, near Bumpstead Heylon'. Almost certainly as a mark of respect to Margaret and in an attempt to secure further patronage, the college appointed Fisher as its master in 1505. Margaret made a personal visit to Cambridge in 1505, where she was received with much honour at the college. This visit paved the way for Henry VII's own successful visit in 1506, when Fisher was able to persuade the King to donate funds to complete the building work at King's College Chapel. Margaret accompanied her son on this visit, and it was around this time that her stepson, James Stanley, was made Bishop of Ely (whose diocese included Cambridge), presumably at his stepmother's request. Margaret is also recorded to have taken an interest in Corpus Christi College at Cambridge when she attempted to secure a fellowship there for a scholar named Thomas Maunfeld, although it appears that she was not successful in this appeal.

By the early years of the sixteenth century, Margaret had become a figure of major importance to Cambridge, and the university asked her to arbitrate in a dispute between it and the town:

Most noble and excellent princes our special good and gracious lady, humbly we recommend us to your highness shewing that notwythstonding the composicion devised and ordaynde by your most wyse concayle betwen thys our soverayn lorde the kyngs universite and yours and the mayer and the burgeysys of Cambryg for unite [unity] and peas [peace] to be had finally between us and them and the mor restfulnes of our mynds to study to the supporting of crists ffaythe, they nothyng, as yt semyth, regardyng your blessed mynd and gret labours ne the high pleasure of Allmighty God in thys behalf dayly cessyth nott to renew our Trobles, insomuche that refusing and willing utterly the cesse of justice among us ne acceptyng our vicechancellor for their juge in a personall action agenste them comensed by certayne scholars the parte playntife, they now of late before ony sentence definitive or any other just cause of complaynte mynystered by us unto them hath uncharytably to the vexacyon of the sayd scolers not only procuryd a prevy seale, but hath sued them with oon of our bedellys oonly for doyng of hys office at the commyn lawe to the poynte of owtlawry, plainly infringing the sayd composicion not in thys alone but in other artycles, as now we have by a specyall byll remembered and thys berar can more largely declare.

The university, well aware of Margaret's interest in learning, begged her to intervene, insisting that, otherwise, those scholars who were required to present themselves in court to answer the townsmen's cases would fail to satisfy the residency requirements of their degrees and so 'shal be compellyd by long tarryng owt not only to lese [lose] their lernyng, but also ther place, exhibicion and living, and as we soe fere thys the lay menys audacyte not repressed shal be herafter owr gret decay'. Margaret's reply to the university's appeal does not survive, but she responded favourably, with the university again writing to her to commend her as 'owrer speciall good lady and singular benefactrice'. Margaret evidently told the university to draw up a list of articles setting out areas of dispute with the townsmen so that she could 'se good direction and dew reformacion be made'. She listened to what the arbitrators had to say, before affixing her seal to an agreement that was reached on 11 July 1502. A list of thirty articles were finalised in May the following year, and it appears that Margaret, who, on occasion, acted in a judicial capacity on behalf of her son, was happy to intervene on behalf of the university.

Whilst Margaret was, at first, content to benefit an existing college in her patronage of Queen's, and the university as a whole, with Fisher's encouragement, she soon decided on a considerably more ambitious scheme. Margaret's former brother-in-law, Henry VI, had been an enthusiastic patron of learning and founded both Eton College near Windsor and King's College, Cambridge. He was also involved in the foundation of another college at Cambridge, God's House, which was founded in 1439 by William Byngham, the parson of St John Zachary of London. Byngham's petition to the King for a licence for his college survives and sets out his aim that it be used to support scholars of grammar, with lands granted up to a value of £50 a year. Byngham had lofty ideals for his foundation, but in reality, it was never sufficiently endowed. Henry VI showed a personal interest in God's House. It was originally intended that sixty scholars would reside there, however, due to the college's poverty, there were never more than four in residence at any time. For Margaret, the college's Lancastrian links must have been an attraction, and it may well have been Fisher who pointed out that it was ripe for refoundation. At Margaret's request, on 1 May 1505, Henry VII granted her a licence to expand the college to sixty members, as originally intended. He confirmed that the members of the college were to study the grammatical sciences, other sciences and liberal faculties or holy divinity. It was also confirmed, again at Margaret's request, that the members of the college were required to pray for Margaret, Henry, his children, Edmund Tudor, Margaret's parents, Elizabeth of York and Henry VI. In the same document, Henry gave his mother permission to change the name of the foundation to Christ's College. Margaret was enthusiastic in her support of her new college, and only three days after the licence was granted, she settled the advowson of the church of Malton in Cambridgeshire on Christ's. She persuaded Henry to grant her the Abbey of St Mary de Pratis at Creyke in Norfolk in 1507, which she immediately assigned with its revenues to her college. She made a number of other grants of property to Christ's, taking a great personal interest in the foundation. From the first, she reserved rooms at the college for her own use when she was in Cambridge, and there is some evidence that she oversaw the building works at the college. One surviving account, which shows something of Margaret's strong character, relates that, whilst she was visiting the unfinished college, she looked out of the window to see a student being punished by the dean for his poor scholarship. Margaret leaned out of the window, crying out *'lente, lente!'* (gently, gently!). For the King's mother, a lazy scholar should not escape punishment entirely, but she was determined that he should not be treated too harshly. Margaret expected her scholars to work hard, as she had high expectations for her college. In her Will, she left her foundation the manor of Malton to ensure that the members of her college had somewhere to stay and continue their work even when there was plague in Cambridge. Margaret was determined that her college should be a credit to her, and she left much of her plate to Christ's, including two great gilt crucifixes, two chalices and a gilt foot for a cross for an altar. She also appears to have been a regular visitor to her foundation in the last years of her life, with a woman bringing a cake to the college for her in July 1507, something that suggests that the King's mother was regularly known to be in residence.

Margaret's interest in Cambridge did not cease with her foundation of Christ's, and in 1508, Fisher drew her attention to the poor state of the Hospital of St John the Evangelist in Cambridge. In order to dissolve a religious house and refound it as a secular college, it was first necessary to procure the consent of the Bishop of Ely, who, as Margaret's stepson, immediately complied. She also rapidly obtained Henry VII's licence, although neither the bishop's nor Henry's consent were officially drawn up in Margaret's lifetime. Margaret intended that her new college would support a master and fifty scholars. When it became clear that she would not live to see her foundation, she detailed her wishes in a codicil to her Will; these were diligently carried out by Fisher and her other executors after her death. That it was Margaret's contacts and force of character that ensured that she was able to lay the foundations for her second college was clear from the troubles that beset her executors following her death. John Fisher himself recorded,

Ffirst, my Lorde [Bishop] of Ely wiche thene was, albeit that he hadde promysede my lady his assent for the dissolvyng of Saynte Johns housse, wiche then was a religious housse, unto a College of Students, yett because he hadde not sealide, he wolde not performe his promyse; and so delaide the matters a long seasone till at the last we were fayne to agree with hyme by the advyce of my lord of Winchestre to our grete charge. This was the first sore brounte that we hadde, and like to have quailede all the mattere, if it hadde not ben wiselie handelide; for upon this hong all the reste. Yff this hadde ben clerelie revoikede by hyme, we cudde not have done any thing for that College, according to my Ladys entente and wyll.

Fisher's determination to do Margaret a service, even after her death, drove him on, and he and his fellow executors were beset with further troubles when, due to poor legal advice received, they found that the licence they obtained from the Pope was not fit for purpose and had to send once again to Rome. Finally, they also found they had difficulties from the King, Margaret's grandson, Henry VIII, who was not over-eager to recognise a verbal promise to his grandmother made by his father. Only through Fisher's devoted labour was it possible, finally, for St John's to admit students for the first time, some years after its foundress's death. Margaret did not live to see her second foundation at Cambridge, but both St John's and Christ's remain and stand as memorials to their foundress and her interest in education.

Margaret's interest in education can also be seen in her patronage of printing and her own translation works. Until the late fifteenth century, it was necessary for all books to be written out by hand, and as a result, they were a rare and expensive commodity. In 1476, William Caxton opened a printing press in the almonry of Westminster Abbey. This was a major turning point in education and allowed for the mass production of books for the first time. Following Henry's accession, Margaret turned her attention to Caxton's press, interested in the ability to reach a large audience for the first time, and she became one of his leading patrons. Margaret was a very active patron, advising the printer on what works to publish, and she even provided him with some of her own books for him to copy for his press. Margaret's support certainly helped Caxton's works to receive greater attention in court circles, and his gratitude is clear in a number of his dedications to her. In his dedication to *The Hystorye of Kinge Blanchardyne and Queen Eglantyne his Wyfe*, Caxton flattered his patron by calling her

Duchess of Somerset, a title that Margaret may have felt she was entitled to as the most senior surviving Beaufort:

> Unto the right noble puissant and excellent princess, my redoubted lady, my lady Margaret Duchess of Somerset, mother unto our natural and sovereign lord and most christian King Henry the Seventh, &c. I, William Caxton, his most indign humble subject and little servant, present this little book I late received in French from her good grace, and her commandment withal for to reduce and translate it unto our maternal and English tongue; which book I had long before sold to my said lady, and knew well that the story of it was honest and joyful to all virtuous young noble gentlemen and women, for to read therein for their pastime.

Margaret also requested that Caxton print an English translation of the popular work *The Ladder of Perfection*, and a work called *The Grete Shyppe of Fooles of this Worlde* was printed by the publisher Wynkyn de Worde at her 'enticement and exhortacion'. Margaret further requested that more personal works be printed, and in 1509, she commanded Wynkyn de Worde to publish the text of John Fisher's sermons on seven penitential psalms, which she had heard and evidently enjoyed. More poignantly, she asked Fisher to publish the funeral sermon that he preached for her son following his death in 1509. For Margaret, printing was an excellent way to spread information, and she published her own translations of religious works, including *The Mirroure of Golde for the Sinful* Soule and the fourth book of a *Treatise of the Imitation and Following the Blessed Life of our Most Merciful Saviour Christ*.

Margaret came to rely on John Fisher's advice in the last decade of her life and much of what would become her legacy was suggested by him. She also found herself in a position to benefit her chaplain. Fisher would later claim in a dedication to Henry VII's councillor, Richard Fox, Bishop of Winchester, that the King decided 'of his own mere notion, without any obsequiousness on my part, without the intercession of any, as he more than once declared to myself, he gave me the Bishopric of Rochester' and that 'there are many who believe that his mother, the Countess of Richmond and Derby, that noble and incomparable lady, dear to me by so many titles, obtained the bishopric for me by her prayers to her son. But the facts are entirely different'. In his dedication, Fisher continued that

> I do not say this to diminish my debt of gratitude to this most excellent lady. My debts are indeed great. Were there no other besides the great and sincere love she bore me above others, as I know for a certainty, yet what favour could equal such love on the part of such a Princess? But besides her love, she was most munificent towards me. For though she conferred on me no ecclesiastical benefice, she had the desire, if it could be done, to enrich me, which she proved not by words only, but by deeds; among other instances.

Margaret was fond of Fisher and may not have openly shown him just how involved she was in his appointment as Bishop of Rochester in 1504. However, a letter survives from Henry VII to his mother that, although it does not suggest that it was Margaret who requested the appointment, makes it clear that the promotion was hers to veto if she wished:

And I thought I shoulde not offend you, which I will never do willfully, I am well myndit to promote Master Fisher youre Confessor to a Busshopric; and I assure you Madam, for non other cause, but for the grete and singular virtue that I know and se in hym, as well in conyng [cunning] and natural wisdome, and specially for his good and vertuouse lyving and conversation. And by the promotion of suche a man, I know well, it should corage many others to lyve vertuosely, and to take suche wayes as he dothe, which shulde be a good example to many others hereafter. Howbeit without your pleasure knowen I woll not move hym, nor tempt hym therein. And therefor I beseche you that I may know your mynde and pleasure in that behalf, which shall be followed as muche as God will give me grace. I have in my days promoted many a man unadvisedly, and I wolde now make some recompencion to promote some good and vertuose men, which I doubt note shulde best please God, who ever preserve you in good helth and long lyve.

Unbeknownst to Fisher, his promotion was entirely in Margaret's hands. Even after two decades on the throne, Henry still relied on his mother's counsel as the most disinterested and loyal of everyone about him.

During the years following Elizabeth of York's death, Margaret was less often at court. This may, in part, have been due to the fact that, as the acknowledged first woman in the land, she no longer felt the need to make her presence felt constantly in order to maintain her position. She may also have been feeling her age. She remained Henry's most trusted supporter, however, and continued to assist him in his rule and the best interests of the dynasty they had founded. Henry had made Margaret a grant of Corfe Castle in Dorset early in his reign, and she is recorded to have taken a particular interest in this property, jealously guarding royal rights there. Shortly after receiving the grant, in 1488, she personally ordered an enquiry into what rights belonged to the crown. The enquiry centred on information from as far back as the reign of Richard II, but as far as Margaret was concerned, it had a satisfactory conclusion with it being discovered that 'the whole isle of Purbyk is a royal warren and pertains to the said castle; also that the whole town of Corf pertains to the said castle'. The meadows and pastures there were found to belong to the King. Margaret was pleased with this result, and it served to increase the revenues that she received from the castle. Later that year, she was also able to persuade her son to supply the lead needed for the repairs and other building work that she was carrying out at the castle. Henry has always suffered from a reputation for greed and miserliness, and whilst this was not entirely justified, he was viewed by his contemporaries as acquisitive. This was a reputation that Margaret also held to some extent, although, to her fury, it was Henry that got the better of her over her manor of Woking in 1503, when he forced her to sign it over to him. Woking had been the main home that Margaret had shared with her third husband, Henry Stafford, and it had always been a particular favourite of hers. She was therefore loath to let it go and argued over the terms of the surrender for some years. She returned to Woking within weeks of her son's death, demonstrating that the surrender was not voluntary. This was the first evidence of discord between mother and son. With their similar, strong-willed characters, it was always likely that there would be some disputes and further evidence of a quarrel can be seen in 1504, when she was indicted for keeping an illegal number of retainers. Evidence for a dispute between mother and son is, however, minor, and they continued to work as a partnership.

There is some evidence that Henry relied on Margaret to act in a judicial capacity in his kingdom. In 1525, Margaret's grandson, Henry VIII, received a petition from the people of the north of England complaining that the men in his illegitimate son's household at Sheriff Hutton Castle in Yorkshire had 'been governing the north, hearing and determining causes between party and party'. A note on the outer sheet of this petition recorded that

> Mem. how that the like commission that my lady the king's grandam had was tried and approved greatly to the king's disadvantage in stopping of many lawful processes and course of his laws at Westminster Hall; and also his subjects thereby susteined great losses, mischances, charges and vexations thereby, and none gains commonly by any such commission but the clerks which for their proper lucres doth upon every light surmise make out processes, etc.

Margaret was given the power to hear matters and set up her own courts. This accords with the decision of the University of Cambridge to ask for her judgement in its dispute with the townsmen and, again, is evidence of Margaret's semi-regal powers. Margaret also wrote a letter to her son from Calais in around 1501. Calais was the last English possession on the Continent, and Henry had visited it in 1500 with Elizabeth of York. Although no details of Margaret's visit survive, it may be that she went there specifically on her son's business or in order to provide, once again, a royal presence for the town.

By the last few years of Henry VII's life, his health was visibly failing. As early as 1498, the Spanish ambassador commented that 'the king looks old for his years, but young for the sorrowful life he has led'. The chronicler Edward Hall commented that the King was prematurely aged due to the domestic strife he had faced. A postscript to Henry's letter to Margaret in July 1504, which was written around the time of Lord Stanley's death, also shows that his health was failing:

> Madam, I have encumbered you now with this my long writings, but, methinks, that I can do no less, considering that is so seldom that I do write, wherefore, I beseech you to pardon me, for verily, Madam, my sight is nothing so perfect as it has been; and I know well it will impair daily; wherefore, I trust that you will not be displeased though I write not so often with my own hand, for on my faith, I have been three days or [before] I could make an end of this letter.

The news that Henry's eyesight was deteriorating must have been deeply worrying for his mother, and she was one of the few people he confided in. In the spring of 1507, he fell dangerously ill, and whilst he recovered, he was again unwell early the following year. By July 1508, he appears to have been suffering from consumption. Henry's ill health and his melancholy had increased with the loss first of his eldest son and then his wife, and he came increasingly to rely on his mother and his surviving son. As early as 1504, the Spanish ambassador commented in a letter to Isabella of Castile that

> the Prince of Wales is with the king. Formerly the king did not like

to take the Prince of Wales with him, in order not to interrupt his studies. It is quite wonderful how much the king likes the Prince of Wales. He has good reason to do so, for the Prince deserves all love. But it is not only for love that the king takes the Prince with him, he wishes to improve him. Certainly there could be no better school in the world than the society of such a father as Henry VII. He is so wise and so attentive to everything; nothing escapes his attention. There is no doubt that the Prince has an excellent governor and steward in his father. If he lives ten years longer he will leave the Prince furnished with good habits, and with immense riches, and in as happy circumstances as man can be.

Henry VII was a fond father, and his motives for keeping his only surviving son with him may have been that he was lonely. Both he and Margaret were also deeply afraid for the future of their dynasty and knew that its survival rested only on the life of one boy. To this end, Henry made attempts to remarry in the last few years of his life, apparently first considering his daughter-in-law, Catherine of Aragon, who was conveniently still living in London. He later considered Catherine's cousin, the Queen of Naples, before discounting her due to her lack of wealth. As late as 1507, he induced Catherine of Aragon to write to her father in favour of his suit to marry her widowed sister, who had succeeded their mother as Queen of Castile. This also came to nothing, and Henry was still unmarried when he fell ill again in March 1509.

Henry was at Richmond when he suffered his final collapse. As soon as Margaret heard the news, she moved her household to Coldharbour in order to be close to him and visit him daily. In 1509, Henry was only in his early fifties, but it soon became clear that he was dying. For a woman as religious as Margaret, she must have had mixed feelings on the death of her only child, and whilst she was certainly devastated, she was consoled to some extent by the fact that the King was determined to make a good end. According to *Hall's Chronicle*, as his health grew worse, Henry, 'desiring to exhibit some gratuitie to his people that he might be had in memory after disease [decease]', ordered that a general pardon be granted to all prisoners, save those that had been convicted of murder or theft. He also paid the fees of all prisoners in London and some of the debts of the city. Henry lingered for some days, and likely to Margaret's gratification, public processions were held in a number of parishes in order to pray for his restoration to health.

Henry VII was a pious man, in spite of his reputation for covetousness, and John Fisher, making a sermon in his memory, confirmed that he made a good end:

The sacrament of the auter he receyved at Mydlent, and agayne upon Easterday, with so grete reverence that all that were present were astonyed therat; for at his first entre in to the closet where the sacrament was, he toke of his bonet, and kneled downe upon his knees, and so crept forth devoutly tyl he came unto the place selfe where he receyved the sacrament. Two dayes nexte before his departynge, he was of that feblenes that he myght not receyve it agayn; yet nevertheless he desyred to se the monstraunt wherin it was conteyned. The good fader, his confessor, in goodly maner as was convenyent, brought it unto hym; he with suche reverence, with so many knockynges and betynges of his brest, with so quyche and lyfely a countenance, with so desyrous an harte, made his humble obeysaunce therunto; with so grete humblenes and devocyon kyssed, not the selfe place where the blessed body of our lorde was conteyned, but the lowest parte of the fote of the monstraunt, that all that stode aboute hym scarsly myght conteyn them from teres and wepynge.

Margaret may have been one of those who witnessed the King's piety and wept. She certainly heard all the details of her son's last hours, even if she was not actually present. On the day of his death, Henry asked to hear Mass, and on seeing the crucifix, he 'dyd beholde with grete reverency, lyftynge up his heed as he myght, holdyng up his handes before it, and often embrasynge it in his armes, and with grete devocion kyssynge it, and betynge often his brest'. Henry's thoughts remained with his mother until the end, as, when he made his Will on the last day of March, he appointed her as the first named, and thus the chief, of his executors. To his mother's devastation, he died on 21 April 1509.

It is not recorded whether Margaret was with her only child when he died, but she may have been. She was certainly a regular visitor to his deathbed. For Margaret, the loss was greater than any she had previously suffered. In ill-health herself, she knew that she had only to live long enough to see her grandson, Henry VIII, securely established on the throne before she too could die content in the knowledge that she had helped to preserve the dynasty that she and her son had founded. For Margaret, Henry's death was the cruellest turn of Fortune's Wheel, from which she never recovered.

13

MY LADY, THE KING'S GRANDMOTHER: 23 APRIL-29 JUNE 1509

With Henry VII's death, Margaret was the only adult member of the immediate royal family living in England. Henry's heir, Prince Henry, was immediately proclaimed king as Henry VIII. He did not reach his eighteenth birthday until 28 June 1509 and, although at seventeen, was widely considered old enough to rule, he was legally, at least, still a minor on his accession.

There is no doubt that Margaret, who had devoted most of her life to her child, was devastated at his death. By making her the chief of his executors, Henry VII showed his mother the faith he had in her. He left strict instructions for his executors in his Will, in particular regarding his burial, in which he asked to be buried in the new chapel he had built at Westminster Abbey beside the body of Elizabeth of York. Margaret took her responsibilities as Henry's executor seriously, and she signed warrants for his funeral. She also personally requested that John Fisher preach a sermon in memory of her son at St Paul's Cathedral on 10 May 1509 and was so pleased with the result that she ordered it to be printed, so that the text of the sermon, in which Henry's piety and charitable nature were especially extolled, would be known to as wide an audience as possible.

Although she played a role in the organisation of Henry's funeral, the bulk of the work was left to others. Margaret had made her

Will on 6 June 1508, which suggests that she was in such ill health that she considered herself close to death. She evidently rallied, but at the beginning of 1509, she was again so ill that estimates for her funeral expenses were drawn up. She recovered but, from that date, delegated a number of affairs, allowing John Fisher and two other men who were named as executors in her Will to sign her cofferer's accounts in her place, for example. Margaret's ascetic lifestyle did not help her health, and Fisher recorded in his sermon dedicated to her after her death that she continued to fast on the days prescribed by the Church even though 'for aege and feebleness albeit she were not bounde'. Her one concession to her ill health appears to have been that she would only wear her penitential hair shirts and girdles during weeks when she was 'in helthe'. Otherwise, her strict religious observance continued unchanged, and for a considerable time before her death, her hours at prayer meant that 'her knelynge was to her paynful, and so paynful that many tymes it caused in her backe payne and dysease'. Whilst she was able to physically leave her bed, she continued with her severe routine.

In the weeks following Henry's death, Margaret's health began more rapidly to fail, and it is likely that grief played a part. According to Fisher, it was soon apparent to everyone that she was dying, but like the Biblical Martha before her, she refused to complain of her suffering:

And in lyke maner, the soul of this noble Prynces, which had the Body adjoyned unto it in favour and love, as Syster and Brother, it myghte complayn for the dethe of the body, sythe every part of the same body had ben so occupyed in the servyce of God before. Her eyes in wepynges and teares, sometyme of devocyon, sometyme of repentance; her eares herynge the worde of God and the Devyne Servyce, which dayly was kept in her Chappel with grete nombre of Preests, Clerckes, and Chyldren, to her grete charge and cost; her tongue occupyed in Prayer moche parte of the daye; her legges and fete in vysytynge the Aulters and other holy places, going her statyons customably when she were not let; her handes in gyvynge almes to the poore and nedye, and dressynge them also whan they were syke, and mynystrynge unto them mete and drynke. These mercyfull and lyberall hands to endure the moost paynful cramps, so greveously vexynge her and compellynge her to crye, O Blessyd Jhesu helpe me! O blessyd Lady socoure me! It was a mater of grete pyte. Lyke a spere [spear] it perced the hertes of all her true servants that was about her, and made them crye alsoe of Jhesu for helpe and socoure, with grete haboundence of teares.

Margaret was very aware in the spring of 1509 that her body was rapidly beginning to disintegrate, and again according to Fisher, she lived in fear of losing her sight, her hearing or the use of her legs, 'which thynges sholde have ben mater to her of grete discomforte'. With Henry's death, Margaret finally lost her strong will to live, although she knew that, in order to ensure the safety of her dynasty, she still had one more secular act to perform.

The accession of Margaret's grandson, Henry VIII, was widely welcomed in England, and he was viewed by many as the likely bringer of a new and prosperous future to England. Henry VII had been a capable king, leaving the crown solvent at his death, something that had not been the case for a considerable time. He was never beloved by his people, however. His son, Henry VIII, on the other hand, resembled more his handsome Yorkist forebears than his father and grandmother, and he was welcomed by many in England as a king that they could be proud of. An Italian visitor to Henry VIII's court in 1515 recorded a description of the King that would have been similar to how he appeared on his accession. Henry was athletic and 'above the usual height, with an extremely fine calf to his leg, his complexion was fair and bright, with auburn hair combed straight and short, in the French fashion, and a round face so very beautiful, that it would become a pretty woman, his throat being rather long and thick'. In a Europe that was, in 1509, ruled mainly by old men, Henry was a star. Lord Mountjoy, who notified the scholar Erasmus of Henry's accession, voiced the hopes of many when he wrote,

> I have no fear, my Erasmus, but when you heard that our Prince, now Henry the Eighth, whom we may well call our Octavius, had succeeded to his father's throne, all your melancholy left you at once. For what may you not promise yourself from a Prince, with whose extraordinary and almost divine character you are well acquainted, and to whom you are not only known but intimate, having received from him (as few others have) a letter traced with his own fingers? But when you know what a hero he now shows himself, how wisely he behaves, what a lover he is of justice and goodness, what affection he bears to the learned, I will venture to swear that you will need no wings to make you fly to behold this new and auspicious star. Oh my Erasmus, if you could see how all the world here is rejoicing in the possession of so great a Prince, how his life is all their desire, you could not contain your tears for joy. The heavens laugh, the earth exults, all things are full of milk, of honey and nectar!

The hopes expressed at Henry VIII's accession were almost

impossible to live up to, and it is just possible that Margaret harboured grave concerns about the fitness of her grandson to rule. Margaret's great-nephew, Reginald Pole, who was related to the Yorkist royal family through his mother, later recorded that, at her death, she wept for fear that her grandson would turn away from God. Given Pole's later opposition to Henry and his religious policies, which saw the reformation of the Church and England's break with Rome, it is most likely that these comments were written with the benefit of hindsight and do not accurately represent Margaret's own feelings. However, it is just possible that, seeing her young and pleasure-loving grandson, Margaret was struck with a stab of fear at leaving him alone with the safety of her dynasty in his hands.

Whatever her personal thoughts about her grandson, Margaret was careful not to voice them. The new king was only seventeen at the time of his accession and had no experience of ruling. It therefore fell to Margaret, as her son's chief executor and the most senior adult member of the royal family, to take on the role of ensuring that the transition to Henry VIII was smooth. Although the King was widely recognised to be able to rule alone, Margaret took on something of the role of regent, undertaking to assist her grandson until her reached eighteen. Margaret was aware that she would not be around to guide her grandson in the early years of his reign, and she therefore immediately set about selecting his council for him out of the men that had been most trusted by his father. This was a major undertaking for Margaret, and she knew that the new king would rely heavily on those she suggested. According to Edward Herbert, Henry's seventeenth-century biographer, the King trusted his grandmother's choices, and 'he took their impressions easily, both out of a diffidence of his own strength in the managing of the weighty affairs of his kingdom, and a desire he had to be free to those exercises which most sorted with his youth and disposition'. Margaret took care to ensure that the council was made up of both scholars and soldiers, and it was headed by churchmen: William Warham, Archbishop of Canterbury, and Henry VII's particular friend Richard Fox, Bishop of Winchester. Margaret took the time to brief the council on how she wanted them to act:

> Whom she so disposed, as they might deliberate well among themselves always, before they gave their advice to this young king, as not thinking fit (at that age) he should be distracted by difference of opinions. Neither did they vary much, during her life; though afterward, some smothered jealousies broke out into open faction.

Whilst she lived, Margaret remained a political force to be reckoned with, and by choosing men favourable to herself and her son and ordering them to only present unanimous advice to the King, she hoped that the kingdom would continue to be governed in a way that was acceptable to both her and her son, even after their deaths. She also had a more personal reason for choosing those that had been friends to her son in his lifetime, and the first act of the council was to finalise Henry VII's funeral. Once the council had been appointed, the new king left Richmond Palace for the Tower of London, where he consulted alone with his council for the first time. Although ill health and mourning may have prevented Margaret from joining them there, she was certainly kept apprised of what was happening and, by her force of will alone, kept the council united.

Although young and willing to listen to advice on the governance of his kingdom, Henry VIII was also impetuous, and on 3 June 1509, he privately married Catherine of Aragon, his brother's widow. Henry later claimed that he had done so on the dying request of his father, and if this was the case, Margaret was probably satisfied with the marriage. However, whilst Henry VIII and Catherine had been betrothed soon after Arthur's death in order to preserve the alliance with Spain, Henry VII had never shown any particular inclination towards the match and had, at one point, instructed his son to make a formal protest against his betrothal on the grounds that it had been entered into without his consent and in his childhood. Henry VII had treated Catherine very poorly in the years of her widowhood, and it is perhaps more likely that Henry VIII, seeking to assert himself as an adult ruler, took the initiative in the marriage himself, choosing the most conveniently available princess. Margaret is known to have attended court at Greenwich on 8 June, only five days after the marriage, perhaps to inspect the behaviour of the new queen, and she was apparently satisfied with what she saw.

Another reason for rushing into his marriage was so that Henry could share his coronation with his wife. Margaret and her youngest granddaughter, Princess Mary, stood behind a lattice in a rented house in London to watch the coronation procession as it passed on 23 June 1509. The procession was as spectacular as those that Margaret remembered from her son's reign. Henry VIII wore a fine robe of crimson velvet, furred with ermine and a jacket of cloth of gold. His clothes shone with diamonds, rubies, emeralds, pearls and other rich stones, and he wore a great chain around his neck. The new queen rode in the procession in a litter pulled by two white horses and Margaret may perhaps have been reminded of the coronation of her daughter-in-law, many years before, when Elizabeth of York too had appeared dressed in all her finery and with her fair hair hanging loose around her shoulders.

She may, perhaps, have thought even further back and remembered the earlier coronation of Queen Anne Neville, in which she herself had played a prominent part. Henry and Catherine were crowned the day after the procession in Westminster Abbey. Once again, as she watched the coronation procession, Margaret was seen to weep; although happy for her grandson, she feared another turn of Fortune's Wheel would bring disaster to them all. Margaret was able to attend her grandson's coronation banquet in Westminster Hall, with her ever-faithful Henry Parker acting as her cupbearer and also bringing her own carver. Already unwell, it appears that she may have been unlucky enough to develop food poisoning after eating a cygnet at the banquet. Deeply unwell, she retired to a house in the precincts of Westminster Abbey, aware that she had now done all she could for the future of her dynasty.

Margaret had already chosen her son's chapel in Westminster Abbey as the site of her burial. She had also given charitably to the abbey throughout Henry VII's reign, including in 1508 making indentures with the Abbot of Westminster to ensure that he prayed for her, Henry VII, his children, her last three husbands, Elizabeth of York and her parents, the people who had always been most important to her in her life. This affinity with the abbey is probably why she chose to die within its precincts. Although her grandson's coronation marked Margaret's retirement from public affairs, she was still forced to deal with difficulties in her own household during her last days.

John Fisher was with Margaret constantly as she lay dying. Over the years of their association, he had become very important to her and wielded a considerable amount of power in her household. The anonymous author of one *Life of Fisher*, claimed,

He ordered himselfe so discretly, so temperatly and so wysely, that both she and all her familie [i.e., her household] were governed by his high wisdome and discretion, wherby at last he became greatly reverenced and beloved, not only of the vertuous ladie, and all her houshold, but also of the kinge her sonne.

Fisher wielded a great deal of power in Margaret's household, but there may already have been murmurings about the extent of his influence even during Margaret's lifetime, and he was not as beloved as he thought. According to Fisher's own account,

When my lady was at the poynte to departe out off this worlde unto the mercy off God, I hadde pety off hir poure servaunts, and movide hir that suche as hadde done hir goode service, and was but littill recompenside, that it wolde please hir thei might furst be consideride after the wisdome and descrecion of my lorde of Wincestre and me; and she was well contentyde.

Margaret may have been content to allow the two bishops to decide what her servants should receive, but they certainly were not, and after her death, a group of them went to complain to the King himself. Just how aware Margaret was of the discontent in her household at Fisher's influence and her failure to provide sufficiently for them is not recorded, but she appears to have remained lucid until the end. Fisher recalls that, at the very hour of her death,

When the holy Sacrament conteynyng the Blessyd Jhesu in it was holden before her, and the questyon made untyll her, whether she byleved that there was verayly the Son of God, that suffered his blessyd passyon for her and for all Mankynde upon the Crosse? Many here can bere recorde, how with all her herte and soule she raysed her body, to make answere thereunto, and confessed assuredly, that in that Sacrament was conteyned Chryst Jhesu, the Sone of God, that dyed for wretched Synners upon the Crosse, in whome holly she putte her truste and confydence.

It was the sheer strength of Margaret's will that kept her alive, and her action in support of her grandson was the last service she was able to do for the son to whom she had been devoted.

Margaret prepared herself for death as well as possible. According to Fisher, in his funeral sermon for her, she had been accustomed to charitably keep twelve poor people at any one time in her house, providing them with lodging, food and clothing. When they were ill, she showed her charity by 'vysyntynge [visiting] them and comfortynge them, and mynystrynge unto them with her owne hands: and when it pleased God to call ony of them out of this wretched worlde, she wolde be present, to see them departe, and to lerne to deye'. Margaret died on 29 June 1509, a few weeks after her sixty-sixth birthday and, more pertinently, the day after her grandson's eighteenth birthday. She died surrounded by her household in the presence of her friend John Fisher, who later commented, 'Ah my lorde! yf thou had ben presente, and had herde this sorrowfull cryes of her thy servaunte, with the other lamentable mornynges of her Frendes and Servaunts, thou for thy goodness wolde not have suffred her to dye: But thou wolde have taken pyte and compassion upon her.'

Even in her old age, having survived her only child, three husbands and most of her generation, Margaret's will to live remained strong, and she, along with those around her, wept as she finally gave up the reins of power, leaving England to be ruled by her grandson, Henry VIII: the representative of the Tudor dynasty that she, more than anyone else, had founded.

14

MOTHER OF THE TUDOR DYNASTY

Margaret Beaufort was at the centre of turbulent events throughout her life. It is no wonder that she learned to fear the sudden changes in fortune that she endured, and the concept of Fortune's Wheel could have been developed for her. Margaret's contemporary, the chronicler Edward Hall, summed up the changeability of fortune succinctly when he said, in relation to Margaret's rival and co-conspirator, Elizabeth Woodville:

Suche are all worldly chaunces, nowe in prosperyte and aboundaunce, mutable and chaungeable and full of inconstancy: and in aduersitye often chaunge from euell to good and so to bettre, to the entent that they that be in wealthe and flowe in the aboundaunce of all thinges shall not thynke theim selfes in suretye to tarye styll in that degree and state: and that they that be in misery and calamytie shall not despayre nor mystrust God, but lyue in hope, that a better daye of comfort and gayne wyll once apere and come.

This could have been written for Margaret herself: the mother of the Tudor dynasty always lived in fear that her good fortune would be followed by despair.

Whilst, during Margaret's early life, the Wheel of Fortune turned somewhat indiscriminately, as she grew older, she was remarkable in that she was able to take control of her own destiny. Margaret lived in an age of powerful women, with Margaret of Anjou, Cecily Neville and Elizabeth Woodville all crossing her path at various stages in her life. It can, however, perhaps be said that Margaret Beaufort was the most remarkable of them all. It was Margaret who was able to take her son's very dubious claim to the throne and turn him into a viable rival to the incumbent king. It was also she who arranged for him the marriage that secured the Tudor dynasty's place on the English throne. Margaret's grandson, Henry VIII, and his own children, always prioritised the claims of Elizabeth of York, as the heiress to the House of York when they set out their right to the throne. However, whilst Elizabeth did indeed have a stronger hereditary title, it was Margaret herself who should be seen as the most important ancestress to the Tudor dynasty. It was Margaret who gave her son, the first Tudor, his drop of English royal blood, and it was she who, through her continual efforts, maintained his hopes of returning to England. Eventually, when the political situation was right, her actions paved the way for his triumphant return, at great personal cost to herself. No one was more influential in putting Henry Tudor, an unknown Welsh exile, on the throne of England and the King himself was always grateful to his devoted mother.

Margaret was aware that, in the late fifteenth century, a woman could never have won or held the throne alone, and she was content to transmit her claims to her son. Whilst she allowed herself to be passed over in the succession, however, she certainly did not allow herself to be passed over politically. She saw herself as working in partnership with her son and was a constant rival to his queen, Elizabeth of York, for status and control. By signing her name as 'Margaret R', Margaret set out her own belief in her role. She ably assisted Henry VII in his consolidation of his rule and, on his death, by force of her will, she lived just long enough to see her grandson's eighteenth birthday and hand over the reins of power to him.

Margaret, a Beaufort by birth, was married to her second husband, Edmund Tudor, for a shorter period than any of her other spouses. In spite of this, it was the union that produced her only child, and she prioritised Edmund over her other husbands, significantly always using the title of Countess of Richmond that marriage to him had bestowed on her. The arms of Beaufort, Tudor and Stanley adorn the fine tomb that was built for Margaret in Henry VII's chapel at Westminster Abbey, but there is no mention of Henry Stafford, the husband with whom she was, almost certainly, happiest. For Margaret, the childlessness of her third marriage and the great success of the child of her second marriage made Henry Stafford fade into the background when she adopted her new role of 'My lady, the King's Mother'.

Through her actions in assisting her son on his path to the throne, Margaret helped to ensure that, through him, she has been the ancestress to every subsequent monarch of England. Whilst the direct line of the Tudor dynasty died out in 1603, Margaret's line continued through the descendants of her favourite granddaughter and namesake, Margaret Tudor. Margaret Beaufort was recognised as an important ancestress by the first Stuart king, James I. In the early years of the seventeenth century, the poet Samuel Daniel delivered an address to the King that spoke of his famous great-great-great-grandmother:

Marg'ret of Richmond, (glorious grandmother
Unto that other precious Margaret,

From whence th'Almighty worker did transfer
This branch of peace, as from a root well set)
Thou mother, author, plotter, counsellor
Oh union! that didst both conceive, beget,
And bring forth happiness to this great state,
To make it thus entirely fortunate:

O could'st thou now but view this fair success,
This great effect of thy religious work,
And see therein how God hath pleas'd to bless
Thy charitable counsels; and to work
Still greater good out of the blessedness
Of this conjoined Lancaster and York:
Which all conjoin'd within; and those shut out,
Whom nature and their birth had set without!

How much hast thou bound out posterities
In this great work to reverence thy name!
And with thee that religious, fruitful, wise,
And learned Morton! who contriv'd the same,
And first advis'd, and did so well advise,
As that the good success that thereof came,
Show'd well, that holy hands,
Clean thoughts, clear hearts,
Are only fit to act such glorious parts.

Within a century of her death, Margaret's role in ending the Wars of the Roses and bringing to power the Tudors, a united dynasty combining the claims of both Lancaster and York, had become legendary. Of all the great figures in the Wars of the Roses,

Margaret was one of the last surviving, and she was certainly the victor, however much she feared a further turn of Fortune's Wheel. She did not rule Henry VII, but there is no doubt that he was guided by her. She was the counsellor that he trusted the most, and he allowed her to take up the role and trappings of queenship, even in the lifetime of his wife. Margaret could be domineering at times, and she entirely overshadowed her daughter-in-law, but she was also kind and genuinely thought that she was acting in the best interests of her family and dynasty in everything she did.

For Margaret, the final turn of Fortune's Wheel came in June 1509, and even she, one of the last survivors of her generation, seen by many as a relic from an England that had been left behind, could not cheat death. In her Will, dated a year before her death, she wrote that she had had 'called to our remembrance the unstabilnesse of this transitory worlde, and that ev'ry creatur here lyving is mortall, and the tyme and place of deth to ev'y creatur uncerteyn'. She left John Fisher, the person she trusted most after her own son, as the chief of her executors. He did not let her down, and whilst, with Margaret's forceful character gone, her servants and relatives felt able to challenge her Will and much of what she had done in relation to her colleges and charities, he diligently set out to fulfil her wishes. It was left to Fisher and the other executors to arrange Margaret's grand funeral after her death, and Fisher himself preached her funeral sermon, praising the woman who had done so much for him. Margaret's young servant Henry Parker in his old age extolled the virtues of his former employer, informing her great-granddaughter, Queen Mary, that 'this precious margareyte is past from this worlde, not as other ffloures [flowers] be that to day be fayre, and to morowe withered and drye, but this oure fayre floure as long as the sea hath fyshes, and the skye twinkling starres, untyll the sounde of the last trompet shall call all creatures to Judgment, her fame, her honour, her liberalitye, her prudence, her chastytye, & her excellent vertue shall be comendyd for euer'. Margaret was genuinely loved and admired by those who knew her.

It is left to Margaret's great friend and closest associate, John Fisher, to supply her epitaph. Some years after her death, he wrote, in a dedication to a mutual friend, Richard Fox, Bishop of Winchester,

> As I have spoken her praises in a funeral oration, I will not pursue the subject here, though she never could be praised too much. This only will I add, that though she chose me as her director, to hear her confessions and guide her life, yet I gladly confess that I learnt more from her great virtue than I ever taught her.

Fortune's Wheel was both kind and sometimes unkind to Margaret: the daughter of a probable suicide, the greatest heiress in England, divorced at ten, married to the King's half-brother at twelve, a widow at thirteen, a mother at thirteen, twice more a widow, a plotter, a prisoner, the mother of a king, most of all, Margaret Beaufort can be remembered as the mother of the great Tudor dynasty.

APPENDIX:
MARGARET BEAUFORT IN HER
OWN WORDS

In spite of her political prominence, few letters or other documents survive to attest to Margaret's character. Her surviving letters, which all date to the period after Henry VII came to the throne, are therefore of great interest. Margaret's surviving letters are printed in full below in order to provide an additional insight into the character of this exceptional woman. Some of the letters are of more interest than others, but each is included in order to provide as full an account as possible. In the course of my research into Margaret, I have come across no further letters written by her. The corpus below is therefore as complete as possible. It may be that, in the future, further documents will come to light to extend our knowledge of Margaret. At the moment, at least, the letters provide the only evidence for Margaret Beaufort in her own words.

Some of the letters are written in the formal style used by members of the royal family and give little indication of Margaret's character. Margaret's letters to her son are of great interest, however, as they reveal a depth of emotion not otherwise clearly apparent. Her letters to John Paston, threatening him, demonstrate that Margaret was not a woman to cross. She had been named as one of her kinsman William Paston's executors and took a personal interest in seeing that his estate was properly distributed. Her letter to the Earl of Ormond, complaining that the gloves he had sent her from Flanders were too big for her hands, contains a subtle dig at the greatest lady in Flanders, Margaret of York, by implying that she was on the large side: Margaret Beaufort herself was renowned for her abstinence in food and drink. Her letters to Oxford University demonstrate the interest in education that would eventually lead to her founding two colleges at Cambridge.

Margaret Beaufort to the Bishop of Exeter, 21 March 1488
Right reuerend Fader in God and oure right welbiloued. In our harty

wise, we commaund [commend] vs vnto you, and for asmoche as John Dalkyn, receiuor of oure Lordshippe of Holdernes belonging vnto oure cousin of Bukes hath not commen vp and made his accompt as he ought to doo by raison of his said office, but hath sodenly departed from hous [us] othrewise than according to the trust that was put in hym: We therefore desire and herty pray you to send us by this bringer a pryve seill for the said John after the tenure of this bille whiche we send you herein closed, as our specialle trust is in you and as we may doo for you at your desires hereafter, whereunto we shalbe always redy by Goddes grace who send you right good lif and long.

Yeuen vndre our signet at oure place of Colde Harborowe, the 21st day of Marche. My lord y pray you y may her [hear] of your newes of Flaundyrse.

M. Rychemound

Margaret Beaufort to the University of Oxford

Trust and right welbeloved, we grete you wele; and where oure ful welbeloved master Maurice Westbury hath lately commensed within the Universite there, by reason whereof he, accordyng to the auncient and laudable custumes and status of the same, aught to be resident there duryng oon hole yere next and immediatly folowyng his saide commensement; how be it we desire and hartily pray you – in asmoch as we have ordeined the said master Maurice to applie hym to the erudition & doctrine of certayn yong gentilmen at our findyng for a season – that ye, at this oure instaunte, wille dispense with him in that behalve, any statute or ordinaunce had among you to the contrary notwithstanding. And ye thus doing shal have us youre good lady in any thing reasonable that ye shal desire of us, concernyng the weal of you or the saide Universite hereafter. Yeven undre oure signet at the castel of Windesore, the xii day of January. Margaret.

Margaret Beaufort to the Earl of Ormond, the Queen's Lord Chamberlain, 25 April 1496

My Lord Chamberlain,

I thank you heartily that ye list so soon remember me with my gloves, the which were right good, save they were too much for my hand. I think the ladies in that parts be great ladies all, and according to their great estate they have great personages. As for news here I am sure ye shall have more surety than I can send you. Blessed be God, the King, the Queen, and all our sweet children be in good health. The Queen hath been a little crased [i.e., ill], but now she is well, God be thanked. Her sickness is [?not] so good as I would but I trust hastily it shall, with God's grace, whom I pray give you good speed in your great matters, and bring you well and soon home.

Written at Shene the 25th day of April,
M. RYCHEMOND

Margaret Beaufort to the University of Oxford, 1500
By the King's moder

Right reverende ffader in god, right trusty and welbelovyd, we grete you wele; And this present day have recevyd your right kinde lettres and lovinge tokins by our welbeloved Thomas Pantre, oon of your bedells; for the whiche we thank you in owre harty wise; Wherby we perceyve ye have electe and chosen oon m. Rooper, doctor of divinite, to rede owre lecture there; whereof we be right gladde, and trust with godd's mercy it shalbe to the greate honour and weal of your said Universite; aswele to thynecrease of vertu as lernyng off Students with in the same, whiche we right specially tender, and shalbe gladde to further at altymes to the best we can. Yeven under owre Signett at the manowre of Bukeden, the first day of Juyn.

Margaret Beaufort to the University of Oxford, 1500

Trusty and welbelovyd, we grete you wele; and understonde the Rowme of gentilmen bedell in divinite within youre universite is now voide by deceasse of your late office in the same; wherunto ye in breve tyme intende to electe soome honest and hable person. We specially tendering thonnoure and thincrease of lernyng in divinite, and be credybly enformed by the right reverent fader in god, the bysschopp of Rochestre, and certain other whiche be verray lovers of the said faculte, that one Rychard Wotton is a right hable and convenient person for the said office, Desire therfore and pray you so to owe youre good favores unto hym as rather for oure sake he may be proferryd to the said Rome [room]. Wherby ye schall not oonly do a thing for the grete honowre and weale of youre said universite but also unto us full Singuler plesur. Yeven under signet at the manour of Buckdoone, the xxiii day of Auguste.

Margaret Beaufort to Richard Shirley, 1501
To our servant Richard Shirley, bailiff of our town of Ware.
Richard Shirley,

We send unto you at this time the king's servant, clerk of the market, this bearer for ordinance and devising of victuals, as well for man as beast, within our town there; willing you to help and assist him in the same the best you can, and thereupon to do the execution thereof as you tender our pleasure. Written at the manor of Hatfield, the 23rd day of July.

MARGARET R

Margaret Beaufort to Henry VII, 1501?
My own sweet and most dear King, and all my worldly joy.

In as humble manner as I can think, I recommend me to your grace, and most heartily beseech our Lord to bless you. And my good heart, where that you say that the French King hath at this time given me courteous answer, and written letter of favour to his Court of Parliament, for the brief expedition of my matter, which so long hath hanged; the which I well know he doth especially for your sake, for the which my ......ly beseech your Grace it ...... to give him your favourable ...... thanks, and to desire him to continue his ...... in......e...... me. And, if it so might like your Grace, to do the same to the cardinal; which, as I understood, is your faithful, true, and loving servant. I wish my very joy, as I oft have shewed, and I fortune to get this, or any part thereof, there shall neither be that or any good I have, but it shall be your's, and at your commandment, as surely and with as good a will, as any ye have in your coffers; and would God ye could know it, as verily as I think it. But, my dear heart, I will no more encumber your Grace with further writing in this matter, for I am sure your chaplain and servant, Dr. Whytston, hath shewed your highness the circumstances of the same; and if it so may please your Grace, I humbly beseech the same, to give further credence also to this bearer. And our Lord give you as long good life, health, and joy, as your most noble heart can desire, with as hearty blessings as our Lord hath given me power to give you.

At Colyweston the 14th day of January, by your faithful, true bedewoman [i.e., a person who prays for another] and humble mother,

Margaret R

Margaret Beaufort to Henry VII, 1501

My dearest and only desired joy in this world,

With my most hearty loving blessings and humble commendations I pray our Lord to reward and thank your grace, for that it hath pleased your highness so kindly and lovingly to be content to write your letters of thanks to the French king, for my great matter, that so long hath been in suit, as Master Welby hath shewed me your bounteous goodness is pleased. I wish, my dear heart, an my fortune be to recover it, I trust you shall well perceive I shall deal towards you as a kind, loving mother; and, if I should never have it, yet your kind dealing is to me a thousand times more than all that good I can recover, an all the French king's might be mine withal. My dear heart, an it may please your highness to licence Master Whitstone, for this time, to present your honourable letters, and begin the process of my cause – for that he so well knoweth the matter, and also brought me the writings from the said French king, with his other letters to his parliament at Paris – it should be greatly to my help, as I think: but all will I remit to your pleasure. And if I be too bold in this, or any my desires, I humbly beseech your grace of pardon, and that your highness take no displeasure.

My good king, I have now sent a servant of mine into Kendall, to receive such annuities as be yet hanging upon the account of Sir William Wall, my lord's chaplain, whom I have clearly discharged; and if it will please your majesty's own heart, at your leisure, to send me a letter, and command me that I suffer none of my tenants be retained with no man, but that they be kept for my lord of York, your fair sweet son, for whom they be most meet, it shall be a good excuse for me to my lord and husband; and then I may well, and without displeasure, cause them all to be sworn, the which shall not after be long undone. And where your grace shewed your pleasure for [   ] , the bastard of King Edward's, sir, there is neither that, nor any other thing,

I may do by your commandment, but I shall be glad to fulfil to my little power with God's grace. And, my sweet king, Fielding, this bearer, hath prayed me to beseech you to be his good lord in a matter he sueth for to the Bishop of Ely, now (as we hear) elect, for a little office nigh to London. Verily, my king, he is a good and wise, well-ruled gentleman, and full truly hath served you well, accompanied as well at your first as all other occasions, and that causeth us to be the more bold and gladder also to speak for him; howbeit, my Lord marquis hath been very low to him in times past, because he would not be retained with him; and, truly, my good king, he helpeth me right well in such matters as I have business with in these parts. And, my dear heart, I now beseech you of pardon of my long and tedious writing, and pray Almighty God to give you as long, good, and prosperous life as ever had prince, and as hearty blessings as I can ask of God.

At Calais town, this day of St Anne's, that I did bring into this world my good and gracious prince, king, and only beloved son.

By your humble servant, beadwoman, and mother,

MARGARET R

Margaret Beaufort to the Mayor of Coventry
By the Kinges Moder,

Trusty and welbeloved, we grete you wel. And wher we of late, upon the compleint of oon Owen, Burchis [burgess] of the Cite ther, addressed our other lettres unto you, and willed you by the same and in our name, to call afor you the parties comprised in the same compleint. And therfore to order the Variaunce depending betwixt them according to good conscience. Albeit as it is said, the said Owen can or may have no reasonable aunswer of you in that behalve to our mervall. Wherfor We wol and in the Kinges name commaunde you efsoones to call befor you the said parties, and roundely texamyn them. And therupon to order and determyne the premisses, as may stande with good reson, and the quytie of the Kinges laws. So as no compleint be made unto us hereafter in that behalve. Indevoyring you thus to do, as ye tendre the kings pleasure and ours, and the due ministracon of Justice. Yeven under our signett at our Manoir of Colyweston, the last day of September.

To oure trusty and welbeloued, the Maior of the Citie of Coventry, and his brethren of the same, and to eny of theim.

Margaret Beaufort to Sir John Paston, 10 February 1497-1503

By the Kings Moder

Trusty and right welbeloved, we greet you well. And wher by the meanes of our trusty and right welbeloved Sir Reynold Bray, Sir Thomas Lovell and Sir Henry Heydon, knights, there was a full agreement made and concluded, and also put in writinge, betwen our trusty and right welbeloved Sir John Savile, knight, and Gilbert Talbot, esquier, on th'one partie, and yow on th'other, for divers lands which they ought to have in the right of their wives, daughters and heyers to William Paston, esquier, their late fader deceassed, which lands ye by mighty power kepe and witholde from them without any just title, as they afferme; and albeit the said agrement was made by your minde and consent, yet ye ne doe performe the same, to our merveile if it be so.

Wherefore we desier and also counsell yow without delay upon the sight hereof now shortly to ride to the court to the said arbitrators now ther being, with whom ye shall finde your adverse partie, or other in their names fully authorized, to abide such final ende and conclusion in the premisses as shall be consonant with the said agrement, without further troubles or busines therin herafter to be had; and that ye will thus do in any wise so as we be not driven through your defalte to put to our hands for further remedye to be had in the premisses.

Yeven under our signet at our mannor of Colly Weston the xth day of Februarye'.

Margaret Beaufort to Sir John Paston, 10 April before 1504

By the Kinges modre

Trusty and welbeloved, we grete you wele, and pray you in our name to have the conynve of a bill herin closed in good and deliberate examinacion, and therupon to set such cude and ordinate direction as shalbe consonant to justice, right, and good conscience, so as for lakke therof the partie plaintief have no cause reasounable to pursue furthre unto us in that behalve, as we trust you.

Yeven undere our signet at our manour of Colyweston the xth day of Aprill.

Margaret R.

NOTES

1 A Beaufort Heiress: 1443-1444

The quotes regarding Fortune's Wheel are from Fisher 1840:127. Details of Margaret's maternal family are from Cooper 1874:1-3. Froissart details Katherine Swynford's background and marriage to John of Gaunt (vol. VI pp.190-1). There are two biographies of Katherine that detail the births and legitimisation of her children (Lucraft 2010 and Weir 2007). The quote on John of Gaunt's marriage to Katherine Swynford is from Froissart p.191. The Pope's consent to the Beaufort's legitimacy is noted in Richard II's statute legitimising them (Myers 1969:169). John of Gaunt's Will is from *Testamenta Vetusta* vol. II pp.141-2. Details of the marriage of Henry IV to Mary de Bohun and Henry IV's usurpation of the crown can be found in Norton 2011 (forthcoming). Capgrave 1858 discusses Henry IV. Henry IV's grant to the first Earl of Somerset of £1,000 p.a. is from PRO SC 8/139/6909. There is an account of the Battle of Baugé in John Hardyng's Chronicle (Myers 1969:230). John and Thomas Beaufort's petition to Gloucester in 1427 is in PRO SC 8/141/7018. The agreement with the Duke of Bourbon is from PRO C 47/30/9/14. Margaret's father's dispute with Crowland Abbey over Deeping is related in the *Crowland Chronicle Continuations* pp.398-9. Information on the English rule in France during Henry VI's minority can be found in Griffiths 2004. Details of Somerset's bargaining and service in France are from Griffiths 2004:466-469 and Jones 1981. Somerset's meeting with the Abbot of Crowland, his return to England and suicide is from the *Crowland Chronicle Continuations* p.399.

2 First Marriage: 1444-1453

The grant of Margaret's wardship to Suffolk is printed as an appendix in Fisher (pp.168-9). John and William Merfield's comments about Henry VI are from Myers 1967:264. Jean de Waurin's comments on Henry VI are from Dockray 2000:4. Dockray 2000:1 points out that Henry VI was unlikely to be a simpleton, as he mastered both French and Latin. The instructions to the Earl of Warwick in 1428 are quoted from Dockray 2000:3. Piero da Monte, November 1437 (Dockray 2000:4) notes Henry VI's comments on the evils of women. John Blacman is printed in Dockray 2000 (the quote on Henry's piety is from p.80). Details of Suffolk's background can be found in Neillands 1992:21. Information on Margaret's relationship with her St John half-siblings is from Jones and Underwood 1995:32-34. Henry's marriage to Margaret of Anjou and Suffolk's role in the negotiations are contained in the many biographies of the Lancastrian queen, including Archer 1995, Bagley 1970, Haswell and Maurer 2003. Lee 1986. Laynesmith 2004 also contains details of her life. Cron 1994 specifically considers the relationship between Suffolk and Margaret of Anjou. The quotes concerning Margaret Beauchamp from the *Crowland Chronicle* are from p.400. Quotes from Fisher on Margaret's education are from p.110 and pp.114-5. Caxton's dedication to Margaret of *The Hystorye of Kinge Blanchardyne and Queen Eglantyne his Wyfe* is printed as an appendix to Fisher (p.179). The Duchess of Buckingham's Will is quoted from Walpole 1769:290. Fisher's quote on Margaret's character is from p.109. A number of sources suggest that Suffolk murdered Humphrey of Gloucester, including an English Chronicle written before 1471 (Davies 1856:62). Details of Suffolk's fall are in Storey 1999. The charges used in Suffolk's impeachment are from the Paston Letters vol. I pp.99-105. Suffolk's letter to his son is in the Paston letters vol. I pp.121-2. John de la Pole's sons had a claim to the throne through their mother, who was the sister of Edward IV. There is an account of Suffolk's death in William Lomner to John Paston, 5 May 1450 (*Paston Letters* vol. I p.124).

3 Second Marriage: 1453-1456

Seward 1995:28 describes the summons to Margaret's mother. Details of Catherine of Valois's life can be found in Griffiths 2004, Griffiths and Thomas 1998 and Norton 2011 (forthcoming). Henry VI's act annulling wardships, made in 1455, is printed in *Rotuli Parliamentum* V:330. The date of Edmund and Margaret's marriage is not recorded. They were married during the course of a parliament as an Act against Grants of Wards and Marriages, 1455, refers to Margaret being unmarried and a later Act concerning Richard Duke of York and Others, and the Abbot of Kirkestall, 1455, refers to Margaret as Edmund Tudor's wife (*Rotuli Parliamentum* V:330 and 343). Margaret's vision of St Nicholas is from Fisher p.112. *Whethamstede's Register* (Dockray 2000) describes Henry's mental collapse. Margaret of Anjou's attempts to secure Henry's recognition of her son are from *Paston Letters* vol. I pp.195 and 226. Edmund's epitaph is quoted from Cooper 1874:11. The links between Catherine and the Beauforts after her secret marriage are described in Griffiths 2004:61. Grants to Edmund Tudor of land in Kendal and Weresdale are from an Act of 1454 (*Rotuli Parliamentum* V:253). Griffiths and Thomas 1998:40-46 details Edmund and Jasper Tudor's political activities. The petition by the co-heirs of the Earl of Kent is from PRO SC 8/152/7597. Leyland vol. V records the tradition that Henry VII was conceived at Caldicot Castle. Margaret's concerns about her granddaughter's early marriage are from Don Pedro de Ayala to Ferdinand and Isabella, 25 July 1498 (CSP I no.210).

4 Margaret's First Widowhood: November 1456-January 1458

Leland 1744:74 describes Pembroke Castle. Margaret's letter to Henry reminiscing about his birth is quoted in Wood 1846, vol II. The earlier letter of Margaret's is from Halstead 1839:206-7. Griffiths and Thomas 1998:47 note that Henry was originally baptised Owen. Owen Tudor's background is discussed in Griffiths and Thomas 1998:5. Jasper's Will is from *Testamenta Vetusta* vol. II pp.430-1. Cooper 1874:11 records Henry's commemoration of his father. Henry VII's payments to his uncle, the younger Owen Tudor, are in *Extracts from the Privy Purse Expenses of King Henry the Seventh, from December 1491 to March 1505* (*Excerpta Historica* 1831:119 and 128). The quotes from Fisher comparing Margaret to Martha are from p.109. The *Myrroure of Golde*, which was translated by Margaret, is printed as an appendix in Fisher. Parker's account of Margaret offering to join a Crusade as a laundress is from BL Add. MSS. 12060. Stow 1842:176 notes that she founded an alms house at Westminster.

Notes

5 Third Marriage: 1458-1470

Jones and Underwood 1995:40 relate Margaret and Jasper's visit to the Duke of Buckingham. Buckingham's Will is in *Testamenta Vetusta* vol. II pp.296-7. WAM 5472 f.33 records that William Bailey was sent by Margaret to return books to the Duchess of Buckingham. Henry Stafford's Will is from *Testamenta Vetusta* vol. II p.324. WAM 12181-90 contains Henry Stafford's accounts from 1466 to 1471. F.61 details Margaret and Stafford's journey to London from the Midlands, stopping at a number of places on the way. The same source details their move from Bourne to Woking, suggesting that, in the early years of their marriage, Bourne would have been their main residence. WAM 5472 f.45 notes that medicines for Henry Stafford were fetched from London. Seward 1995:134 suggests that Stafford suffered from 'St Anthony's Fire'. An example of Margaret and Stafford hunting can be found in WAM 5472 f.43. Griffiths 2004:804 notes the grant of Henry's wardship to Jasper and the Earl of Shrewsbury. Warwick's comments on Henry VI and Margaret of Anjou are quoted from Dockray 2000. A number of works detail the Wars of the Roses, and these are listed in the bibliography. York's actions in claiming the throne are recorded in *Whethamstede's Register* (Myers 1969:283-4). His actual claim is set out in a contemporary document printed in Dockray 2000:23. Neillands 1992:17 describes the attempts of Richard, Earl of Cambridge, to make Edmund Mortimer king. Henry VI's comments recorded by John Blacman are from Dockray 2000:38. Griffiths and Thomas 1998:52 describe Jasper Tudor's opposition to Edward IV following his usurpation of the crown. Henry's comments to Philip de Comines are from p.538 of the chronicler's work. Herbert's Will is from *Testamenta Vetusta* vol. I p.305. Margaret and Stafford's visit to Raglan can be seen in their accounts from WAM 12185 f.35-40. Hall's description of the young Henry VII is from p.414. Milanese State Papers: Newsletter from London, 14 April 1461 (Dockray 1999:9) notes the jubilation on Edward's accession. *Gregory's Chronicle* (Dockray 1999:9-10) and Hearne's *Fragment of an Old Chronicle* (Giles 1845:9-14) describe Edward's attempts to be reconciled with Somerset and the duke's defection. Seward 1995:131-3 records the grant to Margaret and Stafford of Woking and their lives there. WAM 12189 f.58 describes fresh fish purchased for Woking, for example. A purchase of hogsheads of white wine is recorded in WAM 5472 f.5. The record of Henry Stafford's long gown of velvet is also from f.5. Margaret's purchases of clothes are described in WAM 32407 f.13v. Margaret's purchase of New Year's gifts from a goldsmith is from the same source. Fisher p.113 describes Margaret's asceticism. Jones and Underwood 1995:47 note that Margaret secured Henry's admission to the Order of the Holy Trinity at Knaresbrough. The letter from John Paston is from vol. I p.389. WAM 5472 f.5 to f.5v details the visit to London during the parliament. The earlier visit to London, with Margaret's visit to the Bishop of Chichester, is from WAM 5472 f.5v. Seward 1995:135 describes Edward's visit to Woking. Margaret's clothes for the visit are described in Jones and Underwood 1995:47. Edward IV's collection of books is detailed in his Wardrobe Accounts (published in Nicolas 1830).

6 The Fall of the House of Lancaster: 1469-1471

There are two recent biographies of Elizabeth Woodville, which detail her marriage and life: Baldwin 2002 and Okerlund 2005. Her life is also detailed in Laynesmith

2004. The quote from Mancini is from p.61. *Annales Rerum Anglicarum,* in January 1465 (printed in Dockray 1999) records the marriage of John Woodville. Warwick and Clarence's proclamation is from Dockray 1999. Jasper's activities are in Griffiths and Thomas 1998:60-62. *Warkworth's Chronicle* (Giles 1845:108) describes Henry VI's capture. Corbet's account of his rescue of the young Henry Tudor is from his petition to Henry VII (Owen and Blakeway 1822:248). Margaret and Stafford's activities in trying to locate Henry and then secure his wardship are from WAM 5472 f.43-47. Margaret's attempts to negotiate for Henry's return are from Jones and Underwood 1995:49 and Seward 1995:173. Margaret of Anjou's response to Warwick's terms is contained in 'Touching the manner of the treaty of marriage between the prince and the earl of Warwick's second daughter, with the answer of Queen Margaret' (Giles 1845:232). The quote on Henry VI's release from *Warkworth's Chronicle* is from Giles 1845:118. *Warkworth's Chronicle* also describes Henry VI's parliament following his restoration (p.121). Griffiths and Thomas 1998:69 describe Margaret's reunion with Henry Tudor. The quote from Polydore Vergil on Henry Tudor's meeting with Henry VI is from p.135. Seward 1995:175 describes the visit of Edmund Beaufort to Woking. Edward's return to London is noted in 'History of the Arrival of Edward IV in England, and the final recovery of his kingdoms from Henry VI, 1471' (Giles 1845:56). Bernard Andreas's Latin life of Henry VII describes Henry and Jasper's flight from Tenby.

7 A Fourth Husband: 1471-1483

Details of Margaret's fourth marriage can be found in Seward p.208-9 and Bagley 1985. The Act containing Margaret and Stanley's marriage contract is from *Rotuli Parliamentorum* VI:312. Stanley's Will is in *Testamenta Vetusta* vol. II:458. Domville 1899:70 suggests the rivalry between Gloucester and Stanley over Berwick. The quote from Comines on Henry's arrival in Brittany is from p.538. Vergil's comments on Henry's imprisonment are from p.155. Griffiths and Thomas 1998:80 describe Louis XI's attempts to obtain Jasper and Henry. Vergil's comments on Edward's fear of Henry Tudor are from p.159. Griffiths and Thomas 1998:85-8 and Jones and Underwood 1995:60-61 discuss Margaret's negotiations with Edward IV for Henry's return. The draft pardon is on the reverse of WAM 32378. The draft is very faint and water damaged and is made up of a brief five lines of text. The interpretation of this document has been taken from Jones and Underwood 1995.

8 Mother to the King's Great Rebel & Traitor: April 1483-December 1483

Horrox 1995:103 describes Margaret as a kingmaker. The *Crowland Chronicle Continuations* described the council meeting after Edward IV's death. Mancini records that Elizabeth and Dorset attempted to raise an army. Thomas More relates Elizabeth's time in sanctuary. The quote from Comines on Edward's supposed first marriage is from p.537. The fanciful description of Richard is by John Rous (Myers 1969:344). Richard's actions following his brother's death are discussed in great detail in Horrox 1999. Richard's letter to the keeper of his wardrobe is printed in Halliwell 1848:153. Margaret's clothes for the coronation can be seen from 'Wardrobe Account, 1483' (Jeffery 1807). The coronation is detailed in 'An anonymous account of the coronation of Richard III' (*Excerpta Historica* p.380-383). Stow 1615:460

records the plot to rescue the princes from the Tower. Jones and Underwood 1995:62 assert that Margaret was involved in the plot. Buck p.64 discusses Margaret's treason against Richard III. The most detailed account of Buckingham's rebellion and Margaret's role is in *Hall's Chronicle*. Buck's comments on Margaret's involvement in the conspiracy are from p.63-4. The attainders for many of Henry's supporters in Buckingham's rebellion survive, including 'An Act for the Atteunder of the Bishop of Elye and others, 1483' (*Rotuli Parliamentorum* V:250). The Act of Attainder against Margaret is on pp.250-1 of the same source. Bagley 1985:15 suggests Margaret spent her imprisonment at Lathom and Knowsley.

9 Bosworth Field: January 1484-August 1485

Henry Parker's comments are from BL Add. MSS. 12060. Henry's circular letter is from Halliwell 1848:161-2. Richard's attempts to obtain Henry from Brittany are from *Hall's Chronicle* p.402-3. Seward 1995:295 notes that Margaret warned Henry to flee Brittany. Richard's assurance of his nieces' safety is quoted from Nicolas 1830:xli. Hicks 2006 is the only biography of Anne Neville. Further details of her life can be found in Laynesmith 2004, Hicks 1991, Hicks 1992, Norton 2011 (forthcoming), Saul 2005 and Seward 1997. The *Crowland Chronicle Continuations* recounts the rumours surrounding the death of Anne Neville and Elizabeth of York's conspicuous appearance at court. The letter cited by Buck is quoted from Nicolas 1830:xlv. Visser-Fuchs 1993 considers the possible marriage between Elizabeth of York and Richard. Further details of Elizabeth of York's life can be found in her biographies: Harvey 1973, Nicolas 1830 and Okerlund 2009. The quote from the *Crowland Chronicle Continuations* on Elizabeth of York's character is from p.500. *Hall's Chronicle* p.410 notes Henry's attempts to marry a Herbert. Richard's denial that he planned to marry Elizabeth is quoted from Myers 1969:342-3. The *Ballad of Ladye Bessiye* is printed in Hales and Furnival 1868. *Hall's Chronicle* p.410 records that Bray was collecting money for Henry's mercenaries. Richard's proclamation against Henry is printed in Giles 1845:279-280. *Hall's Chronicle* p.411 notes Henry's agreement with Charles VIII and his letters to supporters including Margaret when he landed in England. The *Ballad of Bosworth Ffeilde* is printed in Hales and Furnival 1968. The quote about Richard's concerns about Margaret persuading Stanley to support Henry are from the *Crowland Chronicle Continuations* p.502. *Hall's Chronicle* describes Henry's landing and march towards the battlefield. The *Ballad of Bosworth Ffeilde* describes the meetings between Henry and the Stanleys. *Hall's Chronicle* p.413 notes that Richard had bad dreams the night before Bosworth, and the *Crowland Chronicle Continuations* p.503 describe Richard's disorganised camp. The *Ballad of Bosworth Ffeilde* describes Richard's treatment of Lord Strange. *Hall's Chronicle* and the *Crowland Chronicle Continuations* detail the battle. Jones 2002 analyses the battle.

10 The King's Mother: August 1485-January 1486

Hall's Chronicle p.421 records Henry's time in Leicester. Details of the grants made by Henry to his supporters are from Campbell 1873 vol. I. Edward Woodville's grants are pp.6-7. The quote from the grant to Stanley is on pp.77-8. Details of the hangings from Richard III's tent are recorded in 'A schedule of such goods as shall be left at

Woodhouse for heir loomes to be continued with the house and the estate' (Millar 1986:123). The grant to Margaret concerning Ware is from 11 October 1485 (p.81). Henry Parker relates the visit Margaret received from the Duke of Buckingham in BL Add. MSS. 12060. The grant to John Welles is from 15 October 1485. Bacon's comments on Henry's three titles to the throne are from p.8. The red rose emblem and the Beaufort portcullis were particularly prominent in the decorations prepared for Henry's coronation (listed in the accounts in Legg 1901). An example of the rehabilitation of Henry VI is an 'Act for the Restitution of Henry VI' (Campbell vol. I pp.120-1). The comments on England and London by an Italian visitor are from Andreas Franciscius to Jacobus Sansonus, 17 November 1497 (Williams 1967:188-9). Henry's purchases for his coronation are recorded in 'Emptions and Provisions of stuff for the coronation of Henry VII' (in Legg 1901). Small quantities of scarlet were purchased from a wide variety of sources, suggesting that it was necessary to seek out a number of suppliers. Henry's privy purse expenses are from *Excerpta Historica* 1831. The most complete biography of Henry VII is Chrimes 1999. The king is also discussed in Williams 1994, Rogers 1993 and Lockyer and Thrush 1997. The Act granting Margaret the status of a sole person is printed in a number of works, including Cooper 1874:30-1. Margaret's vow of chastity is also quoted from Cooper 1874. Her vow of chastity is discussed in Cooper 1853. Routh 1924:77 describes Collyweston. Parker's account of Margaret's household is from BL Add. MS 12060. Details of the Orléans ransom and Margaret's efforts to recover it are contained in Jones 1986. Henry's letter to Margaret is printed in a large number of works, including Cooper 1874 pp.209-10. Henry's French expedition in 1492 is discussed in Chrimes 1999:273-283. It is also noted in the *Chronicle of Calais* for 1492. Bacon p.215 claims that Margaret had little political influence. Ayala to Ferdinand and Isabella, 25 July 1498 (Pollard 1914:4) notes Margaret's influence over Henry and Elizabeth of York's disapproval of this.

11 Margaret R: January 1486-July 1504

Margaret's Ordinances are printed in Leland 1774 vol. IV p.179. Elizabeth of York's purchase of cushions in 1503 are from her Privy Purse Expenses p.28. The manuscript containing details of Margaret Tudor's birth is printed in Leland vol. IV p.249. Bacon's comments on the relationship between Henry and Elizabeth are from pp.11-12. The document noting Henry's grief at Elizabeth's death is printed in *The Antiquarian Repertory* vol. IV p.655. There are two biographies of Elizabeth: Harvey 1973 and Okerlund 2009. There is also a detailed memoir of her life in Nicolas 1830. Okerlund 2009:95 discusses Margaret's fondness for Cecily of York. Elizabeth Woodville's Will is from *Testamenta Vetusta* vol. II p.24-6. A contemporary manuscript describing great court occasions and Margaret's attendance there is printed in Leland vol. IV p.206. Henry's letter to the Earl of Ormond dated 13 May 1487 is from Halliwell 1848:171. A contemporary document describing Elizabeth's coronation is printed in Ives 1873. The gifts of the Garter robes to Elizabeth and Margaret by the King are noted in 'Further Deliveries from the great Wardrobe, between 1 March 2nd Henry VII and Feast of St Michael 4th Henry VII' (Campbell vol. II:497). The grant to Farnham for the foundation of a chantry is from Campbell vol. II p.115. The grant of the next presentation to the deanery of St Stephen is from Campbell vol.

II p.218 (21 December 1487). The licence to found a chantry at Guildford is from Campbell vol. I p.278-9 (6 February 1496). Dr De Puebla to Ferdinand and Isabella, 15 July 1498 (CSP I no.202) notes the Spanish ambassador's audience with Henry, Elizabeth and Margaret. Dr De Puebla to Ferdinand and Isabella, 17 July 1498 (CSP I no.203) records Margaret and Elizabeth's request that Catherine learn French. De Puebla to Ferdinand and Isabella, 25 August 1498 (CSP I no.221) describes Elizabeth's letters to Isabella and Catherine. One of the Secretaries of Henry VII to his Nephew, a Clergyman in Spain, 1501 (CSP I no.294) describes Elizabeth's enquiries about Catherine's progress in French. Margaret and Elizabeth's concerns about Princess Margaret marrying young are from Don Pedro de Ayala to Ferdinand and Isabella, 25 July 1498 (CSP I no.210). Herbert p.109 suggests Henry VIII was intended to become Archbishop of Canterbury. Erasmus's Account of his visit to the royal household in 1499 is in Mumby 1913:4. The celebrations that were held when Prince Henry was created Duke of York are described in a contemporary manuscript (Vitellius A XVI) (printed in Kingsford 1905:202). Details of Perkin Warbeck can be found in Seward 1995 and Okerlund 2009. Sir William Stanley's arrest and death are noted in documents printed in Pollard 1914:81 and 86 and in *Wriothesley's Chronicle* for 1495. Elizabeth of York's payments for clothing for her daughters are in her privy purse expenses. Princess Margaret's betrothal is in the contemporary document printed in Leland vol. IV p.262. Details of Catherine of Aragon's journey to England, the celebrations for her marriage and the marriage itself are detailed in a contemporary manuscript printed in Leland 1774 vol. IV. Arthur's death and his parents' reaction are from the same document. Elizabeth's privy purse expenses p.103 note the litter purchased to convey Catherine of Aragon from Ludlow to London. Don Pedro de Ayala to Ferdinand and Isabella, 26 March 1499 (CSP I no.239) notes the danger Elizabeth was in during the birth of Edmund. Okerlund 2009 speculates that Katherine was born prematurely and describes Elizabeth's death. Margaret's ordinances for mourning are from BL Add. MSS 45133 f.141v. 'The fyancells of Margaret, Eldest Daughter of King Henry VIIth to James King of Scotland: Together with her departure from England and journey into Scotland' (Leland IV p.266) describes Princess Margaret's departure for Scotland.

12 A Patroness of Learning: July 1504-April 1509

Henry VII's early visit to Cambridge is noted in 'A shorte and brief memory by Licence and corveccon of the first progresse of our soveraigne lord King Henry' from a manuscript in the Cottonian Library (Leland vol. IV p.186). All the letters to and from Oxford are taken from Anstey 1898. Rex 2003 discusses Margaret's lectureship at Cambridge. Fisher's background is detailed in *The Life of Fisher* (Bayne 1921). His attempts to persuade Margaret to benefit Cambridge and a description of her other good works is from the *Life*, p.10. Baker p.4 details Margaret's preachership at Cambridge. Magrath 1921 details Philippa of Hainault's foundation of Queen's College, Oxford. Searle 1867:133 describes Margaret's interest in Queen's College, Cambridge, after Elizabeth of York's death. Buckingham's grant to the college is quoted from the same work. Cooper 1874:63 describes Margaret's attempts to secure a fellowship for Thomas Maunfeld at Corpus Christi, Cambridge. The letters concerning the dispute between the university and the town are from Cooper 1874:80.

The document describing the foundation of God's House is quoted from Myers 1969:894-5. Nichols 1840:134 describes the poor state of God's House. Cooper 1861:24 details Henry's licence to Margaret to refound God's House. The story of Margaret asking for a poor scholar at Christ's to be chastised less harshly is printed in a number of works, including Nichols 1830:135. Cooper 1861:29 lists Margaret's bequests of plate to Christ's College. Jones and Underwood 1995:222 note that the woman bringing a cake to the college suggests that Margaret was regularly in attendance there. Baker relates the foundation of St John's in his preface to Fisher's funeral sermon for Margaret. Work towards the foundation after Margaret's death is detailed in 'Many suites and greate troubles which the Bishop of Rochester did undergoe in the behalfe of the colledge' (printed in Fisher p.184). Caxton's dedication to *The Hystorye of Kinge Blanchardyne and Queen Eglantyne his Wyfe* is printed in Fisher pp.178-9. The prefaces to *The Ladder of Perfection* and *The Grete Shyppe of Fooles of this Worlde* are also in Fisher. Fisher's seven penitential psalms are in Mayor 1876. Walpole p.291 lists Margaret's translation works. Fisher's comments on the acquisition of his bishopric are in his 1527 work 'On the Truth of Christ's Body and Blood in the Eucharist' to Fox, Bishop of Winchester (printed in Domville 1899). Henry VII's letter to Margaret is from Fisher p.164. Margaret's inquiry into royal rights at Corfe is in 'Document of Maladministration of Justice' (Pollard pp.143-44). 'Grant of 20 November 1488 of the lead from the manor of Woxesey to be used for Corfe' (Campbell vol. II p.364) notes that Henry supplied the lead for Margaret's repairs at Corfe. Jones and Underwood 1995:82 describe Margaret's forced surrender of Woking. Lockyer and Thrush 1997:36 note that Margaret was indited for keeping an illegal number of retainers. The note from 1525 about Margaret taking a judicial role is printed in Pollard 1913:200. The *Chronicle of Calais* for 1500 (p.3) records Henry and Elizabeth's visit to Calais. Comments that Henry looked old are from Ayala to Ferdinand and Isabella, 25 July 1498 (Pollard p.4) and *Hall's Chronicle* p.498. Henry's letter to his mother from July 1504 is quoted from Halsted p.211. Chrimes p.313 notes that Henry was believed to have been suffering from consumption. The Spanish ambassador's comments on Henry's fondness for Prince Henry are in The Duke of Estrada to Isabella of Castile, 10 August 1504 (Mumby 1913:50). Isabella of Castile to the Duke of Estrada, 11 April 1503 records that Isabella had heard rumours that Henry intended to marry Catherine, which she called 'a very evil thing' (Mumby 1913:41-2). Catherine of Aragon to Queen Juana, 25 October 1507 (Mumby 1913:93) notes the princess's support for Henry VII's hopes of marrying her sister. Seward 1995:331 claims that Margaret moved to Coldharbour to be close to Henry in his final illness. *Hall's Chronicle* p.10 talks of Henry's charity when he realised that he was dying. Fisher's funeral sermon for Henry, which was preached in St Paul's on 10 May 1509 is printed in Fisher. The quote is from p.144. Henry VII's Will is in *Testamenta Vetusta* vol. II pp.32-3.

13 My Lady, the King's Grandmother: 23 April-29 June 1509

Routh 1924:124 notes that Margaret signed warrants for Henry's funeral. Jones and Underwood 1995:234 note that estimates for Margaret's funeral expenses were drawn up in early 1509. The quotes from Fisher's funeral sermon on Margaret's health are from pp.113, 120-1, 127. The description of Henry VIII in 1515, by a Venetian diplomat, is taken from Williams 1967:388. Lord Mountjoy's letter is taken from Mumby. Jones and Underwood 1995:237 record Reginald Pole's claims regarding Margaret's deathbed. Herbert pp.110-1 describes Margaret's appointment of Henry VIII's council and her management of them. Jones and Underwood 1995:236 describe Margaret's attendance to watch Henry VIII's coronation procession. *Hall's Chronicle* p.508 describes the coronation and the fine clothes that Henry wore. Parker claims that Margaret was taken ill after eating a cygnet at Henry's coronation banquet (BL Add. MSS. 12060 f.23-23v). Fisher's funeral sermon p.126 notes that she wept at Henry VIII's coronation. The quote from the *Life of Fisher* on Fisher ordering Margaret's household is from p.10. The quote on Fisher's attempts to persuade Margaret to be generous to her servants is from 'Suites and great troubles which the Bishop of Rochester did undergoe in the behalfe of the colledge' (Fisher p.186). The quotes from Fisher's funeral sermon on Margaret's death are from pp.130 and 117.

14 Mother of the Tudor Dynasty

Samuel Daniel's poem is quoted from Chalmers 1810:525. Margaret's Will is from *Testamenta Vetusta* vol. II. The *Life of Fisher* p.28 describes Margaret's funeral. Parker's comments are from BL Add. MSS. 12060 f.23. The quote by Fisher that is something of an epitaph for her is from 'Fisher's dedication in his 1527 work 'on the Truth of Christ's Body and Blood in the Eucharist' to Fox, Bishop of Winchester' (in Domville 1899:187).

Appendix: Margaret Beaufort in Her Own Words

Margaret's letter to the Bishop of Exeter is taken from Campbell vol. II p.284. Her letters to Oxford University are from Anstey pp.614, 665 and 667. The letter to the Earl of Ormond is from Halsted 1839. The letter to Richard Shirley is from Wood 1846 vol. II. Margaret's first letter to Henry VII is from Halsted 1839:206-7. The gaps in the text are where the original letter has been damaged and is now illegible. The second letter to Henry VII is from Wood 1846 vol. II. The letter to the Mayor of Coventry is printed as an appendix to Fisher's funeral sermon (p.167). The first of Margaret's letters to Sir John Paston is taken from the *Paston Letters* vol. III:392 (the Will of William Paston, naming Margaret as his executor, is from the same source, p.469). The second letter to Sir John Paston is from Simon 1982:115.

BIBLIOGRAPHY

British Library has been abbreviated to BL. Public Record Office has been abbreviated to PRO. Westminster Abbey Muniments have been abbreviated to WAM. Place of publication is London unless otherwise stated.

Primary Manuscript Sources

BL Add. MSS. 12060: A Book of Miracles and Examples of Virtue for the Guidance of a Ruler, Dedicated to Queen Mary by Henry Parker Lord Morley.

BL Add. MSS. 45133: Ordinances for Mourning 1502-3.

PRO SC 8/139/6909: Petition by John, first Earl of Somerset to King Henry IV, 1404.

PRO SC 8/141/7018: Petition by John, Earl of Somerset and his brother, Thomas Beaufort to the Duke of Gloucester and parliament, 1427.

PRO SC 8/152/7597: Petition by Richard, Duke of York, Edmund Tudor, Earl of Richmond, Margaret Beaufort, Countess of Richmond and others in relation to the manors of Collingham and Bardsley and the advowson of the church in Middleton, 1455.

PRO C 47/30/9/14: Engagement of the Duke of Bourbon to secure the release of the Earl of Somerset and Thomas Beaufort from their imprisonment in France, 1427.

WAM 12181-90: Household accounts of Sir Henry Stafford, 1466-1471.

WAM 5472: Receipts and expenses of Reginald Bray, receiver of Sir Henry Stafford 1468-1469.

WAM 32407: Receipts and expenses of Reginald Bray, receiver to Lord Stanley 1473-1474.

WAM 32378: Patent of Henry VI creating Edmund Tudor Earl of Richmond, with a draft pardon from Edward IV to Henry Tudor on the reverse.

Primary Printed Sources

Andreas, B., 'Historia Regis Henrici Septimi', in Gairdner, J. (ed.), *Memorials of King Henry the Seventh* (1858)

Anstey, H. (ed.), *Epistolae Academicae Oxon*, vol. II (Oxford, 1898)

Bacon, F., *History of the Reign of King Henry VII*, Lumby, J. R. (ed.) (Cambridge, 1885)

Bayne, R. (ed.), *The Life of Fisher MS. Harleian 6382* (1921)

Buck, G., *The History of King Richard the Third*, Kincaid, A. N. (ed.) (Gloucester, 1619)

Calendar of State Papers Spain, vol. I 1485-1509, Bergenroth, G. A. (ed.) (1862) (abbreviated to *CSP* in the text)

Campbell, W. (ed.), *Materials for a History of the Reign of Henry VII*, 2 vols (1873)

Bibliography

Capgrave, J., *Book of the Illustrious Henries*, Hingeston, F. C. (ed.) (1858)

Chalmers, A. (ed.), *The Works of the English Poets, From Chaucer to Cowper*, vol. III (1810)

Comines, P. de, *Memoirs*, vol. I (1823)

Davies, J. S. (ed.), *An English Chronicle of the Reigns of Richard II, Henry IV, Henry V and Henry VI Written Before the Year 1471* (1856)

Dockray, K. (ed.), *Edward IV: A Source Book* (Stroud, 1999)

Dockray, K. (ed.), *Henry VI, Margaret of Anjou and the Wars of the Roses: A Source Book* (Stroud, 2000)

Excerpta Historica (1831)

Fisher, J., *The Funeral Sermon of Margaret Countess of Richmond and Derby, Mother to King Henry VII, and Foundress of Christ's and St John's College in Cambridge, Preached by Bishop Fisher in 1509 (Including Baker's Preface)*, Hymers, J. (ed.) (Cambridge, 1840)

Froissart, J., *The Chronicle of Froissart*, vol. VI, Berners, Lord (ed.) (1903)

Gairdner, J. (ed.), *The Paston Letters*, 3 vols (Westminster, 1896)

Giles, J. A. (ed.), *The Chronicles of the White Rose of York* (1845)

Hales, J. W. and Furnivall, F. J. (eds), *Bishop Percy's Folio Manuscript, Ballads and Romances*, vol. III (1868)

Hall, E., *Chronicle Containing the History of England* (1809)

Halliwell, J. O. (ed.), *Letters of the Kings of England*, vol. I (1848)

Harris, N. (ed.), *Testamenta Vetusta*, vol. I (1826)

Herbert, E., *The History of England Under Henry VIII* (1870)

Ives, J. (ed.), *Select Papers Chiefly Relating to English Antiquities* (1873)

Jeffery, E. (ed.), 'Wardrobe Account, 1483', in *The Antiquarian Repertory*, vol. I (1807)

Kingsford, C. L. (ed.), *Chronicles of London* (Oxford, 1905)

Legg, L. G. W. (ed.), *English Coronation Records* (Westminster, 1901)

Leland, J., *The Itinerary*, vol. V, Hearne, T. (ed.) (Oxford, 1744)

Leland, J., *Joannis Lelandi Antiquarii de Rebus Britannicis Collectanea*, vols IV and V (1774)

Mancini, D., *The Usurpation of Richard III*, Armstrong, C. A. J., (ed.) (Gloucester, 1984)

Mayor, J. E. B. (ed.), *The English Works of John Fisher Bishop of Rochester* (1876)

More, T., *The History of King Richard III* (2005)

Mumby, F. A. (ed.), *The Youth of Henry VIII: A Narrative in Contemporary Letters* (Boston, 1913)

Myers, A. R. (ed.), *English Historical Documents vol IV:1327-1485* (1969)

Nichols, J. G. (ed.), *The Chronicle of Calais* (1846)

Nicolas, N. H. (ed.), *Testamenta Vetusta: Being Illustrations from Wills*, vol. 2 (1826)

Nicolas, N. H. (ed.), *Privy Purse Expenses of Elizabeth of York and Wardrobe Accounts of Edward the Fourth* (1830)

Pollard, A. F. (ed.), *The Reign of Henry VII from Contemporary Sources*, vol. I (1914)

Riley, H. T. (ed.), *Ingulph's Chronicle of the Abbey of Croyland with the Continuations by Peter of Blois and Anonymous Writers* (1854)

Rotuli Parliamentorum; ut et Petitiones et Placita in Parliamento, vols V and VI (1767)

Stow, J., *The Annales or Generall Chronicle of England* (1615)

Stow, J., *A Survey of London, Written in the Year 1598* (1842)

The Antiquarian Repertory, vol. IV (1784)

Vergil, P., *Three Books of Polydore Vergil's English History, Comprising the Reigns of Henry VI, Edward IV and Richard III*, Ellis, H. (ed.) (1844)

Williams, C. H. (ed.), *English Historical Documents 1485-1558*, vol. V (1967)

Wood, M. A. E. (ed.), *Letters of Royal and Illustrious Ladies*, vol. 2 (1846)

Wriothesley, C., *A Chronicle of England*, vol. I, Hamilton, W. D. (ed.) (1875)

Secondary Sources

Archer, R. E., 'Queen Margaret of Anjou, Queen Consort of Henry VI: A Reassessment', in *Crown, Government and People in the Fifteenth Century* (Stroud, 1995)

Bagley, J. J., *Margaret of Anjou*

Bagley, J. J., *The Earls of Derby 1485-1985* (1985)

Baldwin, D., *Elizabeth Woodville* (Stroud, 2002)

Chrimes, S. B., *Henry VII* (New Haven, 1999)

Cooper, C. H., 'The vow of widowhood of Margaret, Countess of Richmond and Derby (foundress of Christ's and Saint John's Colleges, Cambridge) with notices of similar vows in the 14th, 15th, and 16th centuries', in *Report Presented to the Cambridge Antiquarian Society, at its Eleventh General Meeting* (1853)

Cooper, C. H., *Memorials of Cambridge*, vol. II (Cambridge, 1861)

Cooper, C. H., *Memoir of Margaret, Countess of Richmond and Derby* (Cambridge, 1874)

Cron, B. M., 'The Duke of Suffolk, the Angevin Marriage, and the Ceding of Maine, 1445' (*Journal of Medieval History* 20, 1994)

Domville, M., *The King's Mother: Memoir of Margaret Beaufort, Countess of Richmond and Derby* (1899)

Erlanger, P., *Margaret of Anjou* (1970)

Griffiths, R. A., *The Reign of King Henry VI* (Stroud, 2004)

Griffiths, R. A., and Thomas, R. S., *The Making of the Tudor Dynasty* (Stroud, 1998)

Halsted, C. A., *Life of Margaret Beaufort* (1839)

Harvey, N. L., *Elizabeth of York* (1973).

Haswell, J., *The Ardent Queen* (1976)

Hicks, M., 'Warwick – The Reluctant Kingmaker' (*Medieval History* 1, 1991)

Hicks, M., *False, Fleeting Perjur'd Clarence* (Bangor, 1992)

Hicks, M., *Anne Neville* (Stroud, 2006)

Horrox, R., 'Personalities and Politics' in Pollard, A. J. (ed.), *The Wars of the Roses* (Houndmills, 1995)

Horrox, R., *Richard III: A Study in Service* (Cambridge, 1999)

Jones, M. K., 'John Beaufort, Duke of Somerset and the French Expedition of 1443' in Griffiths, R. A. (ed.), *Patronage, the Crown and the Provinces in Later Medieval England* (Gloucester, 1981)

Jones, M. K. 'Henry VII, Lady Margaret Beaufort and the Orleans Ransom', in

Bibliography

Griffiths, R. A., and Sherborne, J. (eds), *Kings and Nobles in the Later Middle Ages* (Gloucester, 1986)

Jones, M. K., and Underwood, M. G., *The King's Mother* (Cambridge, 1995)

Lander, J. R., *The Wars of the Roses* (Gloucester, 1990)

Laynesmith, J. L., *The Last Medieval Queens* (Oxford, 2004)

Lee, P. A., 'Reflections of Power: Margaret of Anjou and the Dark Side of Queenship' (*Renaissance Quarterly* 39, 1986)

Lockyer, R., and Thrush, A., *Henry VII* (1997)

Lucraft, J., *Katherine Swynford* (Stroud, 2010)

Magrath, J. R., *The Queen's College*, vol. I (Oxford, 1921)

Maurer, H. E., *Margaret of Anjou* (Woodbridge, 2003)

Millar, O., 'Strafford and Van Dyck', in Ollard, R., and Tudor-Craig, P. (eds), *For Veronica Wedgwood These: Studies in Seventeenth-Century History* (1986)

Neillands, R., *The Wars of the Roses* (1992)

Nichols, J., *The History of the University of Cambridge and of Waltham Abbey* (1840)

Norton, E., *She Wolves, The Notorious Queens of England* (Stroud, 2008)

Norton, E., *England's Queens: The Biography* (Stroud, 2011, forthcoming)

Okerlund, A., *Elizabeth Wydeville: Th Slandered Queen* (Stroud, 2005)

Okerlund, A., *Elizabeth of York* (New York, 2009)

Owen and Blakeway, *The History of Shrewsbury Part I* (1822)

Rex, R., 'Lady Margaret Beaufort and Her Professorship, 1502-1559', in Collinson, P., Rex, R., and Stanton, G. (eds), *Lady Margaret Beaufort and her Professors of Divinity at Cambridge 1502 to 1649* (Cambridge, 2003)

Rogers, C., *Henry VII* (1993)

Routh, E. M. G., *Lady Margaret: A Memoir of Lady Margaret Beaufort Countess of Richmond and Derby Mother of Henry VII* (1924)

Saul, N., *The Three Richards* (2005)

Searle, W. G., *The History of the Queen's College of St Margaret and St Bernard in the University of Cambridge 1446-1560* (Cambridge, 1867)

Seward, D., *The Wars of the Roses* (1995)

Seward, D., *Richard III: England's Black Legend* (1997)

Simon, L., *Of Virtue Rare* (Boston, 1982)

Storey, R. L., *The End of the House of Lancaster* (Stroud, 1999)

Visser-Fuchs, L., 'Where Did Elizabeth of York Find Consolation?' (*The Ricardian* 9, 1993)

Walpole, H., *A Catalogue of the Royal and Noble Authors of England, with Lists of their Works* (Edinburgh, 1796)

Weir, A., *Katherine Swynford* (2007)

Williams, N., *The Life and Times of Henry VII* (1994)

LIST OF ILLUSTRATIONS

Integrated Illustrations
1. Margaret's royal descent. © Elizabeth Norton.
2. The Beaufort family. © Elizabeth Norton.
3. Margaret's Links to the House of York. © Elizabeth Norton.
4. Edward III from a drawing in St Stephen's Chapel. Margaret was descended from the king's third surviving son, John of Gaunt. © Elizabeth Norton.
5. Philippa of Hainault, wife of Edward III, depicted in a drawing of a tapestry made during the reign of Edward III and which hung in St Stephens Chapel, Westminster until it was destroyed when the old Palace of Westminster burned down.
6. Richmond Palace. Henry VII built the palace to symbolise the might of the Tudor dynasty. © Jonathan Reeve JR945b20p788 15001550.
7. A line drawing by a French or Flemish artist of Henry VII. Margaret was only thirteen when she gave birth to Henry and they remained close in spite of his long exile in Brittany. © Jonathan Reeve JRCD2b20p764 14501500.
8. Plan of Westminster. Margaret spent much of her life in London and would have recognised many of the sites depicted in this near contemporary plan. © Jonathan Reeve JRCD2b20p769 15501600.
9. A clasp from a prayer book belonging to Margaret Beaufort. Margaret was well known during her lifetime for both her piety and her love of books. © Jonathan Reeve JR1555 fol 01 15001550.
10. A youthful Margaret Beaufort. © Jonathan Reeve JR1179b20p792 14501550.
11. Margaret Beaufort at prayer. © Jonathan Reeve JR1582b61p614B 14501500.
12. A statue of St Nicholas from Westminster Abbey. Margaret was always devoted to St Nicholas and believed that he had directed her to divorce her first husband and marry Edmund Tudor in a vision. © Elizabeth Norton.
13. A statue of Henry VII in his coronation regalia from Westminster Abbey. Margaret wept as her son's coronation, terrified that some misfortune would follow her greatest triumph. © Elizabeth Norton.
14. Edward V shown with his parents and uncle, Earl Rivers. The elder of the princes in the Tower was widely believed to have been murdered by his uncle, Richard III, shortly after he was deposed from the throne. © Jonathan Reeve JR1580 b4fp582 14501500.
15. Perkin Warbeck, who claimed to be one of the missing princes in the Tower was a major threat to Henry VII's rule for a number of years. © Jonathan Reeve JRCD3b20p795 14501500.
16. Coronation of Henry VIII. Margaret made her last public appearance at her grandson's coronation. © Jonathan Reeve JR1161b4p605 15001550.
17. The young Henry VIII. Henry was only seventeen when he succeeded to the throne and he relied on his grandmother's advice. © Jonathan Reeve JR1556 folio 2 15001530.
18. Margaret Tudor. Margaret's eldest granddaughter was named after her and she was always a particular favourite of hers. © Jonathan Reeve JR982b620p837 15001600.
19. & 20. The tombs of Henry VII and Elizabeth of York at Westminster Abbey. Margaret was devastated by the death of Henry VII, her only child, and she survived him by only a few months. © Elizabeth Norton.
21. & 22. Henry VII's Chapel at Westminster Abbey. Henry VII commissioned a fine chapel in Westminster Abbey as his lasting memorial. © Elizabeth Norton.
23. Margaret Beaufort's tomb in Westminster Abbey. At her own request, Margaret was buried near her son Henry VII, in the chapel he built at Westminster. © Elizabeth Norton.

24. Margaret Beaufort in later life. Margaret was well known for her piety and she chose to be depicted in a religious habit. © Jonathan Reeve JR1560b18p686 14501500.

Colour Section

25. Margaret Beaufort. Margaret had a reputation for piety and, in later life, followed an ascetic lifestyle. By kind permission of Ripon Cathedral Chapter.

26. Statue of Margaret Beaufort from Christ's College, Cambridge. Margaret oversaw the foundation of Christ's personally and her statue is proudly displayed over the gate of the college. © Elizabeth Norton.

27. Edward III. The rivalry between the descendants of Edward's sons led to the Wars of the Roses. By kind permission of Ripon Cathedral Chapter.

28. John of Gaunt. Margaret was the great granddaughter of the third surviving son of Edward III through his relationship with Katherine Swynford. Photograph © Gordon Plumb.

29. Henry IV and Joan of Navarre from their tomb at Canterbury Cathedral. Henry IV's usurpation of the crown caused the turbulent Wars of the Roses through which Margaret lived. © Elizabeth Norton.

30. Catherine of Valois - Margaret Beaufort's mother in law - giving birth to the future Henry VI. She shocked contemporaries by marrying Owen Tudor around 1430 (her second husband), her first husband was Henry V. From the *Beauchamp Pageant*. © Jonathan Reeve JR1730b90fp88 14001500

31. Henry VI depicted as a saint. Margaret later claimed that the Lancastrian king had prophesied that her son would rule England and he was widely regarded as a saint. © Jonathan Reeve JRCD JR1561folc06 14001450.

32, 33, & 34. Pembroke Castle. Margaret took refuge in the castle following the death of her husband, Edmund Tudor, and it was there that she bore her only child. The interior images show life as it would have been in the castle during Margaret's residence there.

35. Henry VII and Henry VIII portrayed together in an attempt to show the might of the Tudor dynasty. Henry VII, Margaret's son was the focus of all her ambition and she referred to him as her 'worldly joy'. © Elizabeth Norton.

36. Elizabeth of York. Margaret entirely overshadowed her daughter-in-law and she took to signing her letters as 'Margaret R' to emphasise her queenly role. By kind permission of Ripon Cathedral Chapter.

37. Elizabeth Woodville. Edward IV's widow plotted with Margaret to bring Henry Tudor to the throne as the husband of her daughter, Elizabeth of York. By kind permission of Ripon Cathedral Chapter.

38. Edward IV. The first Yorkist king was suspicious of Margaret and her son and he made strenuous efforts to secure Henry Tudor's return from Brittany. By kind permission of Ripon Cathedral Chapter.

39. Richard III stripped Margaret of all her possessions and placed her in her husband's custody as a punishment for her involvement in Buckingham's plot. By kind permission of Ripon Cathedral Chapter.

40. Margaret of York, duchess of Burgundy. The sister of Edward IV and Richard III was determined to depose Henry VII and assisted pretenders to the throne. © Jonathan Reeve JR JR1565b13p704 14501500.

41. & 42. Greenwich Palace was a favourite residence of Henry VII and Margaret was a regular visitor there. © Jonathan Reeve JR735b46fp186 14501500 and JR944b46fp180 14501500.

43. Richmond Palace gatehouse. Little survives of Henry VII's finest palace today. © Elizabeth Norton.

44. The tomb of Sir David Owen at Easeborne in West Sussex. Henry VII's generosity to the illegitimate son of Owen Tudor demonstrates his affection for his father's family and he was proud of his Tudor blood. © Elizabeth Norton.

45. William Warham, Archbishop of Canterbury was appointed by Henry VII and was known to Margaret personally. © Elizabeth Norton.

46. & 47. Christ's College, Cambridge. Margaret initially intended to patronise both Oxford and Cambridge Universities, but she was persuaded by her chaplain, John Fisher, to focus her energies on Cambridge. © Elizabeth Norton.

48. & 49. St John's College, Cambridge. Margaret did not live to see St John's College and it was left to her friend, John Fisher, to oversee the foundation. © Elizabeth Norton.

50. & 51. Henry VIII at Trinity College, Cambridge and King's College, Cambridge. Margaret's grandson followed her interest in education through his patronage of the University of Cambridge. © Elizabeth Norton.

52. Henry VIII in later life. Margaret selected her grandson's first councillors but died before she could have much influence over his rule. Margaret's grandson resembled his Yorkist mother's family rather than his Beaufort or Tudor paternal family and he was proud of being the grandson of Edward IV. © Jonathan Reeve JR951b53p505 15001550.

53. View of Westminster. © Jonathan Reeve JR729b46fp16 13001350.

54. Great Tournament Roll of Westminster. Margaret's grandson, Henry VIII, was only seventeen when he became king and Margaret took control of affairs, appointing the new king's council for him. © Jonathan Reeve JR1098b2fp204 15001550.

55. Catherine of Aragon. Margaret attended the marriage of Catherine of Aragon to Prince Arthur and she later witnessed the princess marry Arthur's younger brother, Henry VIII. By kind permission of Ripon Cathedral Chapter.

56. London Bridge was one of the major landmarks of London during Margaret's time. Margaret was given a London residence by Henry VII and she spent a large proportion of her time in the capital.© Jonathan Reeve JR1062b10prelims 16001650.

57. Westminster Abbey. Margaret plotted to make her son king and she attended his coronation in the Abbey. © Elizabeth Norton.

58. The Jewel Tower at Westminster Palace. Very little now remains of the medieval palace in which Henry VI prophesied to Margaret that her son would one day become king of England. © Elizabeth Norton.

59. The Tower of London. Margaret's brother-in-law, Henry VI was imprisoned in the Tower following his deposition and he was murdered there soon after the Battle of Tewkesbury. © Stephen Porter and the Amberley Archive.

60. The Tower of London in around 1485, only two years after the mysterious disappearance of the princes in the Tower. © Jonathan Reeve JR992b4p640 14501550.

61. St Paul's Cathedral. Margaret's great-grandfather, John of Gaunt, chose to be buried in the cathedral and it was an important landmark in the London that Margaret knew. © Jonathan Reeve JR715b46fp28 13001350.

62. Mary I was England's first effective reigning queen, something that would have been unthinkable in the late fifteenth century when Henry VII took Margaret's place in the succession. By kind permission of Ripon Cathedral Chapter.

63. Elizabeth I as princess. Margaret's great-granddaughter drew on her as a model of a powerful and political woman. © Jonathan Reeve JR1168b4fp747 15501600.

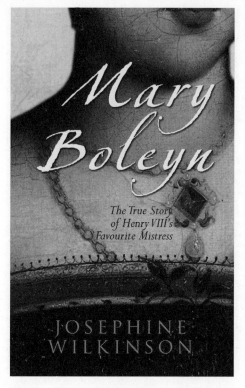

Also available from Amberley Publishing

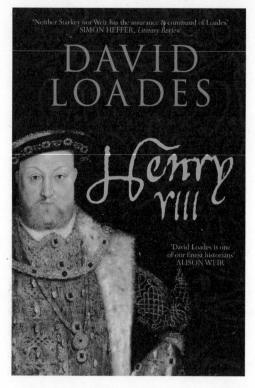

A major new biography of the most infamous king of England

'A triumph' THE SPECTATOR

'The best place to send anyone seriously wanting to get to grips with alternative understandings of England's most mesmerising monarch... copious illustrations, imaginatively chosen' BBC HISTORY MAGAZINE

'David Loades Tudor biographies are both highly enjoyable and instructive, the perfect combination' ANTONIA FRASER

Professor David Loades has spent most of his life investigating the remains, literary, archival and archaeological, of Henry VIII, and this monumental new biography book is the result. As a youth, he was a magnificent specimen of manhood, and in age a gargantuan wreck, but even in his prime he was never the 'ladies man' which legend, and his own imagination, created. Sexual insecurity undermined him, and gave his will that irascible edge which proved fatal to Anne Boleyn and Thomas Cromwell alike.

£25 Hardback
113 illustrations (49 colour)
512 pages
978-1-84868-532-1

Available from all good bookshops or to order direct
Please call **01453-847-800**
www.amberleybooks.com

Available from October 2011 from Amberley Publishing

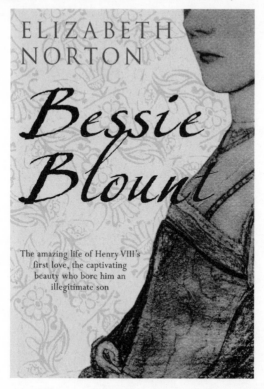

Beautiful, young, exuberant, the amazing life of Elizabeth Blount, Henry VIII's mistress and mother to his first son who came tantalizingly close to succeeding him as King Henry IX

Sidelined by historians until now, Bessie and the son she had by the king are one of the great 'what ifs' of English history. If Jane Seymour had not produced a male heir and Bessie's son had not died young aged 17, in all likelihood Henry Fitzroy could have followed his father as King Henry IX and Bessie propelled to the status of mother of the king.

£20 Hardback
30 illustrations (20 colour)
288 pages
978-1-84868-870-4

Available from October 2011 from all good bookshops or to order direct
Please call **01453-847-800**
www.amberleybooks.com

Also available from Amberley Publishing

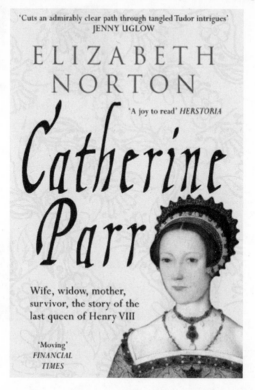

'Cuts an admirably clear path through tangled Tudor intrigues'
JENNY UGLOW

ELIZABETH
NORTON

'A joy to read' HERSTORIA

Catherine Parr

Wife, widow, mother,
survivor, the story of the
last queen of Henry VIII

'Moving'
*FINANCIAL
TIMES*

Wife, widow, mother, survivor, the story of the last queen of Henry VIII

'Scintillating' *THE FINANCIAL TIMES*

'Norton cuts an admirably clear path through the tangled Tudor intrigues' *JENNY UGLOW*

'Wonderful, an excellent book, a joy to read' *HERSTORIA*

The sixth wife of Henry VIII was also the most married queen of England, outliving three husbands before finally marrying for love. Catherine Parr was enjoying her freedom after her first two arranged marriages when she caught the attention of the elderly Henry VIII. She was the most reluctant of all Henry's wives, offering to become his mistress rather than submit herself to the dangers of becoming Henry's queen. This only served to increase Henry's enthusiasm for the young widow and Catherine was forced to abandon her lover for the decrepit king.

£9.99 Paperback
49 illustrations (39 colour)
304 pages
978-1-4456-0383-4

Available from all good bookshops or to order direct
Please call **01453-847-800**
www.amberleybooks.com

More Tudor History from Amberley Publishing

HENRY VIII
David Loades

'David Loades Tudor biographies are both highly enjoyable and
instructive, the perfect combination' *ANTONIA FRASER*

£25.00   978-1-84868-532-1   512 pages HB 113 illus, 49 col

ANNE BOLEYN
Elizabeth Norton

'Meticulously researched and a great read'
THEANNEBOLEYNFILES.COM

£9.99   978-1-84868-514-7   264 pages PB 47 illus, 26 col

THE TUDORS VOL 1
G. J. Meyer

'His style is crisp and popular'
PROFESSOR DAVID LOADES

£12.99   978-1-4456-0143-4   384 pages PB 72 illus, 54 col

THE TUDORS VOL 2
G. J. Meyer

'A sweeping history of the gloriously infamous Tudor era'
KIRKUS REVIEW

£12.99   978-1-4456-0144-1   352 pages PB 53 illus, 15 col

ANNE BOLEYN
P. Friedmann

'A compelling and lively biography... meticulously researched and
supremely readable classic of Tudor biography' *DR RICHARD REX*

'The first scholarly biography' *THE FINANCIAL TIMES*

£20.00   978-1-84868-827-8   352 pages HB 47 illus, 20 col

MARY TUDOR
David Loades

£20.00   978-1-4456-0305-6   352 pages HB 40 illus, 25 col

CATHERINE PARR
Elizabeth Norton

'Norton cuts an admirably clear path through tangled Tudor intrigues'
JENNY UGLOW

'Wonderful... a joy to read'
HERSTORIA

£18.99   978-1-84868-582-6   384 pages HB 40 illus, 20 col

MARGARET BEAUFORT
Elizabeth Norton

£20.00   978-1-4456-0142-7   256 pages HB 70 illus, 40 col

Forthcoming

BESSIE BLOUNT
Elizabeth Norton

£20.00   978-1-84868-870-4   288 pages HB 40 illus, 20 col

CATHERINE OF ARAGON
Patrick Williams

£25.00   978-1-84868-108-8   512 pages HB 80 illus, 40 col

Available from all good bookshops or to order direct
Please call **01453-847-800 www.amberleybooks.com**

INDEX

Tudor History from Amberley Publishing